# Systems and Development

## The Minnesota Symposia on Child Psychology
### Volume 22

# Systems and Development

## The Minnesota Symposia on Child Psychology
### Volume 22

edited by

## MEGAN R. GUNNAR
*University of Minnesota*

## ESTHER THELEN
*Indiana University*

 LAWRENCE ERLBAUM ASSOCIATES, PUBLISHERS
1989   Hillsdale, New Jersey      Hove and London

JB

Lawrence Erlbaum Associates, Inc., Publishers
365 Broadway
Hillsdale, New Jersey 07642

**Library of Congress Cataloging in Publication Data**

Systems and development / edited by Megan Gunnar, Esther Thelen.
    p. cm. — (The Minnesota symposia on child psychology ; v.
22)
    "Papers presented at the 22nd Minnesota Symposium on Child
Psychology, held October 29-31, 1987" — Pref.
    ISBN 0-8058-0409-9
    1. Child psychology—Philosophy—Congresses.   2. Child
development—Philosophy—Congresses.   3. System theory—
Psychological aspects—Congresses.   I. Gunnar, Megan R.
II. Thelen, Esther.   III. Series: Minnesota symposia on child
psychology (Series) ; v. 22.
BF722.S95   1987
155.4'01—dc19                                           88-16529
                                                            CIP

Printed in the United States of America
10   9   8   7   6   5   4   3   2   6-7-91

# Contents

# Preface

This volume contains chapters based on papers presented at the 22nd Minnesota Symposium on Child Psychology, held October 29–31, 1987, at the University of Minnesota, Minneapolis. As has been the tradition for this annual series, the faculty of the Institute of Child Development invited internationally eminent researchers to present their work and to consider problems of mutual concern.

The theme of this volume is systemic approaches to the study of development. The contributors each examined the question of what systemic approaches, generally, and general systems theory, more specifically, can and cannot do to help us in our examination of the ontogeny of human behavior. Systemic approaches to the study of development have had a large impact, at least on our rhetoric, since the late 1970s. The goal of this volume is to assemble a group of scholars with diverse perspectives on systems analyses to examine whether these approaches have had or might have an equally impressive impact on our understanding of development.

We are fortunate to have as contributors to this volume some of the most outstanding current scholars in this area. The contributors are John Fentress; Susan Oyama; Jay Belsky, Michael Rovine, Margaret Fish; and Gerald Patterson and Lew Bank. In addition, Esther Thelan, who served as the co-editor for this volume and co-organizer of the 1987 symposium, also served as one of the contributors. Two distinguished scholars, Francas Horowitz and Arnold Sameroff, have added discussions of these chapters.

Traditionally, each in Minnesota Symposia on Child Psychology the Institute of Child Development faculty have attempted to organize the symposium around issues that are on the cutting edge of the field. This 22nd symposium was no exception.recently there has been a good deal of discussion about a paradigm shift in developmental psychology: A shift from the linear, cause-effect, mechanistic accounts of behaviorism to the biologically based, nonlinear accounts of organismic theories. Of course, as Horowitz (1987) noted, it may be inaccurate to think of this shift as a shift in paradigms: Our field lacks the consensus that the idea of a unified paradigm shift implies. Nonetheless, there has been a move away from simple, stimulus–response accounts of development to explanations that assign to the child an active, constructivist role in his or her own development. Viewing the developing individual as an active agent is one hallmark of organismic theories, a characteristic based on the view that living organisms are open, rather than closed, system.

General systems' concepts applied to the study of development are in the intellectual tradition of organismic theories. Biological systems being open systems are self-maintaining, self-regulating, and self-reproducing (see Laszlo, 1972; Sameroff, 1983). Biological systems have the properties of wholeness and order and thus, although divisible into subsystems, biological systems cannot be understood through a reduction of complex components into simple components. In addition, the development of biological systems involves progressive differentiation, emergent properties, hierarchical organization, feedback and transactions, and equifinality: This last being the idea that similar end-points can be reached from different initial conditions and through different paths (Horowitz, 1987).

As evidenced by the rise in systems rhetoric, at least, these characteristics and properties ring true to our ears. Yes, this sounds more like the organism we study as infant, child, and adult than the robot-like creature of early behaviorist accounts. Furthermore, the general systems approach holds the promise of getting us beyond certain controversies that have stymied the development of our field. For example, as Susan Oyama demonstrates in chapter 1 of this volume, adoption of a systemic, constructivist perspective permits us to avoid the ghost-in-the-machine problem that forces all good interactionists ultimately still to seek "developmental plans" as existing preformed in either the genes or the environment.

If not preformed or predetermined, however, what are the roots of behavioral order?Although this is the title of John Fentress' chapter, Fentress was not the only presenter who grappled with this question. As we move away from linear, mechanistic explanations for development, we confront the problem of increasing the complexity of our explanations at the expense of the clarity of our models. For the researcher, the problem, in part, is that of knowing how to operationalize systems concepts. Because the properties and the characteristics of systems are expected to apply broadly across species and levels of organization, the linkage between systems concepts and operations are, by necessity, vague. What does it mean, for example, to say that a system is self-righting or self-maintaining? What this means must depend on the system under study. For example, self-regulatory processes as understood for hormonal systems cannot be applied directly to our understanding of the self-reglation of emotion, or of cognition, or of affiliative systems. The translation of systems concepts into operations must be worked out anew for each system and set of related systems under study. Although this point may seem obvious and self-evident, it leads to an important and not so obvious point. Simply stated, whether or not systems concepts provide more than rhetoric in any research domain will depend, in part, on the accuracy of the translation in that domain.

The subtitle of Esther Thelen's chapter is, "Can Systems Approach Work?". To the extent that the answer to this question depends on the precision with which systems concepts get translated, then in Dr. Thelen's chapter we have the prototype for how to go about that translation process in at least one area of development. One question worth raising, however, is whether we ever will be able to translate systems concepts with sufficient precision in other domains of development, particularly in the social domains, to have these concepts be useful in either prediction or comprehension. Probably no other aspect of common experience during development has been so widely and frequently linked with the idea of systems as the family. Yet as both the chapter by Jay Belsky, Michael Rovine, and Margaret Fish and the one by Gerald Patterson and Lew Bank demonstrate, the process of translating systems concepts into operations in the study of family relations is not straightforward. At the very least, however, these concepts have led these research groups to ask different questions and to identify different lawful relations in their data than they might have asked and found had they approached their data from a different perspective.

With these remarks as a preface, the reader may now want to proceed to each of the individual chapters and to the two discussant chapters. It remains only for me to conclude by thanking the individuals who made the 22nd Minnesota Symposium on Child Psychology a very special, intellectually rich and exciting experience. Above all, thanks is due to Esther Thelen who played a central role in the selection of speakers and the organization of the symposium. Thanks are due to the speakers and to the discussants, each of whom did an exceptional job. I would also like to thank the individuals who organized and ran the various small discussion groups that were a part of the symposium. These include Alan Fogel, our special guest from Purdue Unviersity; Ann Masten and Alan Sroufe, who led a discussion of systemic approaches to developmental psychopathology; William Charlesworth, who chaired an informal discussion group with Susan Oyama; and Willard Hartup, who along with Lew Bank discussed the problem of statistical analyses appropriate for the examination of systems. Thanks are also due to Lonnie Behrendt and Helen Dickison, who as support staff in the Institute of Child Development saw to many of the administrative details; and to Joan Connors and Louise Hertsgaard, who helped with the editing of the chapters for this volume.

Finally, I would like to acknowledge financial support for the symposium from the General Mills Foundation and the National Institute of Child Health and Human Developement, 2 R13 HD 21906.

*Megan R. Gunnar*

## REFERENCES

Horowitz, F. D. (1987). *Exploring developmental theories: Toward a structural/behavioral model of developmental.* Hillsdale, NJ: Lawrence Erlbaum Associates.

Laszlo, E. (1972). *Introduction to systems philosophy: Toward a new paradigm of contemporary thought.* New York: Harper & Row.

Sameroff, A. J. (1983). Developmental systems: Contexts and evolutions. In W. Kessen (Eds.), *History, theories, and methods.* Vol. II of P. H. Mussen (Eds.), *Handbook of child psychiatry* (pp. 237–294). New York: Wiley.

# 1

# Ontogeny and the Central Dogma: Do We Need the Concept of Genetic Programming in Order to Have an Evolutionary Perspective?

Susan Oyama
*John Jay College*
*City University of New York*

The title of this chapter implies that it is possible to have an evolutionary perspective without the concept of genetic programming (and without any of its surrogates, which proliferate wildly in the psychological and biological literature). This is indeed the case, but before considering how it can be accomplished and why it is important, we would do well to ask why evolution and programming have been assumed to be inextricably joined.

My discussion begins with some remarks on the need to integrate evolutionary and developmental studies, two areas that have been estranged from each other for some time. The rift is hardly surprising; evolutionary theory has been associated with a view of development as centrally controlled and predetermined. It is a view rejected by many who are deeply acquainted with the interactive systems that actually generate living forms, but one that fits an old tradition of preformationist thinking. We look at the standard definition of *evolution* as changes in gene frequencies, a definition that seems to require genetic control of ontogeny. Problems with this way of linking evolution to development are reviewed, along with some inadequate attempts to solve them. The concepts of inheritance and ontogeny are reformulated, and the idea of the developmental system is offered as a way of having an evolutionary perspective without being saddled with an untenable doctrine of one-way flow of developmental "information" from the nucleus to the phenotype.

# KNOWLEDGE AND THE SHADOW BOX

## Seeing

Howard Gruber and Isabel Sehl (1984) have studied the ways people cooperate to construct knowledge that is not available to either of them alone. Pairs of people are presented with a box in which shadows of an object can be seen. Because each looks at the object from a different angle, each sees a different shape. One might see a circle, for example, whereas the other sees a triangle. Together, the partners must construct an object that could project both those shapes. Clearly, some ways of working are more effective than others. Domination is not particularly helpful in moving beyond a one-sided view. Mindless compromise in the absence of real constructive work (the object is partly round and partly triangular) would obviously be inadequate as well.

I suggest that some of the reasons that developmentalists and evolutionists have had difficulty communicating with each other are related to the presuppositions they bring to the shadow box we call science, and thus, what they construct there. Sometimes they have had divergent interests, and the language in which they have communicated has prevented them from realizing it.

Viktor Hamburger (1980) has described the exclusion of embryology from the neo-Darwinian synthesis. The lack of mutual understanding between developmentalists and evolutionists he describes has had its counterpart at the behavioral level; witness the exchanges in the 1950s, 1960s and 1970s between American comparative psychologists and European ethologists (Lehrman, 1953, 1970; Lorenz, 1965). To some extent these groups talked past each other because they were interested in different matters. But I think they also had genuinely different conceptions of development.

## Four Points of View: Chaos at the Shadow Box

The ethologist Niko Tinbergen (1963) suggested that when people ask why an animal does something, there are four possible biological interpretations of the question. Many students of animal behavior have been guided by his explication of the "four whys": (a) the evolutionary history of the behavior, (b) its survival value, (c) the mechanisms by which it occurs, and (d) its development. Tinbergen thought that failure to distinguish these questions had caused considerable confusion. It still does. Developmental psychologists have not traditionally thought about the first two: when they have, they have not always kept their "whys" straight, nor have they necessarily been helped by their colleagues in biology. Too often, the price of admission to the biological brotherhood has been a view of development marked by reliance on essentially preformationist assumptions – assumptions decidedly uninformed by systems thinking, despite a vocabulary liberally sprinkled with systems terms (e.g., Fishbein, 1976; Scarr & McCartney, 1983). The notions of genetic programs and instinct, for instance, draw some of their authority from their associations with evolutionary thought, but carry all sorts of other implications about mode of development and kinds of mechanism: autonomy, internality, spontaneity, naturalness, and resistance to perturbation. They neatly tie together the four "whys" that Tinbergen distinguished. (He did not claim that they were unrelated, just different. He even discussed some ways of relating them, 1963; see also P. Bateson, 1985.)

Imagine for a moment two people at a shadow box. This time they have been given different instructions: One is to discern the object's shape, the other must determine whether it is moving. Imagine also that they must use an ambiguous vocabulary. "Rooving," for instance, means both "round" and "moving." One partner reports the object's rounded contour, and the other concludes that it is mobile. I am suggesting, in this crude way, that their plight resembles that of scientists who must work with ambiguous terms like *inherited, genetic, biological, maturational,* and so on.

The ambiguity of these terms permits the blurring of Tinbergen's "whys." If one worker discovers that a bit of behavior is present in phylogenetic relatives, for instance, the other may conclude that it will be developmentally stable. If one claims that a pattern is adaptive, the other may deduce that it develops independently of experience. Evidence for one "why" masquerades as evidence for another. If aims and terms were clarified researchers might conclude that they were pursuing separate projects, and that they had nothing to say to each other. But it is not separatism that is the goal: rather, the recognition of differences that is the prerequisite to fruitful collaboration. A great deal of conceptual work is required as well. Integration, after all, is not the same as conflation. Furthermore, because these notions of "biological bases" seldom segregate neatly into developmentalists' and evolutionists' heads, coherence within fields suffers even if there is no interest in interdisciplinary work.


## EVOLUTION AND THE CENTRAL DOGMA

### The Argument

The usual way of construing the relationship between ontogeny and phylogeny involves several interrelated ideas. First, evolution is defined by changes in gene frequencies. The genes are thought to produce phenotypes by supplying information, programs, or instructions for the body and for at least some aspects of the mind. Some genes produce better phenotypes than others and are differentially passed on. Although in this view the environment is necessary for proper development, its effects on the phenotype are evolutionarily irrelevent because only inherited traits are transmitted in the DNA. Causal power and information are carried in that DNA, and living things are created by an *outward* flow of causality and form from the nucleus.

This conception of the ontogeny–phylogeny relationship seems to require a dual view of development, one kind for inherited traits and one for everything else. This is true even though statements are routinely made about the interaction of nature with nurture and the impossibility of attributing traits completely to one or the other. Despite their reassuring ecumenical ring, such statements either retain the dichotomy or turn it into a continuum. Emblematic of a trendy but failed interactionism, they appear in response to a multitude of developmental observations that call traditional formulations into question; their shortcomings are examined later. (For critiques of this kind of well-intentioned but conceptually misguided interactionism, see Lewontin, Rose, & Kamin, 1984; Oyama, 1981, 1982, 1985; Tobach & Greenberg, 1984.) Although they scornfully dismiss "extreme views" that attribute behavior *entirely* to the genes or *entirely* to the environment, the devotees of this popular interactionism mistake compromise and relabelling for conceptual resolution.

Many have expressed their unhappiness with the contradictions and faulty inferences that accompany these accounts of the ontogeny–phylogeny relationship. They have tried to formulate a unified conception of ontogeny (P. Bateson, 1983; Gottlieb, 1976; Johnston, 1987; Klopfer, 1969; Lehrman, 1970; Schneirla, 1966; Tobach, 1972). Not surprisingly, they have often had difficulty communicating effectively with colleagues who hold the dominant dualistic view. Indeed, it can be argued that the nature–nurture dichotomy will continue to dominate our theories and research as long as we continue to speak of traits, programs, or encoded potential, as being *transmitted*.

## The Goal

We need to alter our conceptions of ontogeny and phylogeny before we can bridge what Hamburger (1980) called the "nucleocytoplasmic gap." We do not need more conciliatory declarations that nature and nurture are both important, but rather a radical reformulation of both. The conventional model equates nature with the genes and nurture with experience. *Experi-*

*ence* is usually taken to mean learning, so many other factors are automatically ignored (Lehrman, 1962). (Hence the interchangeability of "innate vs. learned" with "genes vs. environment," as in Gould, 1982, p. 250, 1985.) This model should make it impossible to refer to any aspect of the phenotype as *nature*. To do so would be either to confuse genotypic and phenotypic levels or to rely on a conception of development in which some parts of the phenotypes are contained in, or formed by, the genes. Nevertheless, both errors are commonly made, for it is with *phenotypes* that we are ultimately concerned. People become obsessed with genotypes insofar as they think that genotypes prefigure phenotypes. In the face of the conceptual disarray that accompanies the use and misuse of this model, I propose the following reconceptualizations, in which genes and environment are part of a developmental system that results in phenotypic nature:

1. *Nature* is not transmitted but constructed. An organism's nature — the characteristics that define it at a given time — is not genotypic (a genetic program or plan causing development) but phenotypic (a product of development). Because phenotypes change, natures are not static but transient, and because each genotype has a norm of reaction, they are not unitary but multiple.
2. *Nurture* (many levels of developmental interactions) is as crucial to typical characters as to atypical ones, as necessary to universal characters as to variable ones, as basic to stable characters as to labile ones.
3. Nature and nurture are therefore not alternative sources of form and causal power. Rather, nature is the *product* of the *process* of the developmental interactions we call nurture. An organism's nature is simply its form and function. Because nature is phenotypic, it depends on developmental context as profoundly and intimately as it does on the genome. To identify nature with that genome, then, is to miss the entire developmental story in much the same way that preformationist explanations have always done.
4. Evolution is thus the derivational history of developmental systems.

## Conduits and Messages

George Lakoff and Mark Johnson (1980), a linguist and a philosopher, present an "experientialist" alternative to objectivist and subjectivist theories of knowledge. Properties of objects are produced in interaction, rather than residing in the objects or being completely arbitrary and subjective, and metaphor plays a central role. Their attempt to provide a third way, a synthesis that transcends a traditional antithesis, provides some striking parallels with my attempt to use constructivist interaction[1] to move beyond nativism and environmentalism.

They describe the "conduit metaphor" for language, in which ideas or meanings are objects that can be placed in the containers we call *words* and sent along a conduit (communication) to a hearer. The meanings then reside in the sentences and are independent of speaker or context (pp. 10–12, citing Reddy). The objectivist theory of communication is based on this conduit metaphor: Fixed meanings are sent via linguistic expressions (p. 206). In a similar way, I suggest, natural selection is thought to place knowledge about the environment (or instructions for building organisms) into the genes, which are the vehicles by which these biological meanings are transmitted from one generation to the next. The context-independence of meanings in the conduit metaphor is consistent with the connotations of autonomy and necessity that accompany the ideas of instinct and genetically driven development. (On context-sensitivity in systems theory, see Valsiner, 1987.) The details of the communication metaphor tend not to be well worked out in biological discourse (Johnston, 1987; Oyama, 1985), but I think the objectivist (and preformationist) overtones are robust (Cohen, 1979).

Perhaps biologists' propensity to speak of molecular letters, words, and sentences, of genetic codes and grammars, is partially due to these notions of life as language. The genes become the repository of true nature; molecular meanings are contained in a phenotypic vessel, which is some-times treated with so little regard as to render it virtually transparent. Witness some psychologists' willingness to bypass the phenotype by speaking of people responding to children's "genetic propensities" and "genetic differences" rather than to the children themselves (Plomin, 1986, pp. 110, 129). Similarly, Scarr and McCartney (1983, p. 433) refer to experiences that "the genotype would find compatible." They use the term, *developmental system* but insist that genes and environment play different roles in it: The genes, of course, play the determining role. (Despite the importance of both, that is, some causes are more equal than others. For contrast, see Fogel & Thelen, 1987, and Valsiner, 1987, on systems dynamics and Goodwin, 1982, and Oyama, 1981, on phenocopies.)

---

[1]In the past I have not always distinguished clearly between the kind of interactionism I criticize as being inadequate and the kind I think overcomes those inadequacies. The former I often call *traditional* or *conventional* interactionism, the latter, *real* interactionism. But sometimes no modifier is used, and I have ungenerously expected the reader to know which meaning I intend. Others have avoided this problem by using another label (Lewontin et al., 1984; Tobach & Greenberg, 1984). Although I shrink at coining yet another term, I offer *constructivist interactionism* as a name for my approach.

The notion of construction has its own problems, one of which is that it is often associated with environmentalism, and so implies arbitrary and unlimited variation. That is clearly not what is intended here; what I wish to emphasize is the emergence of the phenotype, as well as its own active role in that emergence. (See Oyama, in press, for comments on construction.)

## THE CENTRAL DOGMA: HYPOTHESIS AND METAPHOR

The genes appear to link evolution and development in two ways. They are the material link that promised to make sense of heredity. A conceptual link was forged by the adoption of Francis Crick's Central Dogma of the one-way flow of information (from genes to proteins, never from proteins in toward the genes, Crick, 1957) as the ruling metaphor for development. The metaphor takes many forms (programs, blueprints, instructions; see Newman, 1988; Oyama, 1985), but they always involve the emanation of basic developmental causation from the DNA. An outward flow of information and power achieves the translation of the genetic message in ontogeny.

A subtle transition is thus made from "messages" about molecules to messages about bodies and minds, quite a different thing, whether we realize it or not. The shift is from transmission of *genes* to transmission of *traits*. Focus on the gene as prime mover of ontogeny leads to all sorts of assumptions about genetic control of development as the defining characteristic of certain traits (biological, inherited, programmed); this in turn leads to the need for another kind of process to explain everything else.

The more reductionist one is, the harder it is to appreciate the gap between the molecular and the organismic levels. The kind of reductionism I am speaking of here is not the provisional single-mindedness that allows detailed investigation of a mechanism. It is rather the desire to interpret the whole world in terms of that mechanism, or at least, in terms of the level at which it was studied. It is the failure to shift levels or point of view, whether from inability or from some conviction that to do so would be soft-headed. The genetic program holds a fatal attraction for such minds.

Crick's Central Dogma has come to have the quality of an unquestionable truth. We forget that it is, in fact, an hypothesis about specific molecular interactions, one that is open to empirical support or refutation. But what could challenge the "plain truth" that development is controlled by a genetic program? What would count as evidence for or against such control? One biologist told me that "the whole of molecular biology" demonstrated the reality of the genetic program—hardly the language of normal scientific inference. Programs have so dominated mainstream thinking that people have rarely been called on to defend them. They have functioned as an "enabling concept," important not only in research but in the legitimation of a kind of reductionist explanation (Yoxen, 1981, p. 105). Dawkins (1986, p. 111) spoke of DNA as *programs, instructions* and *algorithms,* and explicitly denied that these terms are metaphors: Of airborne seeds he says, "it is the plain truth [that it is raining instructions]. It couldn't be any plainer if it were raining floppy discs." Organisms become "natural-technical objects structured by logics of domination," "biotic components in a technological communications system," "command-control systems" (Haraway, 1981–1982, pp. 247, 259, 271). When "system" is simply shorthand for "machine governed by a program," this usually signals a preoccupation with static centralized control rather than the sort of distributed, dynamic, contingent control described by Fogel and Thelen (1987; see also Oyama, 1985; Valsiner, 1987. For an analysis of the popular use of "systems" and its links to a preoccupation with control, see Rosenthal, 1984, chapter 13.) Thus, we have the uneasy association of systems terms with a style of explanation that is, as previously noted, uninformed by the kind of systems theory that offers the most to developmental studies.

In addition to asking what kind of evidence is relevant to program explanations, one could ask another question: Does the notion of the program add anything to the understanding gained by analysis of developmental processes? I submit that it does not, and worse, that it usually imports extraneous and misleading implications. The Dogma-as-metaphor helps make intuitive sense of observations, fitting them into a particular world view. Metaphors are not mere embellishments to thought, but are fundamental to knowing itself. I would hardly argue, therefore, that we should give them up. But not all metaphors are equally useful, and one that encourages us to see development as fulfillment of a plan or transmission of a message may not always direct our attention in useful ways. In addition, it supports some of the more troublesome aspects of the nature–nurture opposition. Despite the comfortable fit between the idea of evolution as evolution of genes and the idea of genetically programmed development, there are profound problems with this formulation.

## WEAKNESSES OF THE METAPHOR

### Two Strategies

There are two general strategies one can use in arguing for a genetic program. One is to say that some features develop in this way, whereas others do not. This is the conventional dualistic formulation. The other is to say that all development is in some way controlled by the program. This I call "genetic imperialism," because it seems to be an attempt to include in the genes' purview both the "innate" and the "acquired," to subdue the environment and the organism's history in it. It, too, is dualistic in attributing to the genes and the environment rather different causal roles.

*Conventional Dualism.*    The problem with attributing some parts of the phenotype to the genes and some to the environment is that developmental processes and products are simply not partitionable in this way. In addition, the various criteria for making the distinction is not consistent. Although the concerns motivating any particular instance of the nature–nurture distinction may be interesting and important, casting the question in terms of nature and nurture immediately joins it to a multitude of other questions that have radically different empirical bases. For example, presence at birth, appearance without obvious learning, longitudinal stability, reliable timing, and susceptibility to pertubation are quite distinct developmental issues, and adaptiveness, phylogenetic relationships or distribution in a population are not developmental questions at all. Lumping them all as *instances of the same thing,* namely genetic nature, guarantees that conceptual chaos at the shadow box will be veiled by a common vocabulary.

Thus, one finds blithe cross-inference from populations to individuals and back again, from development to evolution and vice versa, from adaptiveness to mechanism, from phylogenetic similarity to necessity and naturalness, and so *ad infinitum,* all because terms like *biologically based, genetically encoded,* and *inherited* give the illusion of movement within a coherent theoretical system. Jacobson, Boersma, Fields, and Olson (1983, p. 436), for example, declare that if adults' tendency to address infants in high-pitched voices is species-typical and adaptive, then it is "biologically programmed in the adult speaker" and is thus neither learned nor responsive to feedback from the infant. Conversely, if experience *can* influence a behavior, Connor, Schackman, and Serbin (1978) conclude it is *not* "biological," and Frodi and Lamb (1978) reason that certain human sex differences are not biological because the behavior changes over the life span. But the multiple properties attributed to "biology" are not inherently linked to each other and therefore cannot be inferred from each other. Beards, breasts, and reproductive behavior are not present at birth, some learning is species-typical, adaptive characters are not necessarily unchangeable and universal characters do not show much heritable variability. Characters shared with phylogenetic relatives do not necessarily appear early and are not always difficult to change. And so on.

Assuming we have an adequate definition of learning, we can certainly ask whether a given behavior is learned or not, or whether it is influenced by prior learning or not. To answer such questions, however, we need to look at the *development* of the behavior, not ask whether it is difficult to change or is universal. Traits that are reliably found in a species can be distinguished from those that are not on the basis of the reliability of the various aspects of the developmental systems that produce them. Species-typical influences may be typical because they are passed on in the germ cell, because they are part of a reproductive system, because they are created or sought by the organism itself, supplied by conspecifics or other organisms, or are otherwise stable aspects of the niche. These associations must be investigated if we wish to understand the differences between universal and variable traits; our understanding is not improved by the circular tactic of explaining observations or conjectures by varying amounts of programming. The prediction of the future presence of a trait, which is often the issue in the nature–nurture debate about humans, is not properly accomplished by identifying the trait with the genes (by computing heritability coefficients, by detecting it in baboons or in hunter-gatherers, by declaring it adaptive, and so on) but by understanding the *developmental system* well enough that we can say whether the entire system will inevitably be present in the future. Careless inference not only hinders investigation of the question at hand, it also prevents the proper integration of development with evolution. Although errors like these are sometimes discovered and corrected by vigilant scholars, what is needed is correction of the conceptual system that generates them in the first place. Later, I point out the missed opportunity that such confusion represents, and argue for a radical reconceptualization.

*Genetic Imperialism.* Conventional dualism fails, then, because it rests on an incoherent mix of ideas; there is no consistent way of distinguishing features that are programmed from features that are not. Replacing the dichotomy with a continuum (some traits are more genetically programmed than others) does not solve the conceptual problems; the same inconsistencies are found in such conciliatory-sounding formulations as in strictly dichotomous ones. The other way of construing the genetic program is to declare that the genes determine the range of possibilities. They set the limits on development. As in conventional dualism, the mechanisms whereby the genes supposedly do this are obscure. At any rate, the genes are claimed to determine the norm of reaction (Freedman, 1979, p. 150; Mayr, 1961). Scarr (1981) said the range of reaction is the "expression of the genotype in the phenotype" (p. 16) and that the "genotype has only those degrees of freedom that are inherent in its genes" (p. 17). Although she claimed that it is incorrect to say that "heredity sets the limits on development" (p. 17), that is exactly what is entailed by the notion of genetic degrees of freedom. This is all quite ironic, because the array of phenotypes that could be associated with a given genotype is just the array in which all differences are environmentally determined. The environment, after all, is seen as "selecting" the particular outcome. The norm of reaction is therefore a nice demonstration of the joint determination of the phenotype. Every organism incorporates "information" from genes and environment, in a complex that cannot be partitioned as variance is partitioned. But such mundane truths do not seem to be the point here, but rather a kind of metaphysical urge to contain ontogenetic variety within genetic boundaries.

The problem with this imperialistic version is that it is vacuous: A genotype has just those developmental possibilities that it has. Used this way, the program no longer has empirical content, but is more like a symbol of ultimate faith. Or it may only be a fancy way of saying that potential is finite. In fact, one variant of this idea is "programmed potential" (Mayr, 1961, claimed that "the range of possible variation is itself included in the specifications of the code" of the genetic program, p. 1502). But because the range of possible phenotypes is defined by the set of genotype-environment pairings, what is the point of attributing that range to just one member of the pair? And why insist that the range be fixed at fertilization? Potential must be a *developmental* concept if it is to be useful. It cannot be treated as a fixed quantity somehow inscribed in the genome (Horowitz, 1969; Lewontin, 1984). As many have noted, it is just this idea of fixity that has led people to draw conclusions about intellectual potential, for instance, from heritability figures.

A given genome may certainly have several developmental possibilities. But those possibilities vary with developmental state and context. Traditional notions of maturation, readiness, and embryonic competence turn on the realization that possibilities must emerge in ontogenesis. A bee larva has at one moment the potential to become a queen or a worker. A short time later the worker-to-be may no longer aspire to royalty. Its genes are the same, but its effective potential has changed. Similarly, a dominant female cleaner fish ordinarily looks forward to an entire life as a female. Should the male in her group die, however, she becomes a fully functional male within weeks (Lerner & Libby, 1976). Potential does not always diminish over time. A phenotype *develops,* a fact that the concept of genetically programmed potential purports to explain but actually ignores..

One can, of course, attribute to the genome a higher level potential for all these potentials, but as previously noted, this is simply to affirm that all possible developmental outcomes are possible. (It is worth noting that this cannot distinguish adaptive outcomes from nonadaptive ones, normal ones from pathological or idiosyncratic ones.) The claim that the genes circumscribe potential reminds me of a ploy used by the powerful when they realize that power must be shared, if only minimally: Delimit the scope of choice, then let the other choose within fixed, non-negotiable boundaries. "It's time for bed; which pajamas do you want to wear?"[2]

---

[2]The notion of programmatic control probably reflects the technocratic zeal of early systems thinkers (Haraway, 1981–1982; Taylor, in press; Yoxen, 1981) better than it does the

## DEEP PROBLEMS, SUPERFICIAL SOLUTIONS

The difficulties with these conceptions of development have not gone unnoticed. Changes have tended to be cosmetic, however, for a number of reasons.

### Shared Beliefs

Evolution, first of all, is so firmly identified with the genes—gene pools, selfish genes, genetic information—that any attempt to call attention to other aspects of evolution or to question conventional definitions of inheritance are immediately seen as some sort of Lamarckian attack on scientific biology. (See Sapp, 1987, on geneticists' success in imposing genocentric definitions of evolution and heredity. He showed how they used the image of a genetic control center simultaneously to describe cellular activity and their own powerful position in science.)

In addition, so much thought and research are rooted in the nature–nurture tradition that it is difficult to think in different ways. There is a shared belief that it is proper, even necessary, to contrast inner genetic sources of form and change with outer environmental ones. "The biological" is seen to be more real, more basic, more normal, more difficult to change then "the psychological" or "the cultural." We have already seen that the various criteria for designation as biological or inherited do not form a coherent set, although their incompatibilities are easily glossed over when they are referred to by the same terms.

We continue to distinguish necessary inner essence from contingent outer appearance. Consider the oppositions that have been so important in the behavioral sciences: instinct versus learning, maturation versus experience, inborn personality traits versus acquired ones, to name a few. Kenneth Kaye (1982, p. 4) listed some of the "great issues" that psychologists have attempted to resolve by studying human infancy. They range from the pedagogical to the theological, and they are all cast in traditional nature–nurture terms. If one such distinction is questioned, minor local adjustments may ensue, but the complex interweavings of these ideas in our thought and practice make more serious change unlikely. Frequently, the "versus" is changed to "and" or "interacts with" and the problem is considered solved. (Many examples of this are found in Magnusson and Allen, 1983, where authors refer to combinations of innate and environmental factors, the interaction of biology and learning, and so on, all in the

---

reciprocal, distributed control that characterizes a dynamic system. For descriptions of the latter, see M. C. Bateson (1972) and Fogel and Thelen (1987).

service of an "interactional perspective.") Although the cooperation these phrases imply is more pleasant than the oppositional tone of earlier formulations, the dichotomy remains. Hence, the need to distinguish my views from this kind of conventional interactionism. Given the age and ramification of those habits of thought, it is no wonder that small changes to vocabulary or theory are so easily assimilated to dichotomous views.

Two kinds of phenomena raised serious questions for the logic of programming explanations. One was species-typical learning and the other was adaptive variation. As we see here, however, these "bugs" in the genetic program were integrated into traditional thought with minimal discomfort.

## Programmed Variation

Complex behavior that is difficult to account for by learning (e.g., instinct) has traditionally been "explained" by the genes. So has reliable, closely orchestrated development (e.g. maturation). Although the concept of instinct has often been questioned, that of internally driven maturation has largely escaped scrutiny, probably because nativists and empiricists alike shared basic beliefs about physical development (Oyama, 1982). The most rabid behaviorist, after all, requires a body and a reliable set of operants and reflexes to begin a conditioning story. Still, researchers eventually realized that some learning was species-typical, and indeed, was crucial to many "instincts" (avian imprinting is the classical case, but see also Hailman, 1969).[3] This threatened the traditional rendering of instinct as unlearned and of learning as arbitrarily variable. The resolution proposed by some theorists, however, involved *not* a reconsideration of the notion of genetic programming, but an *increase* in the scope of the program. Not only are bodies and unlearned behavior in the genes, but now some learning is in there, too.

Attempts of some theorists to replace the innate-acquired distinction with closed and open programs or with inherited ranges of possible forms (Lorenz, 1965, 1977; Mayr, 1961), or innate, genetically determined epigenetic rules (Lumsden & Wilson, 1981) only blur the distinction between traditionally conceived nature and nurture when they should be questioning the very basis of that distinction. Typical of this approach is Fishbein's (1976) description of "canalized" learning as genetically preprogrammed development, but many others have made similar attempts to reconcile

---

[3]Instinct belongs to a whole set of concepts that mix evolutionary issues (the behavior is the product of natural selection) with developmental ones (it arises spontaneously, with no guidance from the environment, is resistant to variations in experience). One of my prime concerns is to show that an evolutionary perspective does not require this conflation.

species-typical learning with the ideal of genetic control (Freedman, 1979; Gould, 1982; Shatz, 1985; see Johnston's, in press, critique of innate templates in avian song learning). Perhaps these efforts are unsurprising in light of the fact that "species-typical," and more often, "species-specific" became euphemisms for "instinctive" and "innate" in the discourse of workers who did not realize that conceptual improvement takes more than an adjustment of the lexicon. (An even more recent example of such hedging is the ubiquitous term, *constraint.)* Such maneuvers unfortunately tend to be seen as the leading edge of developmental theory, where an "evolutionary perspective" too often means making more and more refined nature–nurture distinctions while attributing more and more to the formative, directive powers of the genes. These theorists claim to be eliminating the nature–nurture dichotomy, but in reality they are simply renaming it and shifting phenomena from one side of it to the other.

In parallel to the inclusion of some learning in the concept of instinct, some investigators (Lorenz, 1977; Mayr, 1961, 1976; see Oyama, 1985, chap. 4 and 5, for critique) saw that any idea of species-typical development would have to include the possibility of branching pathways, to accommodate certain kinds of adaptive variation (alternative morphologies or behavior patterns). External events, that is, often intrude into the supposedly autonomous maturational sequence to move the organism onto one or another path.

So we see that learning can be necessary for the development of behavior usually defined by the absence of learning (instinct) and branching is inherent in development usually considered unilinear (maturation). This shows the impossibility of consistently categorizing developmental phenomena as innate or learned. Putting them on a continuum defined by varying amounts of genetic control does not solve the problem, but rather multiplies it. The hazards of switching from one definition of innateness to another were pointed out in the discussion of Tinbergen's "whys"; in some of the work cited previously we see the consequences of confusing innate-as-species-typical, innate-as-predetermined, innate-as-conferring-survival-advantage, innate-as-unlearned, innate-as-having-an-evolutionary-history, and innate-as-independent-of-the-environment. These failures of consistency could have challenged the conceptual framework of developmental dualism. Instead, the offending phenomenon in each case was simply assimilated to the old system. Thus, we now had genetically programmed learning and genetically programmed developmental branching. The apparent adaptiveness of these violations of ontogenetic autonomy, as well as their selectivity and presumed evolutionary histories, all compelled workers to find a way to attribute them to the genes, even though this necessitated finessing the Central Dogma of development (that biology is created exclusively by the outward flow of genetic information). These efforts, however well-meaning, are finally just superficial responses to profound conceptual problems. That such phenomena can be treated nondualistically is evidenced by Caro and Bateson's (1986) analysis of alternative tactics.

## Local and Global Change

We need to rethink certain phenomena as well as the reasons for, and meanings of, different kinds of inquiry. Even minimal rethinking can help, but piecemeal progress is risky. The unexamined assumptions we sweep under the rug will trip us up as soon as we turn around.

Eliminating the kinds of erroneous cross-inference just described would be an example of low-level improvement. Although Lamb, Pleck, Charnov, and Levine (1985) characterize their research on parenting in human males as biological, for instance, they emphasize variation with context, not fixity. They rightly deny that evolution must bring invariance and immutability. One wishes for more, however. They do not abandon the notion of "hardwired predispositions," and term them *physiological* (p. 886). What happens when sex differences, for instance, are discovered by methods like hormonal assays or evoked potentials? Are they then "hardwired" because physiological? Unanalyzed terms like these are the lumps lurking under their carpet, inviting us all to stumble.

Local improvement, then, is of local utility. Progress on a broader front involves reworking whole networks of concepts and whole patterns of reasoning, not just refining a term here and there. This involves going beyond the dualism that allows Lamb et al. (1985) to comment that social conditions can either "override" biological predispositions or "reinforce" them (p. 888), and to present biology and the environment, as so many do nowadays, as "complementary" (p. 886). It also involves clarifying the scope of one's research. These authors claim to be following Tinbergen, but by treating behavior as "decisions" made in some context and based on the goal of maximizing fitness, they treat a function as a proximate cause, an error Tinbergen (1963) explicitly warned against. They give no evidence that fitness is actually maximized by the variations in human parenting they review, and do not make clear just what they hope to establish. Having relinquished the definition of biology as fixity, they seem to be uncertain about just what it does mean. Evolved behavior may indeed vary with context; this certainly does not mean that all behavior that varies with context is evolved.

In a more sophisticated account, Kaye (1982) spoke of aspects of the social environment being inherited by an infant. He noted that much

experience is ensured by evolutionary history, and described early development as being intensely social. He asserted that it is often more informative
to look, not at the child as an isolated individual, but at the child as a part
of a larger system, in which an adult may play "cognitive" roles that the
child is not yet ready to perform. (See also Rogoff & Wertsch, 1984, on
Vygotsky's concept of "zone of proximal development.") He sees many
universal skills as constructed in interaction, rather than revealed in
maturation. Yet Kaye is quite happy to speak of the abilities the infant
brings to early infancy as innate, maturing "according to the designs of the
genetic program" (p. 17). He explicitly excluded from psychology the study
of maturation, which is "guaranteed by the genotype" (p. 28). (The problem
is not that he attributed the wrong things to maturation, but that he
attributed maturation and innateness to a genetic program.) He also
criticized those who liken development to a train ride "in which the very
process of the journey is determined by its destination. . . . because it
suggests that the child knows where he is headed" (pp. 15–16). Ironically
enough, the intrinsic genetic program is an explanation-by-destination in
which it is not the child who knows where he is headed, but his genes.

Kaye rejected some nativist accounts of human development, charging
that those who overestimate the functions present at birth "try to explain
away some of the mysteries that have led so many psychologists to begin
looking at infants in the first place" (p. 31). But the concept of innateness
does just that. (Kuo, 1922, also made this point about the concept of
instinct.) Kaye's assertion that infants "inherit certain aspects of their social
environments as much as they inherit their nervous systems" (p. 8),
although a provocative step in the right direction, revealed the problem.
In my terms, he has mixed developmental *influences* (what I call
"interactants") with developmental *products*. Genes and social environments are inherited interactants. Nervous systems and social skills,
being phenotypic, must develop.

Kaye associated evolution with innateness and so was forced to circumscribe his interactionism. ("Innate behavior" is cross-referenced under
"Evolution" in the index.) The "genetically determined behavioral tendencies" of parents, then, are inherited biologically, while the rest is inherited
by the mechanisms of cultural evolution (pp. 24–25). Kaye's attempt to
reconcile the role of experience in development with evolution is a com-
mendable one. If he had applied his constructivist thinking to the concepts
of innate behavior and maturation as well as to social development, his
book would not have required the developmental dualism that now
permeates it. Later, I mention some nondualistic research on the developmental role of naturally occurring experiences. It is true, as Kaye said, that
developmental psychologists seek a set of "givens" with which to begin their
inquiries, but there is a difference between taking a set of abilities as given

at some age and attributing them to a particular kind of developmental process.[4]

## DEVELOPMENT AND EVOLUTION

Evolution is change in the constitution and distribution of developmental systems. The study of ontogeny is not a poor relative that must be lent evolutionary legitimacy by genetic hook or crook, but rather the very heart of evolution. Transgenerational stability and change are of the essence in evolution. They depend on the degrees of reliability of developmental processes and a large array of means for repeated ontogenetic constructions. Research on transgenerational continuity should thus be central to evolutionary studies.

When constructive interaction is seen to be fundamentally important for the formation (not just the support) of *all* features, including "biological" ones, then the role of the environment is not complementary to that of biology. It is constitutive of it in much the same way the genes are. This allows a more global reorientation to living organization, one that goes far beyond the local improvements just cited. Attention can be focused on the way any influence is (or is not) integrated into a developmental system, rather than on partitioning the organism according to the role "biology," however construed, is imagined to play in forming it. West and King (1987) have developed an idea of the "ontogenetic niche" that is very close to my developmental system (Oyama, 1982, 1985; see also Johnston, 1982, and the "developmental manifold" of Gottlieb, 1971). They suggest, "ask not what's inside the genes you inherited, but what the genes you inherited are inside of," and advocate studying the niche as a link between generations.

For those who want to approach evolution by linking development with another of Tinbergen's whys, the usual markers of inheritance and innateness will not suffice, for they are part of a tradition of reasoning that has outlived its usefulness (see Klama, 1988, on the relations between the biological and social sciences). No more attempts to distinguish features formed in phylogeny from those formed in ontogeny. No more searches for genetic plans for morphology or behavior.

Both these strategies, looking at developmental links between generations and relating development to the questions of function or evolutionary history, can generate interesting research. They are not mutually exclusive,

---

[4]Not too long ago I heard a developmental psychologist say that certain cognitive abilities of young children were "maturational." I asked her what she meant by that word. Evidently thinking I was objecting to an "extreme" position, she said, "Well, nothing's *completely* maturational." When I persisted in asking what the word *meant,* she finally retorted, with exemplary candor, "I mean it's present by the age of one, it's very complicated, and I don't want to think about it!"

and both involve a willingness to investigate phenomena that tend to disappear when the language of programming is used. Indeed, one could say that whenever a program is invoked, a developmental question is being ignored, or worse, being given a spurious answer.

## Links among Generations

Later, I describe the successive levels of developmental systems, from the nucleus out. Any research that sheds light on the way variations at any level originate could potentially help us understand how systems come to be. Any research that shows how processes can be faithfully repeated across generations could help us understand how systems persist. Most of a developmental system, after all, remains unchanged in the face of evolutionary alteration. The genetic links between ontogeny and phylogeny mentioned earlier in this essay are necessary but not sufficient: The genes alone cannot give rise to the next generation. Although most life cycles narrow to a single cell (Bonner, 1974), and although theoretical accounts often reduce that cell to naked DNA, the developmental system is much more extensive. Its ramified complexity is just what allows such drastic narrowing of the organismic part of the cycle.

A first step in extending the developmental system beyond the gene is appreciating the inheritance of complex cellular structures and constituents (Sapp's, 1987, history of research on cytoplasmic inheritance is called *Beyond the Gene*). Recognizing the integration of mammalian embryonic development into the maternal physiological system is a second (Cohen, 1979; Hofer, 1981b, p. 224, on the mammalian mother as "an external physiological regulatory agent"—external to the infant, but a crucial and very reliable part of the developmental system). Looking at the dependence of development on the organism's own activity and its interactions with conspecifics takes us even further out. Biochemical and even social interaction with parents or siblings can begin before birth or hatching (Gandelman, vom Sall, & Reinisch, 1977, on the influence of fetal position on development of mice and Gottlieb, 1978, on the effect of prehatching experience in ducklings) and can obviously be of great importance later as well (Johnston & Gottlieb, 1985; Lickliter & Gottlieb, 1985).

Of great utility here is Gottlieb's (1976) concept of bidirectional relationships among gene action, physiology, function and social influences. The principle is nicely demonstrated in Vandenbergh's (1987) account of the regulation of mouse puberty by other mice. Vandenbergh's paper also serves as a model for relating individual and population levels. A good account of many infant-parent relationships is found in Cairns' (1979) text, which shows the multiple ways investigators may fruitfully move among different fields. The same book is full of illustrations of the social embeddedness of development, and thus, of the ways that similarity across generations may be maintained or compromised. This is also true of research on the transgenerational perpetuation of behavioral sex differences in rodents (Moore, 1984) and of food preferences and other behavioral patterns in a wide range of species (Galef, 1976). Similarly, Trevarthen (1982, p. 77) showed how human infants' "mental partnership with caretakers" extends their abilities to act. He commented ironically on the idea of the "isolated thinker" and declared that infants "must *share* to know" (p. 81). These are all examples of developmental research that highlights the *connectedness* of the emerging organism to its surroundings, not its insulation from them.

It seems to me that much of this research comes from an appreciation of systemic complexity and a realization that one must move an investigation beyond the boundaries of the organism in order to understand the organism fully. This ability to see links and intimate interchanges with the surround as developmentally fundamental is not part of developmental psychology's conventional focus on individuals, despite frequent references in the literature to "transactions" between children and the environment (or between genotypes and environment, Scarr, 1981, or between nature and nurture, Plomin, 1986, p. 20.) Often, such work on developmental interactions is seen as environmentalist or behaviorist, and thus opposed to "biological" approaches (Furth, 1974; Gould, 1982, 1985; Lockard, 1971; Lorenz, 1965, pp. 3–4). These charges obviously rest on developmental dualism. Although it is true that such research shows the importance of environmental structure, as well as highlighting many possibilities for developmental variation, it is in no way anti- or nonbiological. On the contrary, it illuminates the very phenomena that programming language "explains away"; it shows some of the many ways biology *works*. It certainly does not signal a belief in blank slates. Indeed, in order to move toward a systems view one must realize how bad this metaphor of a slate really is. The conflict over whether it is environmental features or genetic messages that are impressed on the organism reveals the profound similarities between empiricist and nativist views. Both are committed to a notion of development as imposition, not interactive emergence.

The association of biology with necessity and uniformity is indeed mistaken, as the believers in programmed variation realize. To understand how uniformity and variation are constructed in real lives, however, the metaphor of the program, the internal inscription, is no substitute for real investigation. I doubt that the sorts of research mentioned here could have been conceived by people who were still in thrall to dualistic thought. Although they vary in the consistency with which they avoid nature–nurture oppositions, these workers have all acknowledged the fundamental role of organism–environment interchanges in the most basic developmental processes.

## Links to Function and Evolution

We turn now from ecological, physiological, and behavioral links between the generations to theoretical links among Tinbergen's four whys. If questions about immediate causation and development are clearly distinguished from questions about evolution or survival advantage, it is possible to seek ways to relate them to each other. Ronald Oppenheim (1980), for instance, showed the functional significance of many ontogenetic phenomena (see also Turkewitz & Kenny, 1982). Patrick Bateson (1979, 1984, 1987; Caro & Bateson, 1986) has persistently interpreted development functionally, as have most of the workers cited in the preceding few paragraphs.

Knowledge of the natural history of the species in question is clearly useful in making such functional connections. When we are the species in question, however, special problems arise. Not only is human variability notorious, but the whole notion of a single natural history for our own species is equivocal. Charting a path through contemporary and historical variation in ways of living is simple only if one is willing to ignore a great deal and to make some arbitrary choices. The preoccupation with reliable life cycles has too often been part of a desire to discover a single, transcultural, and ahistorical human nature, a "biological base" that would unify diversity. But Voorzanger (1987, p. 51) pointed out that evolutionary history does not provide a conception of human nature or give us moral guidance. Instead, "we have to know ourselves in order to give an evolutionary reconstruction of our behavior."

Seeing natures as developmental products, and thus phenotypic rather than genotypic, turns us away from the search for transcendent reality, back to the processes and products of development. Much work remains to be done on the proper relationships between data and constructs in these investigations, and it is my conviction that the nature–nurture opposition, long a dominant heuristic in many fields, is more often a hindrance than a help in this endeavor.

## INTERACTION IN ONTOGENY:
## SOURCES OF VARIATION,
## SOURCES OF FORM

Current notions of genetic information are unable to account for single developmental pathways, much less alternative phenotypes. Under developmental analysis, any ontogenetic course resolves to multiple pathways at the cellular level. In normal embryological differentiation a single genotype is involved in the development of many types of cells and organs; again we have a "norm of reaction." The variation in cell types is largely environmentally determined (involving the immediate environment of the genes and cells), and all outcomes are jointly determined as developmental processes generate a multitude of transient environments. The genotype–phenotype mapping is complex, contextually and developmentally contingent and indeterminate.[5]

Similar problems exist with the notion of information in the environment. A given event carries different "information" for different organisms, and for the same organism in different states. The tenderly proprietary smile is at one moment a welcome sign of love, whereas a year later it threatens entrapment. On one day a gaping chick provokes parental feeding, whereas a month later the same gape stimulates a reaction that means, loosely, "Go feed yourself." In each case the "information" conveyed by one organism depends on the context and on the history and state of the organism that is interpreting it.

The only way to use the idea of developmental information effectively is to detach it from the notion that ontogenesis is a conduit for the transmission of messages. Developmental interactants are informational not by "carrying" context-independent messages about phenotypes, but by having an impact on ontogenetic processes—by making a difference. Sometimes those differences are perceptible in a naturally occurring array, as they are in a set of clones in different environments. In other cases the arrays must be created experimentally; this is the way contributions to normal development are usually investigated. The research of Gilbert Gottlieb and his colleagues (1976; Johnston & Gottlieb, 1985; Lickliter & Gottlieb, in press) on nonobvious influences on development, including self-stimulation, shows how inadequate it is to regard the developmental environment as supportive but not formative of species characteristics. Much earlier in development, electrical currents generated by the embryo seem to be an important form of self-stimulation (Jaffe & Stern, 1979).

Information is a difference that makes a difference (G. Bateson, 1972, p.

---

[5]Wilhelm Johannsen's genotype–phenotype distinction was intended to be an antidote to the deterministic, particulate notions of heredity as "transmission" (Sapp, 1987, pp. 37–50). Traits were not inherited, genes were. Johannsen opposed "the Weismannian mechanism and reductionism concealed within the corpuscular theory of heredity." Ironically enough, his distinction "offered geneticists the conceptual space or route by which they could bypass the organization of the cell, regulation by the internal and external environment of the organism, and the temporal and orderly sequences during development" (p. 49). With hindsight, I suggest that this misuse of Johannsen's idea was virtually inevitable in light of his limitation of heredity to only part of the causal system needed for development.

315). The concept of the developmental system allows us to distinguish between genetic and environmental variation that makes a difference (generates developmental "information") and variation that does not. But the distinction can only be made with reference to the rest of the system, and thus may vary with it.

We can speak, then, of genetically or environmentally determined variation, but not of genetically or environmentally determined traits. The fact that the difference between two cell types is due to extracellular conditions does not make the cells "environmentally determined" any more than a trait that shows heritable variation in a population is "genetically determined." Phenotypic "messages" are constructed in interaction. This is true whether we study species-characteristic development, as Piagetians do, or species-variable ones, as students of temperament or personality do. Constructivist interactionism, that is, should not be associated only with variability or mutability. It is not, as previously noted, a codeword for environmentalism; nor does it signify some overarching preoccupation with "plasticity."

Interactions between chemicals, between tissues, between organisms, and between an organism and the inanimate environment are parts of the developmental system, and the immediate context of the interaction may be as important as the identity of the interactants. For some animals, "context" is not restricted to physical environment. Interpretation of the situation is crucial. Consider the change in effective context when a subject of the television program Candid Camera realizes what is going on. Or think of the dilemma of the psychologist who wonders whether subjects simulating some social process are a good model for what occurs outside the laboratory. The question is really about what situation the subjects are in, and inspection of the room, even through a one-way mirror, will not necessarily give the answer.

The vocabulary of interactionism has been widely adopted, but the full implications of a constructivist interactionism have not been accepted nearly as readily as its terminology. Taking interactionism seriously means rejecting the Central Dogma as a metaphor for the control of development, even for development of the body. (Notice that this metaphorical notion of information flow is quite independent of the question of reverse translation in molecular biology.) The one-way causation it implies is inconsistent with the reciprocal, multiple causation actually observed in vital processes. Interaction requires a two-way "exchange" of information: Genetic and organismic activity are informed by conditions, even as they inform those conditions. This is nothing more than the bidirectionality so commonly invoked by developmental psychologists today. My complaint is not with the concept, but with the fact that often it is not taken seriously enough.

## WHAT IS INHERITED?

Traditional gene-for-trait language implies a kind of preformationist embryology, and so do updated, facelifted versions. But does the inheritance of discrete genes require the inheritance of traits, in what Cohen (1979) called the "jigsaw" model of development?[6] My answer is obviously that it does not, but the language of selfish genes, of genetic programs and encoded traits, tends to collapse the distinction. It does so by treating the gene as a homunculus that makes body parts and mental structures according to a prior plan.

Some have suggested that we handle the growing dissent over these issues by further separating evolutionary from developmental questions (Dawkins, 1983). It is true that questions about evolutionary adaptiveness are not the same as questions about how a particular adaptive structure is constructed in ontogeny. But the fields have been estranged for too long. The solution is not to keep them apart even more assiduously, but to synthesize them by shifting our focus from the gene as the unit of evolution and the agent of programmed development to the concept of the evolving developmental system. That is, we must widen our concepts of inheritance and of ontogeny, to include other developmental interactants as well; no organism can develop without them all. Evolution involves change in the system constituents and their relations within it.

### Transmission

A major step in this opening out of crucial concepts is the reconsideration of the notion of transmission. Accounts of gene-culture coevolution (Boyd & Richerson, 1985; Durham, 1979; Lumsden & Wilson, 1981) use the model of trait transmission for culture as well as for biology. They seek to remedy the shortcomings of purely genetic theories. By adding a second transmission channel, however, they also continue the tradition of developmental dualism that ensures those shortcomings. In addition, they retain, and extend, the population geneticists' habit of taking genes out of organisms and placing them in mathematically manageable "pools": They concentrate on the countable while taking for granted the processes that generate and regenerate these countable entities. (See Keller, 1987, on the way this tactic

---

[6]Modern evolutionists rely heavily on Weismann's separation between transmission and development. Brian Goodwin (1985) described Weismann's "radically dualist" conception of the organism: a "generative and immortal germ plasm and a transient, mortal somatoplasm which was effectively the adult organism." Transmitted germ particles "stood in a specifically causal relation to a particular part of the organism" (p. 46). Goodwin also observed that with the advent of molecular biology this atomistic view was perpetuated with the concept of the genetic program.

serves the ideology of individualism.) Now we have pools of culture as well, and the repeated and varying life cycles of the organisms themselves are treated as virtually epiphenomenal *effects* of the differential propagation of units from these two pools. But as I have insisted, traits are not transmitted, developmental influences are (Oyama, 1988, in press). Our inheritance does include culture, not as a second set of traits, transmitted via an extragenetic conduit, but as aspects of the developmental context. Hofer (1981a) pointed out the inadequacy of the ideas of genetic and cultural evolution in accounting for all sorts of prenatal effects, and Voorzanger (in press) maintained as do I, that an evolutionary theory that included a rich enough account of development would have no need of a second transmission system. In fact, the very idea of transmission would be transformed, since an adequate account of development renders the conventional conceptions meaningless.

The transmission metaphor denies development. If it is development that we are interested in, then we should choose a vocabulary that takes it seriously. Other people's ideas, actions, values, habits, and beliefs are part of the rich complex of developmental influences from which lives are constructed. So are the genes, and so, as noted here, is much, much more. Whether any given *trait* will be reconstructed in any particular generation is a contingent matter, for it depends on the constitution and functioning of an entire system. Stability of species characteristics is due to stability of developmental systems. This does not depend on absolute reliability of all interactants; some processes are stable despite considerable variation in their constituents, and some outcomes may be stable despite variation in process. Developmental systems are hierarchically organized. They can be studied on many levels, and interrelations among the levels are crucial. (See Salthe, 1985, for an attempt to formalize relationships among levels.)

Developmental biologists speak of cytoplasmic inheritance, of extragenetic changes in cell structure that can be propagated in a lineage, just as certain genetic changes can (Cohen, 1979; Sapp, 1987). Even though variations in a cell can be inherited in this way, invariant features of cell structure are passed on, too, just as the genes common to an entire species are passed on. The rest of the normal environment is also quite reliably present (that is what it *means* to be a normal environment), and when it is not present, some other environment is.[7] Biologists also speak of cell state

---

[7]It is our genocentrism that forces us to group phenomena of such different scale as "the environment." When DNA is the center of the universe, everything else is just surround. Cohen (1979) spoke of the indifference of "DNA-is-God-and-RNA-is-his-prophet molecular biologists" and geneticists to the complexity of the egg; they tended to consider it merely a passive haploid awaiting penetration by another haploid. Embryologists were more impressed by the role of egg structures. We see again the depth of Hamburger's nucleocytoplasmic gap. Cohen is interested in *reproduction,* and it is not an interest that can be satisfied by the equations of

being stably "inherited" (Alberts et al., 1983, p. 835); the key here is not change in genetic material, but transgenerational stability of the cell type. There are, in other words, both species-typical aspects of developmental systems and variations in those systems, both genetic and nongenetic, and an organism inherits the entire complex. The fact that we daily acknowledge the indispensability of both genes and surround to the development of all characteristics and yet continue to attribute some of that development mostly to the genes and some to "other factors" suggest that our theoretical vocabulary has not kept up with our observations. Both evolutionary and developmental studies remain largely genocentric (Goodwin, 1984).

What passes from one generation to the next is an entire developmental system. Heredity is not an *explanation* of this process, but a statement of that which must be explained (see previous discussion of links between generations). The concept of evolving developmental systems gives us a unified view of development while integrating it with evolution. Dualism is no longer required; the inherited-acquired distinction, *as long as it is construed as a distinction between kinds of developmental processes or sources of form,* can be eliminated — not modified or turned into a matter of degree, but eliminated.[8]

Ontogenetic means are inherited, phenotypes are constructed. This enlargement of the idea of inheritance seems outrageous to minds trained to identify it with the genes, but I am only making explicit what is routinely taken for granted. No one claims that genes alone are sufficient for development, or denies that environments, organic and inorganic, microscopic and macroscopic, internal and external, change over organismic and generational time. What is missing from most accounts is the synthetic processes of ontogenetic construction.[9]

---

population genetics. It is just the rich complication of reproductive processes, Keller (1987) argued, that population genetics manages to ignore. In fact, the disembodying of genes facilitates the elision of some of the messier aspects of reproduction, among them the fact that organisms very rarely "reproduce themselves" — biparental contributions make "reproduction" a misnomer.

The integration of developmental processes renders problematic even the experimental separation of environment from genes. Raising genetically dissimilar organisms in the "same" environment and attributing their differences to the genes alone either ignores the effects of the different *effective* environment or manages to see them as proof of the organizing power of the genome (see footnote 9).

[8]Wimsatt (1986) presented a developmental version of the distinction, but he performed rather radical surgery on the concept in order to do so.

[9]It is important to avoid the genetic imperialist impulse here. Scarr and McCartney (1983) point out the importance of experience in development, as well as the role of the child in influencing and selecting its experiences. Then they virtually eliminate the child by attributing agency to its genes: "genotypes are the driving force behind development"; the "impetus" for the experiences necessary for development comes "from the genotype" (p. 428). Ironically, they

Inheritance is not atomistic but systematic and interactive. It is not limited to genes, or even to germ cells, but includes developmentally relevant aspects of the surround, and "surround" may be narrowly or broadly defined, depending on the scope of the analysis. Inheritance can only be identified with "nature" if it embraces all contributors to nature, and nature does not reside in genes or anywhere else until it emerges in the phenotype-in-transition. Nature is thus not properly contrasted with nurture in the first place; it is the product of a continual process of nurture.

Having redefined inheritance in this way, we must also redefine ontogeny. This is difficult for behavioral scientists, who are used to squabbling over degrees of biological programming of personality or behavior but who tend to take programming of the body for granted. (Recall the incomplete interactionism discussed in the section on "Superficial Responses.") Although there may be doubt, that is, about whether sex roles or aggression are in the genes, there is usually no doubt at all that sex organs, teeth and claws are. But the unidirectional flow of genetic information doesn't account for a tooth or a claw, red as it may be, any better than it accounts for the most idiosyncratic behavior. The developmental system, on the other hand, accounts for the emerging phenotype in a way the naked genome cannot.

## Developmental Systems

People sometimes fear that the concept of the developmental system requires them to give up too much, but in fact it only eliminates a confused set of assumptions and inferential habits. Many of the issues formerly associated with the false opposition between nature and nurture (or biology and culture) can still be addressed, but this time clearly formulated and properly distinguished from others. Some are largely evaluative (many concepts of normality, for instance) and are answerable not solely by empirical investigation but by moral discourse as well. If this conceptual unpacking is performed, we will be less likely than we have been in the past to make faulty predictions, to draw illegitimate conclusions from our data, to posit distinctions where there should be none.

The developmental system is a mobile set of interacting influences and entities. It includes all influences on development, at all levels of analysis. Any particular investigation will obviously focus on a limited portion of the system. For an embryologist, the scale of cells and organs defines the investigative field, and higher level aspects of the system can generally be taken for granted. In some cases, as we have seen, it becomes useful to pay attention to other factors as well, for the wider environment may also

---

employ the phrase, "developmental system" (p. 433) while insisting on the primacy of the gene, describing a "system" that is radically different from the one I present.

intrude; witness the effects of radiation or of various chemicals on embryogeny, or other ways in which the experience of a mother may affect her offspring or even grandoffspring (Denenberg & Rosenberg, 1967; Hofer, 1981b, chap. 10).

Even though it is easy to think of many perturbations of this early developmental system (often mediated through the parents), it is essential to realize that the aspects of the environment that do *not* vary are hardly rendered developmentally irrelevant by virtue of their reliability. Gravity usually does not vary, but in its absence, bone and muscle may atrophy, possibly because the pituitary produces insufficient growth hormone. The relevance of this finding to the possibilities of life in space are obvious ("Results of rat tests" Oct. 15, 1985). Many of these broader ecological factors (topography, atmospheric composition, patterns of vegetation, temperature, and humidity) have changed over evolutionary time, sometimes as a result of their interaction with life forms. The system changes over the life cycle and is reconstituted in successive generations in ways that are similar to, but not necessarily identical with, preceding ones. This is the only way to have inheritance of genetic material (and other interactants) without being stuck with inheritance of traits.

Examples of interactants in developmental systems include:

1. The genome, whose parts interact and even more about in ways now being described by molecular biologists (see papers in Milkman, 1982; Dillon's, 1983, book is called, *The Inconstant Gene).*
2. Cell structure, including organelles, some of which have their own distinctive DNA, and may originally have been internal symbionts (Margulis, 1981).
3. Intracellular chemicals, some of which (messenger RNA from previous generations, for instance) may allow considerable developmental progress before the organism's own genes are transcribed at all (Raff & Kaufman, 1983).
4. Extracellular environment — mechanical, hormonal, energetic — parts of which, like the extracellular matrix, are created by the cell itself or by other cells.
5. Parental reproductive system, both physiological and behavioral; prenatal effects are common, and cross-fostering experiments can show dramatic effects of parental behavior, sometimes to the extent of producing behavior quite atypical of the strain or species (Hofer, 1981b, chap. 11).
6. Self-stimulation by the organism itself.
7. Immediate physical environment, including provisions left for young, as when eggs are laid on or in a food source.
8. Conspecifics and members of other species with which important interactions take place.

9. Climate, food sources, other aspects of the external environment that may influence the organism, initially through the parents and later directly.

In many life cycles, a variety of factors can bring about the major branchings of the developmental pathway discussed earlier. Other influences contribute to less dramatic variations, including variations in learning and anything else that helps define the norm of reaction. These factors are also part of the developmental systems of these organisms.

## CONCLUSION: NAILS FOR SHOES, NAILS FOR BATTLES, OR WHY WE NEED THE CONCEPT OF THE DEVELOPMENTAL SYSTEM

An old rhyme goes, "For want of a nail the shoe was lost, for want of a shoe the horse was lost, for want of the horse the rider was lost. . . ." Loss of a particular rider could even lead to losing an entire battle. To know whether that nail makes the difference between losing and winning the battle, shouldn't we know what kind of battle it is, on what terrain it is being joined, what the command structure is, and who the opponent is? Even if it could be shown that the loss of a battle were traceable to a lost nail, this would not make the nail an adequate causal explanation for the entire complex of events that constituted the battle. Indeed, it is the entire complex that defines the nail's role.

The nail can only become a nail "for" losing battles in a world that is sufficiently stable and integrated that the entire battle—to say nothing of the geopolitical circtcumstances that led to it—can be recreated with some regularity. A gene is only a gene "for" a given phenotypic difference if other aspects of the ontogenetic complex (not to mention population structure) are fairly stable. Similarly, an environmental feature can only act as a developmental trigger if the system is competent. If these various conditions are reliable, one can take them for granted and predict outcomes with some certainty even without understanding the developmental processes involved. Much nature–nurture questioning may be translated into queries about the constitution and degree of reliability of developmental systems. But a system that is well integrated in some worlds, and that thus tends to appear as a unit in those worlds, may not be similarly unified in others. Prediction, furthermore, is not the same as comprehension.

Evolution is only partly a matter of changing gene pools. It is also a matter of changing developmental contexts, and one cannot be understood without the other. Niches evolve in several senses. Geological, climatic and organic features of an area change over time, partially as a result of the resident organisms. Niches, furthermore, are not definable apart from their organisms (Johnston & Turvey, 1980; Lewontin, 1982), and as a lineage evolves so do its relations with its surround. The niche is the effective, the developmentally or functionally significant environment; an organism may exploit the "same" environment differently at different times.

We return, then, to the struggling, squabbling scientists peering into the shadow box, trying to make sense of their conflicting accounts. If an ambiguous vocabulary and confused concepts are hindering our communication, we must at least clarify our terms. Eventually the goal is the integration of diverse points of view, both within and among people, by cooperative construction. As useful as it often is to use and reuse a heuristic, sometimes it is necessary to break set, restructure the cognitive field and move on.

We must relinquish the Central Dogma's one-way flow of causality, information and form as our guiding metaphor for development. The same is true of the programming metaphors we have taken from computer technology. We must also give them up as the principal framework for our research and interpretation. They do not do justice to any developmental process one investigates with care, whether at the level of macromolecules or of individuals. Although they provide a familiar and comfortable way of interpreting the world, they have outlived whatever usefulness they may once have had.

Just because it is so deeply rooted in our thought and practice, the nature–nurture complex, more than other faulty scientific frameworks, has significant political and moral repercussions far beyond the research community. It has multiple sources in our philosophical history. It influences the classification of individuals in ways that profoundly affect their future. It influences our view of what is possible for individuals and for the species as a whole. Thus, it has an impact on the manner in which we mobilize for maintenance or for change—indeed, whether we mobilize at all. The dichotomization or ranking of traits by the amount of influence the genes are supposed to have implies some traits have special status. More or less unchangeable, independent of experience, apt to appear in all environments, they are thought to define the real, the basic, the inevitable, even the desirable for us.

Viktor Hamburger (1980) said embryology had not been integrated into the neo-Darwinian synthesis that had apparently unified so much of biology. He offered three principle reasons. First, he suggested, evolutionists tended to focus on the outward flow of influence from the nucleus, whereas embryologists focused on the cytoplasm as crucial in determining differential gene activation. Second, the preformationist implications of the notion of particulate inheritance made embryologists uneasy. Third, evolutionists emphasized trait transmission across generations and neglected trait elaboration over the life cycle.

These are still barriers to effective communication between at least some developmentalists and some evolutionists, and they raise thorny problems for those who try to be both at once. (As we have seen, this nucleocentrism is problematic even for those who have no interest in evolution.) Hamburger called for an interactive view to bridge the nucleocytoplasmic gapinto which so much misunderstanding and acrimony have been spilled. I believe this need is met by the constructivist approach described here. It offers a way of speaking about complex transgenerational continuity and variability, about stability and change in both species and individuals, while allowing us to acknowledge the intricacy and contingency of the processes observed in ontogeny, a way to think in evolutionary terms without being committed to a developmental dualism in which contingent nurture is pitted against genetically predetermined nature. We do not need the genetic program in order to have an evolutionary perspective.

## ACKNOWLEDGMENTS

This chapter is based on a number of talks delivered between 1985 and 1987. The most fully elaborated one was delivered at the 22nd Minnesota Symposium. I am grateful to Pat Bateson and Tim Johnston for their comments on earlier drafts, to Megan Gunnar for her suggestions for the final version, and to the Minnesota Institute of Child Development for 3 days of stimulating exchange.

## REFERENCES

Alberts, B., Bray, D., Lewis, J., Raff, M., Roberts, K., & Watson, J. D. (1983). *Molecular biology of the cell*. New York: Garland.

Bateson, G. (1972). *Steps to an ecology of mind*. New York: Ballantine Books.

Bateson, M. C. (1972). *Our own metaphor*. New York: Knopf.

Bateson, P. (1983). Genes, environment and the development of behaviour. In T. R. Halliday & P. J. B. Slater (Eds.), *Animal behavior, Vol. 3, Genes, development, and learning* (pp. 52–81). Oxford: Blackwell Scientific Publications.

Bateson, P. (1987) Biological approaches to the study of behavioural development. *International Journal of Behavioral Development, 10*, 1–22.

Bateson, P. P. G. (1979). How do sensitive periods arise and what are they for? *Animal Behaviour, 27*, 470–486.

Bateson, P. P. G. (1984). Genes, evolution, and learning. In P. Marler & H. S. Terrace (Eds.), *The biology of learning* (pp. 75–88). Berlin: Springer–Verlag.

Bateson, P. P. G. (1985). Problems and possibilities in fusing developmental and evolutionary thought. In G. Butterworth, J. Rutowska, & M. Scaife (Eds.), *Evolution and developmental psychology* (pp. 3–21). Sussex: Harvester Press.

Bonner, J. T. (1974). *On development*. Cambridge, MA: Harvard University Press.

Boyd, R., & Richerson, P. J. (1985). *Culture and the evolutionary process*. Chicago: University of Chicago Press.

Cairns, R. B. (1979). *Social development: The origins and plasticity of interchanges*. San Francisco: Freeman.

Caro, T. M., & Bateson, P. (1986). Organization and ontogeny of alternative tactics. *Animal Behaviour, 34,* 1483–1499.

Cohen, J. (1979). Maternal constraints on development. In D. R. Newth & M. Balls (Eds.), *Maternal effects in development* (pp. 1–28). Cambridge: Cambridge University Press.

Connor, J. M., Schackman, M., & Serbin, L. A. (1978). Sex-related differences in response to practice on a visual-spatial test and generalization to a related test. *Child Development, 49,* 24–29.

Crick, F. (1957). On protein synthesis. *Symposium of the Society of Experimental Biology, 12,* 138–163.

Dawkins, R. (1983). *The extended phenotype.* Oxford: Oxford University Press.

Dawkins, R. (1986). *The blind watchmaker.* New York: W. W. Norton.

Denenberg, V. H., & Rosenberg, K. M. (1967). Nongenetic transmission of information. *Nature, 216,* 549–550.

Dillon, L. I. (1983). *The inconstant gene.* New York: Plenum Press.

Durham, W. H. (1979). Toward a coevolutionary theory of human biology and culture. In N. A. Chagnon & W. Irons (Eds.), *Evolutionary biology and human social behavior: An anthropological perspective* (pp. 4–39). North Scituate, MA: Duxbury Press.

Fishbein, H. D. (1976). *Evolution, development, and children's learning.* Santa Monica, CA: Goodyear.

Fogel, A., & Thelen, E. (1987). Development of early expressive and communicative action: Reinterpreting the evidence from a dynamic systems perspective. *Developmental Psychology, 23,* 747–761.

Freedman, D. G. (1979). *Human sociobiology: A holistic approach.* New York: The Free Press.

Frodi, A. M., & Lamb, M. E. (1978). Sex differences in responsiveness to infants: A developmental study of psychophysiological and behavioral responses. *Child Development, 49,* 1182–1188.

Furth, H. G. (1974). Two aspects of experience in ontogeny: Development and learning. *Advances in Child Development and Behavior, 9,* 47–67.

Galef, B. G. (1976). Social transmission of acquired behavior: A discussion of tradition and social learning in vertebrates. In J. S. Rosenblatt, R. A. Hinde, E. Shaw, & C. Beer (Eds.), *Advances in the study of behavior* (Vol. 6, pp. 77–100). New York: Academic Press.

Gandelman, R., vom Sall, F. S., & Reinisch, J. M. (1977). Contiguity to male fetuses affects morphology and behavior in female mice. *Nature, 266,* 722–723.

Goodwin, B. C. (1982). Genetic epistemology and constructionist biology. *Revue Internationale de Philosophie. No. 142–143,* 527–548.

Goodwin, B. C. (1984). A relational or field theory of reproduction and its evolutionary implications. In M-W Ho & P. T. Saunders (Eds.), *Beyond neo-Darwinism* (pp. 219–241). London: Academic Press.

Goodwin, B. C. (1985). Constructional biology. In G. Butterworth, J. Rutowska, & M. Scaife (Eds.), *Evolution and developmental psychology* (pp. 45–66). Sussex: Harvester Press.

Gottlieb, G. (1971). *Development of species identification in birds.* Chicago: University of Chicago Press.

Gottlieb, G. (1976). Conceptions of prenatal development: Behavioral embryology. *Psychological Review, 83,* 215–234.

Gottlieb, G. (1978). Development of species identification in ducklings: IV. Change in species-specific perception caused by auditory deprivation. *Journal of Comparative and Physiological Psychology, 92,* 375–387.

Gould, J. L. (1982). *Ethology: The mechanisms and evolution of behavior.* New York W. W. Norton.

Gould, J. L. (1985). Reply to letters from readers. *The Sciences, 25* (6), 15.

Gruber, H. E., & Sehl, I. A. (1984). Transcending relativism and subjectivism: Going beyond the information I am given. In S. Callebant & S. Cozzens (Eds.), *Communication and*

*Cognition* (pp. 57–60). Ghent: George Sarton Centennial.

Hailman, J. (1969). How an instinct is learned. *Scientific American, 221*(6), 98–106.

Hamburger, V. (1980). Embryology and the modern synthesis in evolutionary theory. In E. Mayr & W. B. Provine (Eds.), *The evolutionary synthesis* (pp. 97–112). Cambridge, MA: Harvard University Press.

Haraway, D. J. (1981–1982). The high cost of information in post-World War II evolutionary biology: Ergonomics, semiotics, and the sociobiology of communication systems. *The Philosophical Forum, 13*(2–3), 244–278.

Hofer, M. A. (1981a). Parental contributions to the development of their offspring. In D. J. Gubernick & P. H. Klopfer (Eds.), *Parental care in mammals* (pp. 77–115). New York: Plenum Press.

Hofer, M. A. (1981b). *The roots of human behavior.* San Francisco: W. H. Freeman.

Horowitz, F. D. (1969). Learning, developmental research, and individual differences. In L. P. Lipsitt & H. W. Riesen (Eds.), *Advances in child development and behavior* (Vol. 4, pp. 83–126. New York: Academic Press.

Jacobson, J. L., Boersma, D. C., Fields, R. B., & Olson, K. L. (1983). Paralinguistic features of adult speech to infants and small children. *Child Development, 54,* 436–442.

Jaffe, L. F., & Stern, C. D. (1979). Strong electrical currents leave the primitive streak of chick embryos. *Science, 206,* 569–571.

Johnston, T. D. (1982). Learning and the evolution of developmental systems. In H. C. Plotkin (Ed.), *Learning, development and culture* (pp. 411–442). New York: Wiley.

Johnston, T. D. (1987). The persistence of dichotomies in the study of behavioral development. *Developmental Review, 7,* 149–182.

Johnston, T. D. (in press.). Developmental explanation and the ontogeny of birdsong: nature-nurture redux. *Behavioral and Brain Sciences.*

Johnston, T. D., & Gottlieb, G. (1985). Effects of social experience on visually imprinted maternal preferences in Peking ducklings. *Developmental Psychobiology, 18,* 261–271.

Johnston, T. D., & Turvey, M. T. (1980). A sketch of an ecological metatheory for theories of learning. In G. H. Bower (Ed.), *The psychology of learning and motivation* (Vol. 14, pp. 147–205). New York: Acadmic Press.

Kaye, K. (1982). *The mental and social life of babies.* Chicago: University of Chicago Press.

Keller, E. F. (1987). Reproduction and the central project of evolutionary theory. *Biology and Philosophy, 2,* 73–86.

Klama, J. (1988). *Aggression: The myth of the beast within.* New York: Wiley.

Klopfer, P. (1969). Instincts and chromosomes: What is an "innate" act? *American Naturalist, 103,* 556–560.

Kuo, Z-Y. (1922). How are our instincts acquired? *Psychological Review, 29,* 344–365.

Lakoff, G., & Johnson, M. (1980). *Metaphors we live by.* Chicago: University of Chicago Press.

Lamb, M. E., Pleck, J. H., Charnov, E. L., & Levine, J. A. (1985). Paternal behavior in humans. *American Zoologist, 25,* 883–894.

Lehrman, D. S. (1953). A critique of Konrad Lorenz's theory of instinctive behavior. *Quarterly Review of Biology, 28,* 337–363.

Lehrman, D. S. (1962). Interaction of hormonal and experiential influences on development of behavior. In E. L. Bliss (Ed.), *Roots of behavior* (pp. 142–156). New York: Harper & Brothers.

Lehrman, D. S. (1970). Semantic and conceptual issues in the nature-nurture problem. In L. R. Aronson, E. Tobach, D. S. Lehrman, & J. S. Rosenblatt (Eds.), *Development and evolution of behavior* (pp. 17–52). San Francisco: Freeman.

Lerner, I. M., & Libby, W. J. (1976). *Heredity, evolution and society* (2nd ed.). San Francisco, CA: Freeman.

Lewontin, R. C. (1982). Organism and environment. In H. C. Plotkin (Ed.), *Learning, development, and culture* (pp. 151–170). New York: Wiley.

Lewontin, R. C. (1984). *Human diversity.* San Francisco, CA: Freeman.

Lewontin, R. C., Rose, S., & Kamin, L. J. (1984). *Not in our genes.* New York: Pantheon.

Lickliter, R., & Gottlieb, G. (1985). Social interaction with siblings is necessary for visual imprinting of species-specific maternal preferences in ducklings. *Journal of Comparative Psychology, 99,* 371–379.

Lickliter, R., & Gottlieb, G. (in press). Social specificity: interaction with own species is necessary to foster species-specific maternal preference in ducklings. *Developmental Psychobiology.*

Lockard, R. B. (1971). Reflections on the fall of comparative psychology: Is there a message for us all? *American Psychologist, 26,* 168–179.

Lorenz, K. (1965). *Evolution and modification of behavior.* Chicago, IL: University of Chicago Press.

Lorenz, K. (1977). *Behind the mirror* (R. Taylor, Trans.). New York: Harcourt, Brace & Jovanovich. (Original work published 1973)

Lumsden, C. J., & Wilson, E. O. (1981). *Genes, mind, and culture.* Cambridge, MA: Harvard University Press.

Magnusson, D., & Allen, V. L. (Eds.). (1983). *Human development: An interactional perspective.* New York: Academic Press.

Margulis, L. (1981). *Symbiosis in cell evolution: Life and its environment on the early Earth.* San Francisco: Freeman.

Mayr, E. (1961). Cause and effect in biology. *Science, 134,* 1501–1506.

Mayr, E. (1976). Behavior programs and evolutionary strategies. In E. Mayr (Ed.), *Evolution and the diversity of life* (pp. 694–711). Cambridge, MA: Harvard University Press.

Milkman, R. (Ed.). (1982). *Perspectives on evolution.* New York: Sinauer.

Moore, C. L. (1984). Maternal contributions to the development of masculine sexual behavior in laboratory rats. *Developmental Psychobiology, 17,* 347–356.

Newman, S. A. (1988). Idealist biology. *Perspectives in Biology and Medicine, 31,* 353–368.

Oppenheim, R. W. (1980). Metamorphosis and adaptation in the behavior of developing organisms. *Developmental Psychobiology, 13,* 353–356.

Oyama, S. (1981). What does the phenocopy copy? *Psychological Reports, 48,* 571–581.

Oyama, S. (1982). A reformulation of the idea of maturation. In P. P. G. Bateson & P. H. Klopfer (Eds.), *Perspectives in ethology* (Vol. 5, pp. 101–131). New York: Plenum.

Oyama, S. (1985). *The ontogeny of information.* Cambridge: Cambridge University Press.

Oyama, S. (1988). Stasis, development and heredity. In M-W. Ho & S. Fox (Eds.), *Process and metaphors in the new evolutionary paradigm.* (pp. 255–274) London: Wiley.

Oyama, S. (in press). Transmission and construction: Levels and the problem of heredity. In G. Greenberg & E. Tobach (Eds.), *Critical analyses of evolutionary theories of social behavior: Genetics and levels.* New York: Shapolsky Publishers.

Plomin, R. (1986). *Development, genetics, and psychology,* Hillsdale, NJ: Lawrence Erlbaum Associates.

Raff, R. A., & Kaufman, T. C. (1983). *Embryos, genes, and evolution: The developmental-genetic base of evolutionary change.* New York: Macmillan.

Results of rat tests stir concern for astronauts. (1985, Oct 15). *New York Times,* p. C8.

Rogoff, B., & Wertsch, J. V. (Eds.). (1984). *Children's learning in the "zone of proximal development".* San Francisco: Jossey-Bass.

Rosenthal, P. (1984). *Words & values.* Oxford: Oxford University Press.

Salthe, S. N. (1985). *Evolving hierarchical systems.* New York: Columbia University Press.

Sapp, J. (1987). *Beyond the gene: Cytoplasmic inheritance and the struggle for authority in genetics.* Oxford: Oxford University Press.

Scarr, S. (1981). Genetics and the development of intelligence. In S. Scarr (Ed.), *Race, social class, and individual differences in I. Q.* (pp. 3–59). Hillsdale, NJ: Lawrence Erlbaum Associates.

Scarr, S., & McCartney, K. (1983). How people make their own environments: A theory of genotype→environment effects. *Child Development, 54,* 424–435.

Schneirla, T. C. (1966). Behavioral development and comparative psychology. *Quarterly Review of Biology, 41,* 283–302.

Shatz, M., (1985). An evolutionary perspective on plasticity in language development: A commentary. *Merrill-Palmer Quarterly, 31,* 211–222.

Taylor, P. J. (in press). Technocratic optimism and the partial transformation of ecological metaphor after World War Two. *Journal of the History of Biology.*

Tinbergen, N. (1963). On aims and methods in ethology. *Zeitschrift fuer Tierpsychologie, 20,* 410–433.

Tobach, E. (1972). The meaning of the cryptanthroparion. In L. Ehrman, G. S. Omenn, & E. Caspari (Eds.), *Genetics, environment and behavior* (pp. 219–239). New York: Academic Press.

Tobach, E., & Greenberg, G. (1984). The significance of T. C. Schneirla's contribution to the concept of levels of integration. In G. Greenberg & E. Tobach (Eds.), *Behavioral evolution and integrative levels* (pp. 1–7). Hillsdale, NJ: Lawrence Erlbaum Associates.

Trevarthen, C. (1982). The primary motives for cooperative understanding. In G. Butterworth & P. Light (Eds.), *Social cognition: Studies of the development of understanding* (pp. 77–109). Brighton: Harvester Press.

Turkewitz, G., & Kenny, P. A. (1982). Limitations on input as a basis for neural organization and perceptual development: A preliminary theoretical statement. *Developmental Psychobiology, 15,* 357–368.

Valsiner, J. (1987)., *Culture and the development of children's action.* New York: Wiley.

Vandenbergh, J. G. (1987). Regulation of puberty and its consequences on population dynamics of mice. *American Zoologist, 27,* 891–898.

Voorzanger, B. (1987). No norms and no nature—the moral relevance of evolutionary biology. *Biology and Philosophy, 2,* 39–56.

Voorzanger, B. (in press). Methodological problems in evolutionary biology VIII. Biology and culture. *Acta Biotheoretica.*

West, M. J., & King, A. P. (1987). Settling nature and nurture into an ontogenetic niche. *Developmental Psychobiology, 20,* 549–562.

Wimsatt, W. C. (1986). Developmental constraints, generative entrenchment, and the innate-acquired distinction. In W. Bechtel (Ed.), *Integrating scientific disciplines* (pp. 185–208). Dordrecht: Martinus-Nijhoff.

Yoxen, E. (1981). Life as a productive force: Capitalising the science and technology of molecular biology. In R. M. Young & L. Levidow (Eds.), *Studies in the labour process* (pp. 66–122). London: CSE Books.

# 2
# Developmental Roots of Behavioral Order: Systemic Approaches to the Examination of Core Developmental Issues

John C. Fentress
*Dalhousie University*

## INTRODUCTION: THE DEVELOPMENTAL ORDER

The concept of order is ubiquitous in our views of nature. Where are the important similarities and the important differences in the events we observe? How do these events succeed in showing properties of intrinsic order while also being receptive to their surrounds? By what means do we link levels of order together into a more comprehensive picture? Perhaps most fundamentally, how do we put our views about order into a framework that is in itself dynamically ordered?

There is no more eloquent testimony to the mysteries of such questions than the emergence of order in behavior. Throughout development, the child or animal refines properties of its expression, combines previously isolated properties together into new packages, and opens up new windows of receptivity to its world while closing other windows on the way to establishing a unique individuality. Development is a miracle in the deepest sense of that term. As a middle-aged parent of young children I have had the pleasure to watch this miracle of behavior unfolding in ways that I could neither have predicted nor dictated. As an ethologist working with mammals ranging from mice to wolves, I am continually astounded by the "wisdom of nature" in producing effective and diverse creatures. As an individual who also on occasion wears the hat of neuroscientist, or at least waves the banner of integrative neuroscience, I remain flabbergasted that brains can put themselves together at all—especially under imperfect developmental conditions that often compel the organism to "go beyond the information given" (Bruner, 1974; cf. Chomsky's, 1980, "poverty of the stimulus"). I am equally impressed by the sensitivities of developing systems to environmental events. Even insect nervous systems are sensitive to experience as measured by neuroanatomical, neurophysiological, and behavioral methods (Murphey, 1986). Development is, in brief, a "Grade A" miracle worked out through millions upon millions of years of evolution: trials, successes, and errors. Furthermore, it is a miracle that we are beginning to understand.

There is, of course, a "catch-22" in this understanding. We must recognize in our models of development that it is we, the investigators, who are constructing the rules of order. The ordering of our own brains imposes order on, as well as reflects order from, the developmental events that we study. There is simply no way around this fact. We do not "mirror" in a direct one-to-one sense the order of nature any more than the developing organism "mirrors" in a simple one-to-one fashion the developmental experiences through which it passes (Fentress, 1987b, in press). Both we and our young friends are constantly amplifying, distorting, and elaborating upon those events to which we are exposed. Sometimes it is useful to try out alternative models of order, and to see where the chips fall. This is what I plan to do.

My primary emphasis, by necessity, is that of an ethologist or animal behaviorist. The biases I bring to the study of behavioral development thus are different from many developmentalists. We can see where our ideas clash, where they appear to support one another, and where they are simply moving down separate channels.

## FORMALIZATIONS OF ORDER
## IN BEHAVIOR

### General Perspectives

Fundamental problems related to our concepts of order have occupied philosophers and scientists for centuries. In essence, these problems reflect the difficulties we have in thinking concurrently about separations and cohesions in nature (Fentress, 1987b), and in deciding when we are *reflecting* rather than *imposing* order on nature. Most, if not all scholars, have come to the conclusion that our models of order most often conform to a delicate mixture of the two cases of reflected and imposed order.

Unfortunately, we may have to accept order as derived both from the world outside ourselves and from the world within. The boundary between these two sources of order may never be fully established. I recently attended an exciting conference in Stockholm (Fentress, in press), sponsored jointly by The Neurosciences Institute at The Rockefeller University and the Wenner Gren Institute in Sweden, where a number of prominent neuroscientists attempted to grapple with these problems of intrinsic and extrinsic order and what they might mean for models of the human brain. It was noted at this conference that in the first part of this century the charismatic philosopher, A.N. Whitehead (1978), tried to come to grips with order in process (i.e., the flow of events through time). The French philosopher, M. Foucault (1970) explored problems of order from a broad perspective of the human sciences. The French Nobel Laureate in molecular biology, F. Jacob (1976), wrote compassionately on the topic of how our taxonomies of order in living systems reflect both cultural expectations as well as the analytical tools we bring to our studies. The theoretical physicist, D. Bohm (1980), has explored deeply the issue of how we relate levels of order — such as those that confront us when we talk about nerve cells, brains, or children at play.

Even in the arts there are deep concerns with problems of order and what it means. Thus, Eshkol and Wachmann (1958), two masters of human choreography, remark on how our views of order in human movement reflect the descriptive frames that we employ in our studies (a point to which I return later). The classic text of my late friend and colleague, D.O. Hebb (1949) on the *Organization of Behavior* was devoted explicitly to what ideas of order and organization mean. In his terms, "The difficulties of finding order in behavior are great enough to require all one's attention" (1949, p. XV). Hebb was concerned not only with relations of brain and behavior, but with the developmental progressions that occur at each of these levels (Fentress, 1987a). Obviously, order is a fundamental and difficult concept. The developmental unfolding of biological and behavioral systems and their relations brings these problems of order from the conceptual world to the analytic world (Fentress, 1986). As Davidson (1986) has remarked in his recent text on *Gene Activity in Early Development,* "the crucial causal links between genome and embryo remain largely undescribed" (p. 2; cf. Oyama, this volume).

## Polarities of Order

I have become convinced that there are two fundamental polarities of order that exist at whatever level we choose to examine nature (e.g., see also Fentress, 1984, 1986, in press; Fentress & McLeod, 1986; Fig. 2.1). The first of these polarities is that of relative continuity versus relative discontinuity. Does nature move in gradations or in steps? This is a question that relates to our descriptions as well as to our analyses of behavior. All readers of this volume are of course aware of debates among continuity and discontinuity enthusiasts in the developmental sciences. The second funda-

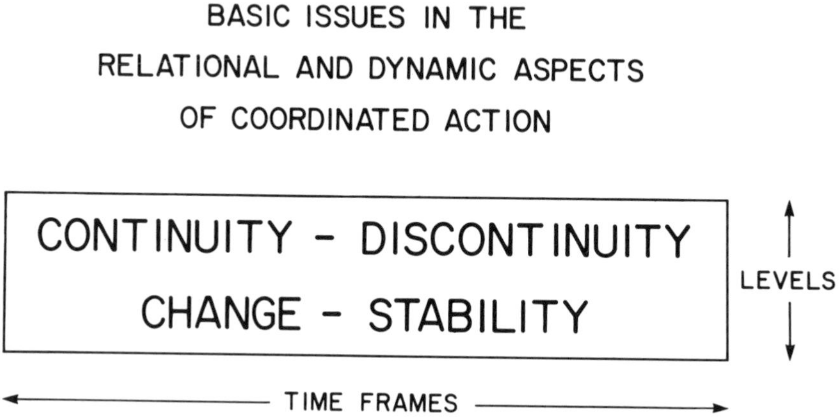

BASIC ISSUES IN THE
RELATIONAL AND DYNAMIC ASPECTS
OF COORDINATED ACTION

| CONTINUITY - DISCONTINUITY |
| CHANGE - STABILITY |

LEVELS

◄──────────── TIME FRAMES ────────────►

FIG. 2.1. Abstracted polarities of order that apply equally to a number of time frames and levels. (Note: From "The Development of Coordination" by J.C. Fentress, 1984, *Journal of Motor Behavior, 16,* p. 101. Reprinted with permission of the Helen Dwight Reid Educational Foundation. Copyright 1984 by Heldref Publications.)

mental polarity is that of change versus stability. Both behavior and its development are described by change (dynamic order), but there must also be rules of change that are in themselves constrained. No one has ever made a wolf behave like a mouse, nor has anyone turned a chimpanzee into a freely speaking child (Premack, 1986). These two polarities of order together reflect a dynamic and relational ordering of behavioral systems in development (Fentress, 1984, 1986, in press).

TOWARD A *D*YNAMIC *N*ETWORK *A*PPROACH
TO BEHAVIORAL DEVELOPMENT:
THE TRUE "DNA" OF OUR MISSION

The classic nature—nurture issue in psychology and biology has still not been resolved due to our inability to grasp fully what it means to be both self-organizing and interactive within a dynamically ordered context (Fentress, 1976). It would be an injustice to previous generations of competent scholars simply to dismiss the nature—nurture issue as a problem without solution (or worse still, as a problem with obvious solution!). We need better tools of analytical as well as conceptual analysis (cf. Oyama, this volume and comments by Sameroff). A major task is to develop tools for thinking about self-ordering (organizational) processes as these operate within the more broadly defined context of sensitivities to the surround.

In this chapter, I argue that dynamically ordered *networks* of behavioral expression may provide the key to what we all seek to understand. My argument, in brief, is that we can all too easily become sidetracked by the apparent elegance of studying events in isolation. Just as organisms are intimately connected to their environments, so too are different properties of behavioral expression and their control intimately connected. Although the experimental isolation of individual events is clearly essential to our analytical procedures, it is often too easy to use this isolation procedure to ignore the broader contexts within which events occur.

## Issues of Context, Cooperation, and Compensation

Let me illustrate this problem with a simple example. In a recent series of experiments, Kent Berridge and I asked what would be the consequences on grooming and other actions in rodents of removing facial somatosensory information (Berridge & Fentress, 1986). The answer to this apparently simple question was context dependent. There were certain phases and expressive contexts in which trigeminal deafferentation produced dramatic changes in behavior; there were other phases and contexts in which the same lesion had no measurable effects even for the same abstracted actions (Fig. 2.2). Now think of developmental events in the expression of behavior. Might not these events also be context sensitive, both in terms of their influences and in terms of their measured effects? The literature relevant to the exploration of such questions is remarkably incomplete.

The issue goes much deeper. Changes in one property of behavior may have consequences on other properties of behavior. Effects can be either synergistic or antagonistic, and may cross over traditional taxonomic categories. For example, different sensory modalities do not necessarily have independent developmental histories. Knudsen and Knudsen (1985) have shown that for barn owls, plugging one ear initially causes the animals to misorient to auditory cues by about 10 degrees due to changes in interaural timing and intensity. Electrophysiological data also indicate a mismatch between auditory and visual maps. However, after several months these maps come back into register and the animals orient properly to auditory cues. If the ear plug is removed the animals now misorient in the opposite direction with a subsequent recorrection. Surprisingly, however, the key ingredient in reorganization is vision. If the owls are prevented from seeing they persist in making auditory localization errors. Visual prisms that displace the perceived location of objects by 10 degrees will also, over weeks, "re-educate" the auditory system. Thus, different sensory channels can be "co-ordered" in development, providing the animal with a unified picture of its world.

This multisensory co-ordering can also be seen in compensatory factors where reduction in the salience of one class of events can increase the

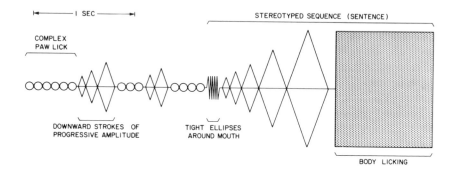

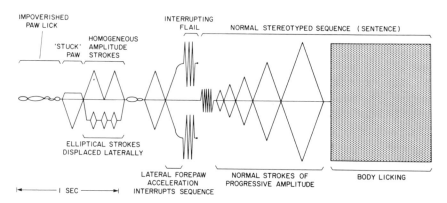

FIG. 2.2. Variable and stereotyped grooming phases in rats. Top line is a representation of grooming phases in intact rats. Bottom line is a representation of grooming after trigeminal deafferentation. Sensory (trigeminal) lesions that disrupt the variable sequence phase have minimal effect on the stereotyped phase, thus indicating the importance of context (Berridge & Fentress, 1986).

salience of another. The most easily illustrated compensatory co-orderings operate within the framework of sensory interactions. Thus, Rauschecker (1984) found that visual deprivation in cats increased the proportion of cells in the superior colliculus that responded to auditory stimuli. Statements of proportion are, of course, potentially risky as they can imply either an increase along one dimension or a decrease along another. Singer (1986) reviewed a large body of data in the realm of visual processing that suggest activity-dependent changes are often threshold dependent, may involve necessary correlation between activation of pre-and postsynaptic elements (as argued years ago on theoretical ground by Hebb, 1949), and may be efficacious only when the animals employ the signals in active behavior. (For a related behaviorally oriented review on experience and visual development see Tees, 1986). Cross-modality and cross-behavior class interactions during development will certainly prove to be at least as multifaceted and complex.

## Properties of Co-ordering

An important lesson of data such as these is that "co-ordering" of events is not only a problem of behavioral performance (Fentress, 1986; Thelen, 1986), but also its developmental pathways. It has sensory, motor, and higher integrative components. I return to this theme several times. This theme reinforces the fundamentally difficult issue I raised previously: How does the organism achieve and maintain both the necessary separations of behaviorally relevant events and the necessary close rules of connection among these events? In a very simple sense, events that are separate are not interconnected, and vice versa. Yet without separation, the organism would remain homogeneous soup; without interconnections it would remain the harbour of biological and behavioral anarchy. Neither option is very satisfactory. There is also a more subtle problem. Events that are casually connected must influence one another's properties, thus giving something of a developmental and performance bootstrap (i.e., interdependencies rather than more simply framed interactions). This is the strong definition of "co-ordering." I develop the argument here that the only way out of the dilemma is to develop models of relative separation and connection that are also dynamically ordered and multilayered. This applies both to performance and the development of performance. Indeed, one of the appeals of such conceptualizations is they may help us bring studies of behavioral integration and development into a much closer fusion than exists currently. *Dynamic network analyses* (DNA) is simply a shorthand summary of these ideas, designed intentionally to catch the attention of my molecular biology colleagues! They too have been forced to deal with dynamically ordered linkages among previously isolated events to the point where simple "programming" metaphors now appear to have limited utility (Stent, 1981; cf. Fentress, in press; Oya   , this volume).

## Influences of Experiences in Behavioral Order

Even given these complications, we have not yet asked in any precise way what kinds of influences we expect experiences to have during ontogeny. They may be diverse and numerous (cf. Oyama, this volume). Obviously, experiences can "add new information" or "instruct" an otherwise incomplete slate. But at the level of mechanism there is also good reason to believe that experiences can serve to "select among" the alternative developmental pathways that the organism has at its disposal (cf. Edelman & Finkel,

1984). Selection itself can be thought of in two ways: (a) selecting the correct file folder (providing a key to open the drawer), and (b) in the more strictly Darwinian sense, amplifying some messages at the explicit expense (extinction) of others (Fentress, in press). Experience can also maintain behavioral and neural networks (Singer, 1986), and modulate the speed and/or timing of developmental events without changing their course (Tees, 1986). Because networks are defined by interconnected strands, the rules of generalization from any experience may be multifaceted. For example, would we expect developmental influences on some property of motor performance to generalize across movements similar in their form or in their function? Might the rules of generalization themselves be very different for experiences that occur at different ages (e.g., generalizing by form at one age and function at another)? There are surprisingly few studies in which such questions have been asked, thus there are few data on which to base even tentative conclusions.

## DESCRIPTIVE FOUNDATIONS

### General Issues

Biologists, among whom I include ethologists, often take refuge by anchoring onto problems of taxonomy. There are good reasons for doing this. If we cannot describe something we do not know what it is that we seek to explain. F. Jacob (1976) has written convincingly that our models of heredity in the early history of biology often reflected inappropriate attempts at taxonomy, thus leading to confusion about underlying organizational principles. D. Bohm (1980), the physicist, put comments on taxonomy into a somewhat more pungent framework: *"To be confused about what is different and what is not, is to be confused about everything!"* (p. 16). Bohm's views are particularly interesting for behavioral scientists to contemplate for two reasons: (a) he stresses the complementary levels or order in nature, and (b) he focuses on dynamic and relational order. Bohm argued, for example, that "to develop new insight into fragmentation and wholeness requires a creative work even more difficult than that needed to make fundamental new discoveries in science" (p. 24). Similarly, he argued with explicit reference to human communication, "order is more like that of a symphony in which each aspect and movement has to be understood in the light of its relationship to the whole" (p. 41).

Recent Parallel Distribute Processing models in human cognition take on a remarkably similar perspective (Rummelhart, McClelland, & the PDP Research Group, 1986). "The sequential nature of speech poses problems for the

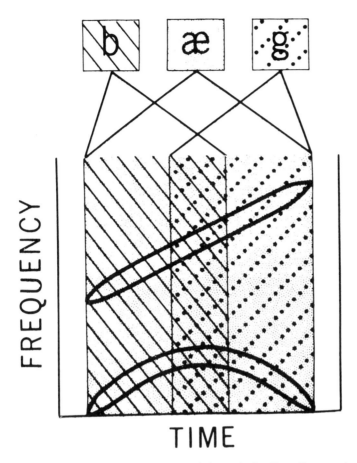

FIG. 2.3. Representation of the word bag, indicating the overlap of successive phoneme "units" (from Liberman, 1970).

modeling of contextual influences, in that to account for context effects, it is necessary to keep a record of the context. It would be a simple matter to process speech if each successive portion of the speech input were processed independently of all of the others. The presence of context effects in speech processing requires a mechanism that keeps some record of that context in a form that allows context to influence the interpretation of subsequent input. Cues to successive units of speech frequently overlap in time. Because of this it is difficult, even counterproductive, to try to divide the speech stream into separate phoneme units in advance of identifying the units." (McClelland & Elman, 1986, p. 60; see Fig. 2.3)

The elegant studies of Esther Thelen on early human leg movements (Thelen, 1986, this volume; cf. Kelso, 1986) also force us to focus on similar issues of dynamic cohesion among action properties, and context as discussed by the authors quoted here. Every abstracted property of behavior at every point in development is co-ordered into a larger unit, the organism. This whole organism approach is not "anti-biological," but it is *anticompartmental* — at least in the excessive (brick-like) sense of that term. We need only remember the insights of Charles Darwin (1872) on the diverse properties of behavioral expression in the animal and human world to appreciate that good biology can also be whole organism biology (cf. Crick, 1984; Hinde, 1982).

## The Classification and Analysis of Movement Sequences in Development

I now turn explicitly to problems of behavioral expression in ontogeny. *Behavioral expression* is defined here as ordered and co-ordered properties of movement. This is what we see. It does not in any way denigrate the importance of sensory, perceptual, attentional, motivational — or any other class of behavioral variables. Rather, movement patterns simply provide a relatively objective anchor point from which we might launch more powerful investigations into these other, psychologically critical, areas of developmental organization.

Ethologists have traditionally made a distinction between form and function in the classifications of behavior. The distinction is simple but important. If I say to you, "this animal is moving its forelegs along a horizontal plane with such and such frequency, amplitude, and so on *(form)*, you would be perfectly entitled to ask me what these movements appear to accomplish *(function)*. Conversely, if I say to you "this animal is fighting (function)", you would be equally entitled to ask whether I am referring to bites, kicks, or scratches, and so forth (form). The link between the morphologies of movement form and their consequences or functions represents one of the enduring challenges for behavioral analysis. Thus, Lashley's (1951) seminal publication on the serial ordering of behavior was designed to remind neurobiologists and psychologists alike that we can obtain the same functional endpoint in behavior through various, and often rich, combinations of individually abstracted movement components or forms. N. Bernstein (1967) from the Soviet Union was also careful to point out that movement functions and forms are two necessarily complementary perspectives. Even at the level of individual muscular contractions, the same basic form of movement may also be accomplished through very different channels (e.g., reviews in Fentress, 1984, 1986, in press; Fentress & McLeod, 1986).

## An Example: How Mice Scratch Their Faces

In 1972 Frances Stilwell and I (Fentress & Stilwell, 1973) abstracted basic movement "units" in the facial grooming sequences of mice and showed how these units were connected together into more broadly defined sequences (Fig. 2.4). We got interested in facial grooming initially because individually abstracted properties *(elements)* of movement not only followed one another within statistically defined sequences, but these elementary properties that we had extracted also often formed different sequential rules of combination with other elements as the sequence as a whole progressed. We thus began to think in terms of analogies to human language, where the same letters compose different words, the same words compose different phrases, and so on. We were also struck by the fact that the rules of sequential connection often appeared "tighter" at the higher than at lower levels of behavioral description. This suggested that the animals might indeed be organized so that they speak biologically coherent phrases even though they may have to change their behavioral wording, and they may

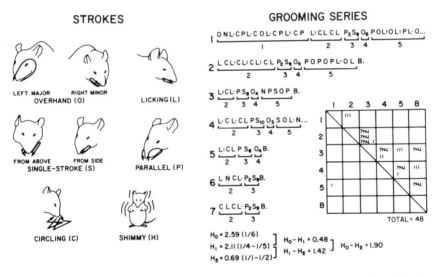

FIG. 2.4. Facial grooming stroke "elements" in mice and their hierarchical rules of connection in time (from Fentress & Stilwell, 1973). "H" values are information measures of sequence structure, where Ho refers to uncertainty assuming each of six face grooming elements are equally probable (1/6), H1 takes into account differential probability (giving a predictability between one quarter and one fifth) and H2 looks for rules of connection between paired elements (giving a predictability of better than half).

speak words even if these words are, by refined analyses, apparently misspelled.

We then became interested in the question of whether young mice, in an admittedly crude analogy to children, develop their abilities to articulate words before phrases, phrases before sentences, and so on. Here we came to a snag. What do we do with imperfectly formed words, phrases, and sentences that we felt we could otherwise classify? Should we give these baby mouse words, phrases, and sentences the same taxonomic label that we found useful to employ in our studies of adult animals? I return to this point in the next section. We also became increasingly uneasy with our language analogy. This was not so much due to fears that our colleagues would grumble about the obvious differences between language performance and mouse grooming, as it was due to the realization that even simple linguistic formalizations can take our minds away from the detailed temporal course of behavior as well as its simultaneous expressive properties. We thus began to turn to music, and especially dance, as more adequate models.

Music is an important model of behavior. There are two primary reasons for this. The first is that in music, as in behavior, the relative timing of events (e.g., rhythm) is basic. The second reason is that in music, as in behavior, we are forced to deal with simultaneous properties of expression (musical chords) as well as the sequential ordering of events (melody lines). As I have suggested previously, the comparisons between behavioral and musical performance can go much deeper, such as might be incurred by our considerations of particular instruments in performance, the role of an abstracted conductor, or the details by which a musical score is written, and interpreted (Fentress, 1978).

## Other General Issues

There are two general issues of particular importance to how we consider developmental taxonomies of abstracted actions and their rules of connection. The first previously alluded to briefly is that action categories designed on the basis of adult behavior may be imperfectly reflected in young animals. Children may say "ba" instead of "ball," target feeding movements imperfectly toward their mouths, and so forth. Often we interpret and classify what they are doing both by some similarities to adult movements in form and consequence, and by broader contexts of expression. In animal behavior studies, similar strategies are employed. This is a reasonable approach, but it can leave one with difficult taxonomic decisions. Sometimes it is not possible to decide whether a young creature's behavior should be classified as an immature form of adult category X, or given a different label. The problems can be especially difficult when, as often happens, the young individual's behavior falls somewhere between two separately categorized adult events. One consequence of ambiguous labels is that our decisions about labeling dictate the course of our models of underlying developmental processes.

The second general issue is that processes of differentiation (separation) and integration (combination) often appear to co-occur as development proceeds, with varying emphases for particular expressive dimensions and different ages (Fentress & McLeod, 1986; Thelen, 1986). There are many debates in the literature as to whether behavioral development is best defined as the progressive refinement of initially more global characteristics or the progressive joining together of initially more fragmented patterns. Perhaps understandably, most reductionistic models of behavioral and biological development have pressed for the view of progressive differentiation from initially imperfectly sculpted global forms. Indeed, terms such as *determination* and *differentiation* are a fundamental part of the developmental biologist's most prized vocabulary; the term *integration* is often absent altogether. In behavior as well, workers such as Coghill (1929) have placed particular emphasis on *individuation* during ontogeny, and there are many data from humans and other organisms that support the position of early diffuse activation followed by more specific patterns (e.g., Gatev, 1972 on human reflexes). Conversely, Windle (1940) argued in favor of the view that isolated reflexes are common in early development of many mammalian species, which then become fused into more complex and coherent patterns. These and related data have been reviewed in detail by Bekoff (1981), Oppenheim (1981), Fentress and McLeod (1986), and Provine (1986).

Of course, there is no logical reason why processes of differentiation and integration must be viewed as opponents rather than cooperative partners in development. Which of these processes appears most dramatic can reflect our taxonomies, their underlying dimensions, their levels of focus, the contexts under which we examine behavior, our theoretical biases and a host of other factors. One of the most obvious of these "other factors" is our technique of measurement. "What you measure is what you get" may be an especially apt slogan for developmental research, apologies to Flip Wilson aside.

## THE DEVELOPMENTAL DANCE OF MOUSE MOVEMENTS: A DETAILED ILLUSTRATION

With my colleague, Ilan Golani, it became possible to pursue such issues in a deeper and empirically explicit manner (e.g., Golani & Fentress, 1985). Golani had previously become involved with potential scientific applications of human dance choreography as proposed by two Israeli colleagues, Eshkol and Wachmann (1958). The notation system of Eshkol and Wachmann is both a simple and profound method for ordering behavioral events in space and in time. At the heart of the "EW" system is geometric representation of movement from complementary descriptive frames. These frames include adjacent limb segments of the individual, fixed points in the environment, or moving social partners (Golani, 1976).

## Descriptive Frames

Eshkol and Wachmann pointed to problems of the definition of even basic movement parameters. Clarification of these basic movement parameters is critical to an understanding of more subtle and dynamic adjustments during the performance of movement sequences, including their developmental profiles. For example, Eshkol and Wachmann note that the ramifications of one movement property can have vastly different consequences on other movement properties as a function of the broader context(s) within which these movements occur. There are thus times when movements of my lower legs have few predictable consequences on the position of my body in space — as I found out recently in my attempts to ice skate! When walking as an adult, however, similar leg movements produce highly predictable trajectories of my entire upper body. In early skating attempts, similar ("bodywise") segmental leg movements may not move my upper body at all, as measured by some external referent — or I might crash "altogether" on the ice, while keeping individual body segments locked together in a fixed manner. There is potentially something very different between descriptions of movement from the perspective of one's own body and the environment. I can "move" in either of these two spheres without moving in the other (cf. Thelen, this volume).

The notion of relativistic "spheres of movement" is at the heart of the whole Eshkol and Wachmann (1958) notational scheme that in turn relates to logically and geometrically defined segmental movement properties. If I choose to move any single limb segment, I am constrained to make this movement in one of three manners: (a) rotations of my limb about its own axis of rotation, (b) movements oriented 90 degrees to the axis of rotation, or (c) conical movements between 0 and 90 degrees. Of course I can move a limb in a straight line, as defined from some environmental reference point, but to do so necessitates a co-ordering of at least two individual limb segment movements that are each defined most basically in terms of their circular (and spherical) properties. Thus Eshkol and Wachmann (1958) apply a strict geometric polar coordinate system to define movements. One can imagine spheres on each joint, and plot the position of a given limb at any one time from the perspective of these coordinates. The numbers can vary whether the coordinates are fixed in space, rotate with externally defined rotations of the limb, and so forth (see Fig. 2.5).

Comparisons can then be made as to the "simplicity" of description when these different coordinate frameworks are compared. My upper arm can move in a regular pattern with respect to my lower arm, but each limb segment can have much more complex relations to environmental referents (e.g., due to movements of other limb segments that "carry along" both my

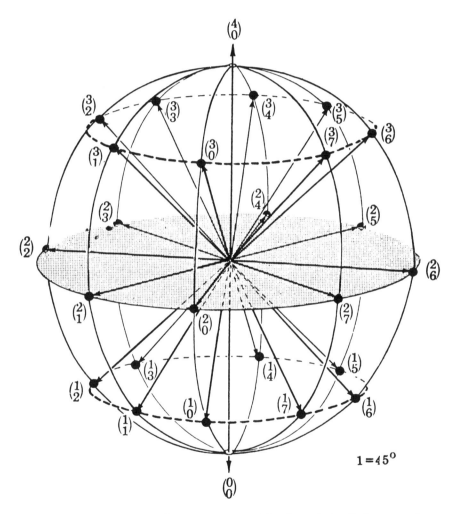

FIG. 2.5. The polar coordinate system used to characterize limb segment movements. Different descriptive perspectives include references to adjacent limb segments, fixed points in the environment, or moving points in the environment; e.g., social partners (from Eshkol & Wachmann, 1958).

upper and lower arm). Or, my upper arm can move in a fixed relation to some external referent, but vary in its movement properties defined by the upper arm's relations to the lower arm (e.g., due to the need to compensate for changes in my lower arm's relation to a given environmental referent). Movement literally becomes a dance: The question is whether and when the primary partner is an adjacent limb segment (or perhaps even more distal limb segment), a fixed point in the environment, a moving point in the environment (e.g., social partner), and so forth. Primary partners can be defined by the regularities of association, and there is no reason why primary partners cannot be changed as movement progresses—in either an integrative or developmental sense.

## Kinematics, Trajectories, and Contact Paths

In a recent study of ontogeny of facial grooming patterns in mice, we (Golani & Fentress, 1985) demonstrated that descriptions of movement from the perspectives of individual limb segment kinematics, trajectories of the limbs in external space, and forepaw to face contacts each provided complementary and nonredundant descriptive perspectives. Changes along one of these dimensions did not provide clear predictions about changes along either of the other two dimensions. This goes back to the everyday observation that we can make similar movements of our toothbrushes across our teeth through variable combinations of head and arm movements, as described from some fixed external reference point. An obvious question is where the relative variances and invariances lie in the organization of movement, and other properties of behavior, as this organization is observed across different phases of development.

One reason this point is critical in the study of behavioral development is that the rules of cohesion and separation among different properties of behavioral expression can change in time. All of this sounds complicated, but is really simple and straightforward. I take for example the development of mouse grooming.[1] I do this to provide a concrete foundation from which I later explore issues in developmental order that are of a necessarily more abstract nature. First, let me provide a sense of the richness of these movements. Note that grooming involves movements of the arms, head, neck, and torso in numerous combinations. This is how we attempted to

---

[1] The purpose of this illustration is to provide a concrete foundation for the broader issues I have outlined. Some readers may prefer to skim this section only, and then return to the more broadly focused parts of the chapter. For other readers, concrete illustrations may help clarify the more abstract issues that form the core of this chapter.

abstract the critical elements in arm movements only (Golani & Fentress, 1985):

Isolated and complete individual grooming cycles start and end with the upper arms dropped, and the forearms slightly flexed so that the forepaws are held below chest level with the back of the paws facing upward. Raising a forepaw toward the face is accomplished through raising of the upper arm in relation to the chest in the sagittal plane, and raising (flexion) of the forearm in relation to the upper arm. As soon as the forepaw reaches the proximity of the chin or earlier, an outward rotation of the upper arm around its longitudinal axis (carrying the forearm laterally, away from the midsagittal plane) is added to the upper arm plane movement. This rotation, sometimes accompanied by upper arm abduction, carries the forearm horizontally sideways, which, when combined with the raising of the forearm, results in a curved path of the forepaw laterad, thereby avoiding direct contact with the face during raising. Toward the end of raising, the forearm supinates, so that the inside of the paw is turned to oppose the side of the face. If the paw is flexed, it aligns with the forearm in midposition. The supination of the forearm continues into the first part of the lowering phase.

Lowering includes an adduction and a rotation of the upper arm that carry the forearm and paw toward the face until paw contact is established. Simultaneously, the forearm is lowered (extension) on the upper arm; when this movement is accompanied by antagonistic raising of the upper arm, the forepaw is transported rostrad along the face. A pronation of the forearm shifts and restricts at this stage the forepaw's contact with the face to the thumb. After the release of paw to face contact at snout tip or at the mouth, the forearm continues to extend, carrying the forepaw to chest level. Sometimes, the forearm is carried along further down by an agonistic lowering movement of the upper arm. (pp. 532–533)

I confess a sense of awe with what the mouse can do, even as represented by this simplified abstraction of arm movements only, in a reasonably simple form of behavioral expression. There is an elegance and artistry here that is but the barest sketch of more complex forms of (e.g., human) behavior. Think now of human infants doing all that they do, the situations they choose either to do or not to do these things, the multiple uses they make of what they do, and so forth, The point is that, in most cases, we do not even know what, in appropriate detail, "they do," *how* infants do what they do, or *how* they develop the capacities for doing these miraculous things — which are not things at all, but complexly orchestrated patterns in both space and time (cf. Thelen's elegant studies of apparently simple kicking movements; Thelen, 1986, this volume). Think even of the "simple mouse" deciding when to groom in conjunction with its other (often much more descriptively complex) actions.

## Precursors and Environmental Supports

Grooming behavior in rodents, as in many human motor actions (Prechtl, 1986) has clear prenatal precursors. Facial grooming strokes can be observed in utero (Agulo ý Gonzales, 1932; Narayanan, Fox, & Hamburger, 1971; Smotherman & Robinson, 1987). Newborn mice, however, express facial grooming behavior only on rare occasions, and this behavior is defined as grooming more by the movements of the forearms than by reliably effective contacts between the forepaws and the face (i.e., they produce grooming movements without achieving grooming function). *Nonfunctional action,* at least as defined by developmental criteria, is a common property of both animal and human development (Fentress & McLeod, 1986).

Part of the problem that young mice have is that they are neither very strong, nor do they have very good balance. These are elementary but fundamental considerations (cf. Thelen, 1986, on human locomotory development). Circuits within the brain for the production of behavioral actions may become established quite early, indeed long before they are manifested in effective overt behavior. This is due to peripheral weaknesses and the like. This is an interesting proposition for it suggests that there must be an ordering of developmental connections that can occur without major benefits from overt practice. There are numerous examples in the ethological and neurobiological literature that support such an argument. Each of these examples must be interpreted with caution, however, a point to which I return later (cf. Fentress & McLeod, 1986).

Recently, we (Golani & Fentress, 1985) attempted to bypass part of these problems of muscular weakness and poor balance by supporting newborn and older mice in a mirrored chamber that also gave orthogonal views of the movements used during grooming. We found that, even shortly after birth, mice that are placed within an appropriately supported grooming posture will groom. Furthermore, once the animals are in this posture, grooming can be elicited by a number of moderately strong peripheral stimuli, such as pinching of the tail. It is as if the animals, once posturally set and supported to groom, need only reasonable encouragement ("activation") to do so. Strong pinches of the tail will block rather than facilitate grooming, so these lines of encouragement must be moderate if they are to accentuate preexisting (e.g., posturally dependent) biases. When stronger, these same peripheral influences may respecify rather than reinforce ongoing predispositions. One can think of dual threshold of effects here: Relatively nonspecific activation (accentuation) of ongoing behavioral states often occurs in response to moderately strong (salient) stimuli that respecify the direction of behavior when these same stimuli are at higher effective strengths (Fentress, 1976, 1986, 1988). Thus, the young mice may squirm rather than groom in response to strong tail pinches. There are dynamically ordered connections between input and output that need much further study, both in their performance and developmental underpinnings (Fentress, in press). This is another point to which I return later.

## Postnatal Movement Phases

For the moment I shall concentrate on descriptive statements, summarized in Tables. 2.1 and 2.2. First, a brief comment on head and neck movements during early grooming ontogeny. In adult grooming these head and neck movements contribute in an often compensatory manner to forearm movements—much like when we eat with an often rich variety of arm and head movements, the sum of which brings food into our mouths. From the first prenatal day the head aligns at the chest at the initiation of grooming cycle, with the lower jaw forming a right angle with

TABLE 2.1
Postnatal Grooming Phases

| | |
|---|---|
| *Phase 1*<br>*(0–100 hrs.)* | • Head held stationary, aligned with chest<br>• Imperfect coupling of forelimb kinematic parameters (wide spatiotemporal variety)<br>• Large spatiotemporal variety of forelimb trajectories with overshoots, excessive pressure, etc.<br>• Rich variety of often fortuitous forepaw to face contact pathways (both symmetric and asymmetric pathways)<br>• Uninterrupted sequences (bouts) of strokes often seen |
| *Phase 2*<br>*(100–200 hrs.)* | • Small head movements<br>• Improved timing and coordination of limb segments<br>• Good intralimb coupling of kinematic components plus bilateral temporal synchrony<br>• Restricted forelimb trajectories with bimanual (symmetrical) coordination<br>• Restricted but consistent contact pathways, sometimes with excessive pressure<br>• Single grooming strokes (bouts rare) |
| *Phase 3*<br><br>*(>200 hrs.)* | • Head actively employed with forepaws; tongue involvement<br>• Continued improvement in kinematic and interlimb coordination<br>• Re-elaboration of trajectories leading to re-emergence of asymmetrical and symmetrical strokes in sequence<br>• Contact pathways begin to form predictable temporal patterns<br>• Adult stroke classes and syntactic structure emerge |

TABLE 2.2
Summary of Grooming Ontogeny Trends (Three Phases)

*Monotonic Trends*

Improved co-ordination of rotational and planar movement properties
Elimination of forepaw-face misses, discontinuous paths, and overshoots
Paws cease becoming stuck, bouncing off face, etc.
Improved bilateral timing

*Developmental Reversals (Phases I-II-III)*

Restriction then extension of contact paths
Disappearance followed by re-emergence of simultaneous asymmetrical paths
Disappearance followed by re-emergence of bouts

*Patterns in Context Following Phase III*

Adult stroke classes with hierarchical and sequential order
Elimination of "motor traps" and emergence of contextual associations with
    other behavioral actions

the neck and the chest. The head arrives at this "start" position from a variety of previous locations. When grooming starts the paws do not have to "search" for the head, because its location is invariant with reference to other body segments. For approximately the first 200 hours postnatally the head remains fixed at the midline until the paws cease contact with the face, after which the head moves up and rotates sideways. This defines an individual cycle, as well as a series of successive strokes. After approximately 200 hours the head begins to contribute to grooming sequences in an active manner, generating a complexly ordered series of paw to face contacts.

These paw to face contacts are rich but also apparently fortuitous through the first 100 hours or so of postnatal development. During this time, forelimb movements have many grooming properties (e.g., rhythmicity and sequencing) but both the kinematic form and the sequential ordering of cycles is loosely structured. The forepaws may, for example, give exaggerated movements in space, bounce off the face, get stuck on the face, or miss the face altogether. As a functional unit, grooming is not very efficient. Kinematic properties within a single limb, or even limb segment, show excessive "degrees of freedom" (cf. Bernstein, 1967, on patterns of coordination change in human development). As illustration, the rotational and lifting components of lower arm movements may occur separately and in different combinations in newborn animals, rather than being fused into the coherent "rotational-lifting" synergy seen later. Each of the two forelimbs may also occupy loosely coupled trajectory spaces, rather than acting as one bilateral unit characteristic of adults (Fig. 2.6). Preliminary data from our laboratory suggest further that the precision of within joint movement parameters migrates in a proximal-distal direction, and that within-limb coordination across individual limb segments precedes that of precise coordination between limbs. These preliminary data support the general model of intrajoint to intralimb to interlimb coordination perfection suggested by Bekoff (1981) on the basis of her elegant studies of early movements in chicks. We (Golani & Fentress, 1985) have demarcated this first rich but loosely constructed 100 hour or so period of postnatal grooming as grooming Phase I (see summary in Table 2.1).

Phase II grooming conveniently occupies the postnatal period of approximately 100 to 200 hours. This is an interesting period for a number of reasons, the primary one being that grooming behavior becomes both simplified and precise. For example, in contrast to Phase I, the forepaws almost always make contact with the face, but in a narrowly localized

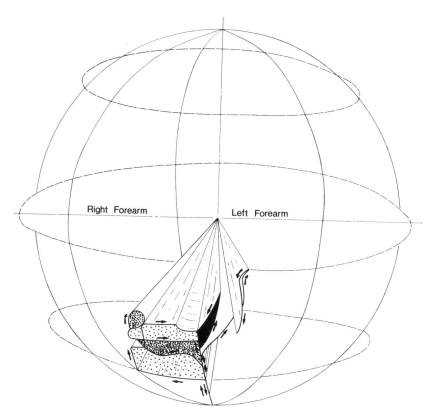

FIG. 2.6. Left and right forelimb trajectories in young (3 day) mouse, Note both obvious lack of symmetry between left and right forelimbs, and also disconnection between limb trajectory properties for a single limb (e.g., as reflected in the "staircase"−discontinuous−nature of certain early limb trajectories).

region near the snout. In Phase I the contact pathways were much richer, covered a much greater region of the face, but were unreliable and unpredictable in detail when they occurred. Phase II behavior also consists of isolated strokes in a greater than ten to one ratio compared with sequentially connected strokes, whereas Phase I grooming exhibited a somewhat greater proportion of sequentially connected strokes than isolated strokes. Many years ago M. Hines (1942) noted that young macaque monkeys also went through a period of retrenchment in the richness of movement as movement precision increased.

We have defined Phase III grooming in mice as that which occurs after postnatal hour 200 or so. There are varieties of concurrent changes that occur during this period. Most generally, the mice maintain the precision of Phase II, while regaining the richness in movement seen in Phase I. Thus, the forepaws always make contact with the face, the face contacts are diverse but also serially ordered in a clear way, and facial grooming consists of an often protracted series of these forepaw to face contacts. In addition, the animals now begin to show an unambiguous ability to make the same contact pathways through an enriched combination of individually defined movements of limb segments. Thus, the animals become more refined in the functional endpoints of movement, while they elaborate upon the means or forms through which these common ends can be achieved. They have now achieved the status of "motor equivalence" discussed by Lashley (1951), where motor equivalence is defined explicitly in terms of the ability to achieve common endpoints through variable means.

## Some Lessons From the Description of Movement

There is an obvious lesson to such statements, once they have been made in explicit terms. One is that even questions of whether behavior becomes more or less "fixed" (cf. the "fixed action pattern" perspective of ethologists) during development can reflect, in very essential ways, the dimensions used to describe behavior. A behavior may become more elaborated along one dimension while becoming more restricted along another. Thus, contact pathway progression is both elaborated and restricted in grooming Phase III in comparison, respectively, to the simple movements of Phase II and the fortuitous forepaw to face contacts seen in Phase I (Tables 2.1 and 2.2). More directly relevant to issues of "formal" versus more "functional" constraints is our observation (Fentress, 1988) that older animals tend to be better at compensating for local limb segment perturbations than are younger animals (i.e., the older animals can maintain common endpoints in behavior even though the maintenance of these endpoints necessitates compensatory connections between movement properties as defined on a more micro measurement scale). It is at such points that we begin to get a strong sense that there are multiple, relativistically ordered, and hierarchically arranged constraining properties in behavioral development that must be considered.

In summary, both monotonic and nonmonotonic changes are seen in the transitions between grooming Phases I, II, and III (Table 2.2). The direction of change depends importantly on the descriptive measures employed. Similar monotonic and nonmonotonic changes also occur in many facets of human development (Fentress & McLeod, 1986; Golani & Fentress, 1985; Prechtl, 1986; Thelen, 1986).

## Sequencing and Compensating in Context

By Phase III (200 hours plus) the mice have crystalized their grooming actions into action categories that can be perceptually distinguished (Fentress & Stilwell, 1973), and these actions begin to show the sequential and hierarchical order characteristic of adult mice. In freely moving mice over their first 2 postnatal weeks there are a number of interesting differences in comparison to adults, however. There are also some interesting parallels ("similarities," to use Bohm's, 1980, term) in these differences and those found in human children compared with adults.

One of these "similar differences" is that both young mice who groom and young children who speak go through a phase where individual movements not only become crystalized into recognizable "entities" (strokes/phonemes-words), but these entities are strung together in often separate temporal packets. They do not exhibit the smooth flow of co-articulated actions seen later (Fentress, 1983; Kent, 1976; see Fig. 2.7). In the case of young mice, the frequency of repeated movements is often less per unit time than that seen for adults, and one might expect this is due to reduced movement velocity in comparison to adults. Although this may be part of the picture, close analysis reveals that what often happens is that movement cycles in young mice are very close to the adult standard, but with pauses interjected between successive cycles. Due to the extreme rapidity of these movements (some of which occur 10 to more than 30 cycles per second) careful frame by frame analyses are needed to clarify where these delay lines occur.

A second interesting feature of immature mouse grooming movements is that although overall sequential integrity of actions over time may be observed, this has to be balanced against an alternative tendency to interject extra elements. Thus, if the adult mouse goes from A to B to C, the young mouse may produce the sequence as A . . xy . . B . . qz . . C . . xz . . . . If we listen carefully to the speech of young children, or observe other actions they perform, we can also witness the interjection of extra elements within

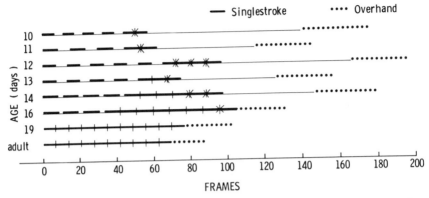

FIG. 2.7. Early grooming sequences are often composed of individual strokes that are adult-like in their timing, but are also separated from one another by pauses. "Single-strokes" (dark bars) are illustrated here. In addition, the transition from "single-stroke" sequences to overhand sequences are often found in young mice, but with frequent interjections of extraneous strokes (from Fentress & Stilwell, 1973). *refers to successive "single-strokes" in which the forelimbs do not show normal alternation of relative amplitude.

a sequence that otherwise has an appropriate sequential construction (i.e., these children often do not go directly from A to B to C).

Thirdly, both young mice and young children may be less adept at compensating for perturbations that occur within their sequentially and hierarchically ordered articulations. For example, if I perturb movements of a particular limb segment during grooming in rodents at different ages, by applying a plastic cuff to adjoining limb segments, older animals are more likely than younger animals to adjust the movements of other limb segments so that the final cohesive expression is conserved (unpublished observations). For younger animals, individual limb segment details in movement are more likely to be maintained even though other participating limb segment movements are perturbed, with the frequent result that the "total effective pattern of action" is eliminated.

A simple human analogue may be helpful at this point. Let us watch young children master the art of eating with a spoon. At the earliest phase (cf. Phase I of our mice), there are certain (albeit still imperfectly defined) similarities in the form of feeding between the infants and adults, although food substances may not always reach the mouth. Later (cf. Phase II of our mice), children tend to restrict their head movements during feeding, and also tend to bring food to their mouths along relatively stereotyped trajectory sequences as defined for any given limb segment or even combination of limb segments. Finally, children reach the conversational stage of feeding during a dinner. At this point they can achieve constant food to mouth sequences through a rich variety of individually defined head and arm movements (cf. Phase III grooming).

In summary, adult mice are often able to compensate for disturbances of one limb segment during grooming so that they preserve the overall integrity of grooming movements more broadly defined. Young mice may fail to make such adjustments, just as young children who move their heads during feeding may fail to track the new position of the mouth as measured by contacts of the spoon on the face!

As a final example, young mammals—whether mice or children—may initiate actions at surprising times. Often this reflects the fact that these young organisms are trapped by either locally occurring motor profiles or concurrent sensory events. They seem less able than are adults to ignore these events, so that they can then preserve the overall integrity of their performance sequence (cf. Fentress, 1984, 1986, and 1988 for more detailed evaluations). To illustrate, young mice may break into a series of grooming events if their forepaws happen to pass near the face, as often happens during poorly coordinated locomotory or even swimming movements. These "sensorimotor" traps, as I have called them, suggest that the constraints in action of young organisms often operate more on the basis of *movement form,* than on more abstract definitions of *movement meaning.* There are a number of interesting parallels here with human actions after neurological damage (Fentress, in press; Posner & Presti, 1987; Teitelbaum, 1977). As illustration, young children may switch suddenly between functionally distinct classes of action if these action classes contain movements that are similar in form (Fentress, 1983). Analogous phenomena are seen in certain types of neurological disorders, where form rather than function again becomes the dominant focus of behavioral expression (Luria, 1980; cf. Teitelbaum, 1977). Such observations also relate much more broadly to our models of hierarchical order in behavior (Fentress, 1983) where, for example, human language is arranged in nested patterns of phonemic, syntactic, and semantic representations (cf. reviews in Rummelhart et al., 1986). In children, the development of more abstract switching rules in speech tends to occur subsequent to the mastery of basic speech elements, the use (and often overgeneralization) of simple rules, etc. (cf. Fentress & McLeod, 1986).

## Hierarchical Structures in the Dynamics of Expression

It is not my intent in this chapter to dwell on issues of brain modeling in behavior and its development (cf. Fentress, in press a). However, a few brief comments are in order to show how even relatively simple action sequences such as rodent grooming can relate to issues of brain organization that may have much broader significance to the construction of future models in developmental psychology. I list main points here. (a) Grooming is a naturally occurring movement sequence that not only emerges early in ontogeny but is to a large extent under subcortical motor control. (b) This is obvious in early ontogeny, because grooming develops prior to the maturation of cortical circuits (although its more complex contextual associations and flexibility may well involve the cortical circuits). (c) Functional decortication in adult rodents, such as through application of KCL on the cortex, often enhances the probability of grooming while reducing its full richness and flexibility (Fentress, 1988). (d) Grooming probability can also be enhanced, while flexibility is reduced, in adult rodents under varying degrees of "stress" (which we can presume to reduce the effectiveness of higher cortical functions). (e) Well-practiced and simple motor actions can also be facilitated in an analogous way by moderate stress. For example, cortically conditioned movement sequences in monkeys are blocked by external disturbances early in their acquisition, but often elicited by these same disturbances once overtrained (cf. Fentress & McLeod, 1986). (f) Recent data in humans suggest that early motor training may involve the critical participation of cortical structures, whereas more highly trained skills may have the major locus of their control diverted to subcortical structures, such as the basal ganglia (Goldberg, 1987). (g) Berridge and Fentress (1987) have found that the corpus striatum (part of the basal ganglia) may participate especially importantly in the most stereotyped phases of rodent grooming sequences. (h) These structures appear to order behavior through a still imperfectly understood combination of movement sequence programming and modulation of afferent signals.

I suspect that each of these points has a potentially important bearing upon how we think about behavioral organization during development and under different contexts of performance, such as I have outlined in previous sections of this chapter.[2] In addition, they may help us work toward a more unified framework for thinking about properties of integrated performance and development together, in a manner that achieves biological (neurological) reality. However, simple reductionism is a trap to be eschewed, for any satisfactory attempts to link developmental neurology and behavior together must take into account species differences, differences in performance characteristics of different classes of action, and most importantly,

---

[2]Analogous issues of behavioral specificity, organization during stress, and physiological mediation of performance are becoming increasingly appreciated in the human literature (e.g., Gunnar, 1987). This emphasizes that fundamental *principles* (and problems!) of behavior may be abstracted across observations, and even species, that obviously differ in their detailed properties.

must rest upon the sophisticated dissection of behavior in its own terms (cf. Kolb, Jacobs, & Petrie, 1987). Therefore, I turn my attention now to clearly "higher order" aspects of behavioral expression and its development: socially coordinated patterns of action. Might there be parallels here with what we observe at the level of the individual?

## FROM SOLO TO SOCIAL DANCES

The issues of separations and co-orderings among properties of behavior discussed thus far have their obvious social analogues (M. Gunnar, personal communication; October, 1987). Here, instead of individual limb segments, we ask about rules of order for individual organisms during their dyadic and higher order interactions. The importance of relational, dynamic, and multileveled perspectives is evident in each case, albeit with emphasis on different dimensions, grid structures and time frames (cf. Fogel & Thelen, 1987).

As illustration from our own animal research, Moran, Fentress, and Golani (1981) elaborated upon the pioneering work of Golani (1976) in a study in which wolves were treated for the most part as straight line vectors. In social behavior, three questions arise immediately, each of which must be defined in terms of relations among these abstracted "vector" animals: (a) How far apart are they?; (b) What is their angle of orientation with respect to one another?; (c) How are points of nearest contact upon the animals' social partners displaced up and down the longitudinal axis of their partners? No one of these measures is contained in the behavior of a single animal; they are each defined "partnerwise." Further, relations among these three partnerwise indices might or might not be independent, nor is it obvious from anything said thus far whether distributions along even one of the three dimensions of social interaction occupy all possible points in space. For adult wolves, at least during aggressive encounters, both individual dimensions of expression and their combinations in time appear to be strictly rule governed (i.e., there are many positions within the abstracted three-dimensional interaction space that are heavily occupied, whereas others are not occupied at all; see Fig. 2.8). That is one definition of dance (Eshkol & Wachmann, 1958).

Consistencies in relations, and consistent modifications of parts that contribute to these relations, have thus far in this chapter been pursued at the level of individual organisms. Here, when different organisms are treated as were individual limb segments within the organism, similar principles appear to apply. Two recent studies support this claim within a developmental context. Havkin (1977) showed that early social interactions among wolf pups exhibited a loose symmetry, which was subsequently

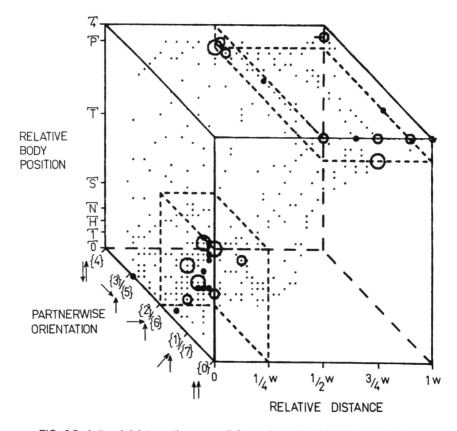

FIG. 2.8. A "social interaction space" for wolves, in which three relational dimensions are represented. The points in this space are clearly nonrandomly distributed (with size of mark representing relative frequency of occurrences). The points shown here are "points of fixation," meaning that the two animals are in a constant relative position, even though each may have moved. Predictable trajectories of change between these points are also observed (from Moran et al., 1981).

replaced by clearly divergent profiles of symmetrical and asymmetrical relations. McLeod (1987) has more recently shown that rules of behavioral connection between individual wolves may peak and then decline, whereas rules of sequential ordering of behavioral "acts" measured from the perspective of the individual animal continue to be refined. McLeod's work is an important example of how similar descriptive frameworks can be applied both to the individual and to social partners, with clear, yet distinct, rules of order applying to each (cf. Havkin, 1981).

There are obviously many other ranges of behavioral expression and its control that might be compared on intraindividual and interindividual dimensions. The fundamental point that I wish to make is that, whether one is speaking primarily about events within or between organisms, both similar questions and similar principles of developmental order in behavior may be found given appropriately and explicitly stated abstractions of the guidelines through which these principles are presumed to operate. Young mice, grooming their faces, at first show rich but poorly coordinated actions, that diverge subsequently into precise patterns of dynamic and hierarchical order. Similarly, wolf social actions go through an initial period of loose symmetry, followed by excessive coupling among particular features of behavior, in turn followed by orderly constructions in behavior that are both wide ranging and connected into consistent higher order expressive frameworks (see Fentress, in press for further details).

## DYNAMIC FOCI
## OF INTEGRATED ACTION

It is clear that we do not yet have a satisfactory framework from which to look at even short-term patterns of behavior in reasonable dynamic and relational terms. The problem is amplified when we begin to consider problems of behavioral development. There are two basic, and conceptually related, aspects of this problem in integrated action. The first concerns dynamic relations among central and peripheral events for any given action. The second concerns relations among different classes of action. Obviously in each case we are circumscribing particular properties of action and also asking how these properties may change within the broader contexts of their expression.

### Dynamic Relations Among Central
### and Peripheral States

There are at least three aspects of the issue of dynamic relations among "intrinsic" (central) and "extrinsic" (peripheral) states. The first is "how powerful" the peripheral states are in determining actions that are otherwise centrally defined. The second is "what routes" these peripheral influences take; (e.g., do they "instruct" or just "modulate" centrally defined activities?). The third is "how necessary" particular routes of peripheral input are in the performance of integrated action sequences at any stage of development. Answers to each of these questions turn out to be contextually dependent. I concentrate only on the first question.

I have already reviewed evidence that the consequences of trigeminal deafferentation upon facial grooming sequences in mice depend on the broader contexts within which elements of facial grooming are viewed. Let

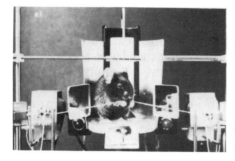
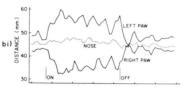
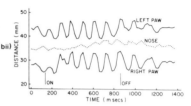

FIG. 2.9. Mouse in filming apparatus that permits application of phasic loads to the limbs during different phases of grooming behavior (from Fentress, 1980). bi and bii show, respectively, horizontal and vertical movements of forepaws and nose, before and after forelimbs pulled horizontally (**ON**) via stretch threads, and after termination of pull (**OFF**). Note continuation of rhythmic vertical movements even though paws no longer contact the face.

me now illustrate that point somewhat further. Woolridge and I developed a preparation where individual mice were placed upon a platform with stretch threads attached to each of their forelegs (Fig. 2.9). These stretch threads were attached to solenoids that could be activated during different phases of grooming. The result of this activation of the solenoids was that the paws were displaced temporarily from their opportunity to contact the face. During slow and variable phases of grooming, activation of the solenoids terminated grooming actions, as one might expect. However, during rapid and stereotyped phases of grooming, the basic vertical cycles of forepaw movements continued even though normal paw to face contacts were no longer possible. This is one of many examples in the animal and human literature that indicate strongly activated behavioral expressions often become both (a) more stereotypically focused and (b) less sensitive to "extrinsic'' sensory influences that may otherwise guide or interrupt them (e.g., reviews in Fentress, 1986, 1988; Fromm, 1987).

## Dynamic Relations Among Action Classes

Careful observations allow one to predict, often with surprising accuracy, when particular actions will occur. For example, grooming is a common transitional behavior that occurs between protracted periods of locomotion and immobility. In infant mice, grooming can be "set" by placing the animal into an appropriate sitting posture. At different ages, different forms of behavior have different priorities. There are a number of pathological circumstances in which one form of action essentially "takes over" (e.g., perseverant motor stereotypies in zoo animals and human autism).

Most obviously for these later cases of perseverant action, but also in other cases, a relatively wide range of stimuli normally associated with other forms of behavior can, on occasion, have a facilitatory influence. This is particularly likely if those stimuli are only moderately strong. Facilitation of the "target" action is often most likely during the early stages of stimulus presentation and shortly after the stimulus is terminated. Low levels of central nervous system stimulation also frequently facilitate a wide range of actions, only to become more focused with increasing activation. This is especially true for young animals, where the "boundaries" that demarcate one integrative system from another may be less precise than they are later; cf. Moran, 1986; Wolgin, 1982).

Such results represent a complex body of literature that together suggests that moderate activation of a variety of behavioral pathways can have a relatively broad band of facilitatory influence (enhance a number of previously "set" activities at low activation levels), only to become more focused at high activation levels (e.g., reviews in Fentress, 1976, 1983, 1984, in press). Further, these quantitative properties are also temporally dependent. For example, stimuli may initially facilitate then block "set" actions, and produce a "rebound" in these actions shortly after the stimulus presentation ceases.

Perhaps the most simple example in the infancy literature is the enhancement of suckling responses by novel stimuli, such as employed by Eimas and his colleagues to test properties of categorical preception (Eimas &

CENTER-SURROUND

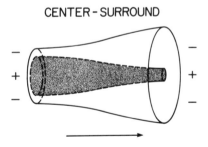

FIG. 2.10. The center-surround model of behavioral organization. A central excitatory core is viewed to be accompanied by an inhibitory surround. Further, the figure provides the suggestion that as the strength of activation in the core area increases (direction of arrows) the range of events that are excited shrinks while the surrounding inhibition expands. (Note: From "The Development of Coordination" by J.C. Fentress, 1984, *Journal of Motor Behavior, 16*, p. 123. Reprinted with permission of the Helen Dwight Reid Educational Foundation. Copyright 1984 by Heldref Publications.)

Miller, in press). As illustration, novel sounds will generate suckling in infants that are "set" by having a bottle nipple placed into their mouths. Sounds that the infant does not treat as novel may be ignored, and obviously sounds that are too loud may block suckling and generate a startle response. To summarize, the point is that relations among behavioral systems have dynamic properties that are a combined reflection of qualitative, quantitative and temporal variables. Simple static "box and arrow" models can be misleading. A more adequate form of conceptualization (Fig. 2.10) can be found in analogy to the "center-surround" models employed in studies of a number of sensory and perceptual systems (e.g., Konishi, 1986). The conceptualization I propose has two basic parts (cf. Fentress, 1984, 1986, in press). First, even higher order integrative systems can be viewed (abstractly) as having an excitatory core and inhibitory surround. Second, as these systems become more strongly activated their core of (abstracted) excitation becomes more restricted into particular functional channels, and their surround of (abstracted) inhibition broadens. There are a number of consequences of the model. Perhaps the simplest to grasp is that strongly activated systems should be more difficult to interrupt (i.e., they have a powerful and broad inhibitory "shield"). This point has been illustrated with the stereotypic phases of rodent grooming. A second consequence of the model is more subtle. It is based on the proposition that organisms can be "multiply activated," with each of these sources of activation being visualized as producing an excitatory core and inhibitory surround. The activations can overlap, as can the inhibitory surrounds. At moderate degrees of activation the central excitatory foci are broad, with the resulting possibility of mutual facilitation (core overlaps). At higher degrees of activation the "excitatory cores" become more narrowly focused, and the "inhibitory surrounds" spread. Overlap between systems would thus be restricted to the inhibitory zones.

The result I wish to emphasize is that ongoing predispositions in behavior may be enhanced by moderate activation of other ("extrinsic") behavioral channels (overlap of excitatory cores). These same predispositions are more likely to be respecified into the extrinsic channels when these channels are strongly activated (due to surround inhibition that blocks the ongoing predispositions). The model provides a relativistic and dynamic alternative to problems of specificity among behavioral control processes that have often otherwise proven difficult to conceptualize (cf. review by Gunnar, 1987, on the specific and nonspecific properties of "stress" as measured at several levels). There are a number of subtleties in the model that we are currently testing that need not concern us here. What I hope to show in the final sections of this chapter is that a similar dynamic conceptualization may apply to the roles of experience in development (i.e., when should experiences enhance versus respecify ongoing developmental sets?).

## TOWARD DYNAMIC MODELS
## OF BEHAVIORAL ONTOGENY

As Susan Oyama (this volume, 1985) has discussed eloquently, it has proven extremely difficult to avoid static dichotomies in our conceptualizations of ontogeny even though we all recognize there is something amiss in these static dichotomies. I have tried to show in previous sections of this Chapter that similar problems occur in our models of integrated action even when development is not a consideration. Conceptualizations of central "versus" peripheral control, specific "versus" nonspecific factors, and even higher "versus" lower levels of control each reflect a topological style of thinking that can only take us so far. Here I hope to show how we might go further.

### The "Crystalization" of Behavior in Development

Ethologists often speak of behavior as being crystalized during development, a metaphor that includes the perfection of individual elements, the linkage of these elements into clear patterns, and the elimination of extraneous events (Marler & Peters, 1982). Harrison (1982) has used the crystalization metaphor somewhat differently to emphasize "kinetically maintained structures" and "self-organizing systems" for the emergence of order during developmental events. Harrison borrowed from earlier work by Mason (1961) on the formation of snowflakes to emphasize that the atomic structure of water is in itself an insufficient predictor of the shape of crystals produced by freezing. This is because flow rates during freezing are also controlled by supersaturation and temperature. Thus, snowflakes grow predictably as plates @ $-1^C$, needles @ $-4^C$ and stars @ $-14^C$ (Fig. 2.11). Compound shapes (e.g., needles with end plates or stars) can be produced by appropriate temperature changes during "development."

This basic physical illustration serves to remind us that simple preprogramming models which suggest inevitability of final product are doomed to failure without appropriate acknowledgment of contextual factors (cf. Stent, 1981). The example also reinforces the position that *once contextual factors are taken appropriately into account,* developmental events in physical systems can be characterized as self-organizing. Thus, sensitivity to environmental context and self-organization are not mutually exclusive alternatives, as is often implied in the literature, but necessary complements.

Obviously biological and behavioral events contain complexities not apparent in simple physical systems, but the polarity of interaction and self-organization represented by the more complex and often interlacing systemsremains fundamental. In recent years a number of developmental theorists (e.g., Gierer & Meinhardt, 1972; Meinhardt, 1982; Willshaw & von

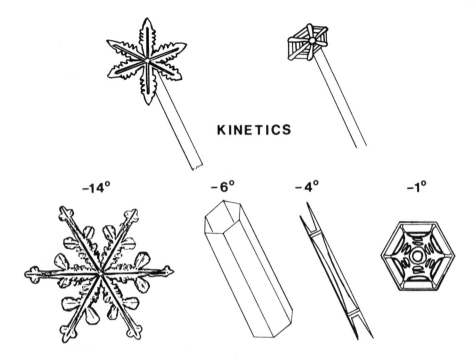

**KINETICS**

−14°          −6°          −4°          −1°

FIG. 2.11. This figure indicates that even simple physical systems can change their developmental properties as a function of the environmental context within which they grow. Therefore it is incorrect to attribute the final form of the snowflake merely with reference to intrinsic properties of water (from Mason, 1961).

der Malsburg, 1976) have demonstrated that models that capture short-range activation with autocatalysis and long-range surround inhibition can sculpt predictable and complex patterns given appropriate knowledge of the biological boundary conditions over which the excitatory and inhibitory processes are produced. As Harrison (1982) pointed out, a major future task is to establish more adequate tools for conceptualizing boundary interactions and dynamics in a biologically (and thus behaviorally) realistic manner.

This realism will be achieved only when we succeed in combining improved formalizations with more detailed knowledge of particular cases. From the brief sketch given here we can already see that simple juxtaposition of intrinsic versus extrinsic events can never suffice. Developing organisms (and their subsystems) must both be receptive to surrounding influences and protect themselves from these influences. That, I suspect, is the hub of the issue. I address some of its ramifications next.

Ontogeny in an Imperfect World

There is a reason for the "central dogma," but Oyama (this volume, 1985) is quite correct in pointing to its limitations. The primary reason to point "centrally," as I see it, is that developing organisms do not "mirror" in any simple isomorphic way the details of the world within which they grow up. And that is fortunate, for this world is itself often both incomplete and distorted. Thus, the developing organism must use the information that is made available externally, and "go beyond" it (Bruner, 1974). The developing organism must also be very selective in the information that it uses. There is, for example, a broad range of studies in ethology that show that developing organisms are selectively tuned to particular features of their environments. Perhaps the clearest illustrations come from the elegant studies by Marler and his colleagues on the ontogeny of bird song (e.g., Marler & Peters, 1982). These studies indicate that song birds are predisposed to make use of a relatively narrow window of auditory experiences in the shaping of their own songs. There are also fascinating species differences uncovered by Marler and his colleagues that we cannot go into here. I use Marler as an example from ethology in part because he has — with considerable success — sought potential links between deeper rules of song acquisition in birds and the developmental processes in human language.

Chomsky (1980) has argued convincingly that children cannot simply mirror the world in their development of language (e.g., his famous slogan of "the poverty of the stimulus"). There are also numerous studies in human experimental psychology that demonstrate how people can abstract from "degraded," "off target," and "incomplete" stimuli in the performance of a wide range of skilled tasks (e.g., Rummelhart et al., 1986). In this literature there are numerous comparisons to the dynamic network analysis (DNA) perspective that I have outlined in previous sections of this chapter. To cite but a single example that may have important developmental analogues, studies of deep dyslexia in humans have indicated that retraining on only a few words within a semantic set can improve performance measured by other untrained words within that set. In development, we can also expect that there will be extrapolations across dynamically ordered networks of current dispositions, but there are at present very few studies designed explicitly to clarify the boundaries of these networks.

Obviously, we cannot do all necessary experiments in humans, but we can, in principle, do many of these experiments in animals. Thus, what if I gave infant mice experience with a subset of grooming movements or their sensory precursors only; might they extrapolate the benefits of this limited experience to other grooming movements — or might they extrapolate down other channels that we do not even anticipate given our present taxonomies of behavior? Or, suppose I gave these mice distorted experiences with grooming, such as might be done with weighted boots. When would the animals show an accentuation of developmental predispositions and when would they respecify the details of their subsequent behavioral expressions? I am not suggesting that such experiments will be easy, but they may be exceptionally important.

For the most part we simply do not know what the rules are for extrapolations from particular experiences during development. Should, for example, we expect generalizations to occur in terms of simple physical scales (cf. Pavlovian conditioning) or in terms of more abstractly defined functional channels of expression that can contain physically quite distinct events? Might the relative importance of generalizations based on form and function also change with age? Recall that young mice may show sudden transitions into grooming if they happen to make movements similar to grooming during locomotion or even swimming, whereas older mice appear able to maintain more abstractly defined functional coherences in behavior (see previous and Fentress, 1988). Experiences might generalize differently at these two different ages.

## A Dual-Threshold Hypothesis

Here I offer a hypothesis that to my knowledge has not been studied explicitly. It is based on the "dual lens" (excitatory core and inhibitory surround) model of integrated action previously outlined. The hypothesis is this. Animals and human infants live in an imperfect world. This world may not only provide incomplete developmental experiences, but also degraded and "off target" experiences. We do not want to victimize either our animals or our children to these flukes of "nurture." Perhaps they have the wisdom to do something along the following lines. They may say to themselves, metaphorically speaking: "If I get some information from my environment that is a bit off target from my present developmental inclinations then let me assume that it is the world and not me that is in error. I shall therefore use this distorted information as a confirmation that I am going down the correct developmental path, and push ahead. However, if the world tells me, in 'strong terms,' that it does not fit with my developmental predispositions, then I might be better off respecifying my future course of action. In brief, I might best operate within a dual threshold framework — facilitate ongoing states first, and respecify these states second."

Now, I am not certain this idea of dual threshold specification in development will work out in detail, but I am willing to bet that clever experiments in the future will give it at least reasonable support. Indeed, there is already some potential, albeit indirect, support. Horn (1985) has summarized data from his laboratory on the dynamic organization of imprinting in chickens, including the biochemcial and anatomical substrates of this imprinting. For my present purposes I highlight only one of the behavioral observations.

First, recall my arguments in previous sections that the "effective strength" of a given stimulus event may decline over time. This is why I have stressed throughout the chapter that qualitative, quantitative, and temporal factors must all be considered together. Next, recall that I have proposed that moderate levels of activation can have a fairly broad band of facilitatory effects, whereas strong levels of activation are more prone to narrow their focus, and thus potentially respecify rather than facilitate ongoing events.

Horn and his colleagues have shown that exposure to either flashing lights or dismembered chicken models within an imprinting context can change preferences in favor of these objects along a short time scale. We might expect this if the animals are saying to themselves: "Aha, I now see that I should follow these weird and mysterious stimuli." Later, however, the chickens do something quite remarkable. They not only no longer show an enhanced preference for the "weird and mysterious stimuli" to which they had been exposed, but they use exposure to these stimuli to reinforce (enhance) their preferences to follow normal chickens. That is, exposure to red lights and chopped chickens now leads the birds to prefer normal chickens even more than they would have without this exposure to red lights and chopped chickens. Horn and his colleagues have also shown that even the opportunity to enhance locomotor activity can accentuate normal developmental (imprinting) preferences. These data are precisely at the heart of my proposition for dynamic network analyses (DNA) of behavioral performance and its development. Although the data that exist presently remain inadequate for fully quantitative modeling, they do suggest directions that future modeling might take.

## CONCLUSIONS: TOWARD A POTENTIAL SYNTHESIS OF INTERACTIVE/SELF-ORGANIZING SYSTEMS IN PERFORMANCE AND ITS DEVELOPMENT

The emphasis throughout this chapter has been on the dynamic, relational, and multilayered nature of behavior, whether examined primarily in terms of moment to moment integration or in terms of development. Indeed, the fundamental issue is how we can join these two perspectives of integration and development together. I perceive that a common issue that we do not yet understand is how we can best conceptualize interactive and self-organizing tendencies within a common package. These tendencies are necessary compatriots, not antagonists. But we need much finer analyses of these dynamically ordered systemic processes and their implications.

Each of the chapters in the present volume provides an important perspective on how we might proceed. Certainly those of us who have been involved primarily in animal research have much to gain from those who have chosen to focus on issues in human development. Indeed, I see a strengthening of our commonality in purpose, which I anticipate and hope will lead to a strengthening and perfection of the obviously inadequate models that we must each now employ.

## ACKNOWLEDGMENTS

The behavioral (ethological) parts of this chapter were supported primarily by grants from the Natural Sciences and Engineering Research Council of Canada; the more neurological and clinical aspects of the chapter reflect research supported primarily by the Medical Research Council of Canada. I thank each of these institutions, and also Dalhousie Graduate Studies, for their generous support. I especially owe thanks to Dr. Megan Gunnar for her invitation to participate in the conference, and to her student and faculty colleagues for providing an unusually stimulating format for the sharing of ideas. Megan's constructively critical comments, along with those of other conference participants, aided me greatly. Wanda Danilchuk once again provided expert assistance during the final stages of preparation of this chapter, and my numerous colleagues at Dalhousie deserve credit for helping me keep my thinking straight about the critical issues in behavioral development.

## REFERENCES

Angulo y Gonzalez, A.W. (1932). The prenatal development of behavior in the albino rat. *The Journal of Comparative Neurology, 55,* 395–442.

Bekoff, A, (1981). Embryonic development of the neural circuitry underlying motor coordination. In W.M. Cowan (Ed.), *Studies in developmental neurobiology* (pp. 134–170). New York: Oxford University Press.

Bernstein, N. (1967). *Co-ordination and regulation of movements.* New York: Pergamon Press.

Berridge, K.C., & Fentress, J.C. (1986). Contextual control of trigeminal sensorimotor function. *Journal of Neuroscience, 6,* 325–330.

Berridge, K.C., & Fentress, J.C. (1987). Deafferentation does not disrupt natural rules of action syntax. *Behavioural Brain Research, 23,* 69–76.

Bohm, D. (1980). *Wholeness and the implicate order.* London: Routledge & Kegan Paul.

Bruner, J.S. (1974). The organization of early skilled action. In M.P.M. Richards (Ed.), *The integration of a child into a social world* (pp. 167–184). London: Cambridge University Press.

Chomsky, N. (1980). *Rules and representations.* New York: Columbia University Press.
Coghill, G. E. (1929). *Anatomy and the problem of behavior.* Cambridge: Cambridge University Press.
Crick, F. H. C. (1984). The function of the thalamic reticular complex: The searchlight hypothesis. *Proceedings National Academy of Sciences, 81,* 4586—4590.
Darwin, C. (1872). *The expression of the emotions in man and the animals.* London: John Murray.
Davidson, E.H. (1986). *Gene activity in early development* (3rd ed.). New York: Academic Press.
Edelman, G.M., & Finkel, L. H. (1984). Neuronal group selection in the cerebral cortex. In G. M. Edelman, W. E. Gall, & W. M. Cowan (Eds.), *Dynamic aspects of neocortical function* (pp. 653—695). New York: Wiley.
Eimas, P. D., & Miller, J. L. (in press). Infant categories and categorization. In G. M. Edelman, W. E. Gall, & W. M. Cowan (Eds.), *Signal and sense: Local and global order in perceptual maps.* New York: Wiley.
Eshkol, N., & Wachmann, A. (1958). *Movement notation.* London: Weidenfeld & Nicholson.
Fentress, J. C. (1976). Dynamic boundaries of patterned behavior: Interaction and self-organization. In P.P.G. Bateson & R. A. Hinde (Eds.), *Growing points in ethology* (pp. 135-169). Cambridge: Cambridge University Press.
Fentress, J. C. (1978). *Mus musicus.* The developmental orchestration of selected movement patterns in mice. In M. Bekoff & G. Burghardt (Eds.), *The development of behavior: comparative and evolutionary aspects* (pp. 321-342). New York: Garland.
Fentress, J. C. (1980). How can behavior be studied from a neuroethological perspective? In H. M. Pinsker & W. D. Willis, Jr. (Eds.), *Information processing in the nervous system* (pp. 263-283). New York: Raven Press.
Fentress, J. C. (1983). Hierarchical motor control. In M. Studdert-Kennedy (Ed.), *Neurobiology of language processes* (pp. 40-61). Cambridge: The MIT Press.
Fentress, J. C. (1984). The development of coordination. *Journal of Motor Behavior, 16,* 99-134.
Fentress, J. C. (1986). Development of coordinated movement: Dynamic, relational and multileveled perspectives. In H. T. A. Whiting & M. C. Wade (Eds.), *Motor development in children: Aspects of coordination and control* (pp. 77-105). Dordrecht: Martinus Nijhoff.
Fentress, J. C. (1987a). D. O. Hebb and the developmental organization of behavior. *Developmental Psychobiology, 20*(2), 103-109.
Fentress, J. C. (1987b). Compartments and cohesions in adaptive behavior. *Journal of Comparative Psychology, 101*(3), 254-259.
Fentress, J. C. (1988). Expressive contexts, fine structure, and central mediation of rodent grooming. *Annals of the New York Academy of Sciences, 525,* 18-26.
Fentress, J. C. (in press). Organizational patterns in action: Local and global issues in action pattern formation. In G. Edelman, W. E. Gall, & W. M. Cowan (Eds.), *Signal and sense: Local and global order in perceptual maps.* New York: Wiley.
Fentress, J. C., & McLeod, P. (1986). Motor patterns in development. In E. M. Blass (Ed.), *Handbook of behavioral neurobiology: Developmental processes in psychobiology and neurobiology* (pp. 35-97). New York: Plenum Press.
Fentress, J. C., & Stilwell, F. P. (1973). Grammar of a movement sequence in inbred mice. *Nature, 244,* 52-53.
Fogel, A., & Thelen, E. (1987). Development of early expressive and communicative action: Reinterpreting the evidence from a dynamic systems perspective. *Developmental Psychology, 23*(6), 747-761.
Foucault, M. (1970). *The order of things: An archaeology of the human sciences.* New York: Random House.

Fromm, C. (1987). Sensorimotor integration: The role of pyramidal tract neurons. In H. Heuer & A. F. Sanders (Eds.), *Perspectives on perception and action* (pp. 13–168). Hillsdale, NJ: Lawrence Erlbaum Associates.

Gatev, V. (1972). Role of inhibition in the development of motor coordination in early childhood. *Developmental Medicine and Child Neurology, 14,* 336–341.

Gierer, A., & Meinhardt, H. (1972). A theory of biological pattern formation. *Kybernetik, 12,* 30–39.

Golani, I. (1976). Homeostatic motor processes in mammalian interactions: A choreography of display. In P.P.G. Bateson & P.H. Klopfer (Eds.), *Perspectives in ethology (Vol. 2, pp. 69–134).* New York: Plenum Press.

Golani, I., & Fentress, J.C. (1985). Early ontogeny of face grooming in mice. *Developmental Psychobiology, 18,* 529–544.

Goldberg, G. (1987). Premotor systems, motor learning, and ipsilateral control: Learning to get set. *Behavioral and Brain Sciences, 10*(2), 323–329.

Gunnar, M. R. (1987). Psychobiological studies of stress and coping: An introduction. *Child Development, 58*(6), 1403-1407.

Harrison, L. G. (1982). An overview of kinetic theory in developmental modeling. In S. Subtelny & P. B. Green (Eds.), *Developmental order: Its origin and regulation* (pp. 3–33). New York: Alan R. Liss.

Havkin, G. Z. (1977). *Symmetry shifts in the development of interactive behaviour of two wolf pups (Canis lupus).* Unpublished masters thesis, Dalhousie University, Halifax, Nova Scotia.

Havkin, G. Z. (1981). *Form and strategy of combative interactions between wolf pups (Canis lupus).* Unpublished doctoral thesis, Dalhousie University, Halifax, Nova Scotia.

Hebb D. O. (1949). *The organization of behavior: A Neuropsychological Theory.* New York: Wiley.

Hinde, R. A. (1982). *Ethology: Its nature and relations with other sciences.* New York: Oxford University Press.

Hines, M. (1942). The development and regression of reflexes, postures, and progression in the young macaque. *Contributions to Embryology, 30,* 153–209.

Horn, G. (1985). *Memory, imprinting, and the brain: An inquiry into mechanisms.* Oxford: Clarendon Press.

Jacob, F. (1976). *The logic of life: A history of heredity.* New York: Random House.

Kelso, J. A. S. (1986). Pattern formation in speech and limb movements involving many degrees of freedom. *Experimental Brain Research Series, 15,* 105–128.

Kent, R. D. (1976). Anatomical and neuromuscular maturation of the speech mechanism: Evidence from acoustic studies. *Journal of Speech and Hearing Research, 19,* 421–447.

Knudsen, E.I., & Knudsen, P. F. (1985). Vision guides the adjustment of auditory localization in young barn owls. *Science, 230,* 545–548.

Kolb, B., Jacobs, W. J., & Petrie, B. (1987). Searching for a technology of behavior. *Behavioral and Brain Sciences, 10*(2), 220–221.

Konishi, M. (1986). Centrally synthesized maps of sensory space. *Trends in Neuroscience, 9,* 163–168.

Lashley, K. S. (1951). The problem of serial order in behavior. In L. A. Jeffress (Ed.), *Cerebral mechanisms in behavior* (pp. 112–136). New York: Wiley.

Liberman, A. M. (1970). The grammars of speech and language. *Cognitive Psychology, 1,* 301–323.

Luria, A. R. (1980). *Higher cortical functions in man (2nd ed.). New York: Basic Books.*

Marler, P., & Peters, S. (1982). Developmental overproduction and selective attrition: New processes in the epigenesis of birdsong. *Developmental Psychobiology, 15,* 369–378.

Mason, B. J. (1961). The growth of snow crystals. *Scientific American, 204,* 120–131.

McClelland, J. L., & Elman, J. L. (1986). Interactive processes in speech perception: The trace model. In D. E. Rumelhart, J. L. McClelland, & the PDP Research Group (Eds.), *Parallel distributed processing* (Vol. 2, pp. 58–121). Cambridge: The MIT Press.

McLeod, P. J. (1987). *Aspects of the early social development of timber wolves (Canis lupus).* Unpublished doctoral thesis, Dalhousie University, Halifax, Nova Scotia.

Meinhardt, H. (1982). Generation of structures in a developing organism. In S. Subtnely & P. B. Green (Eds.), *In developmental order: Its origin and regulation* (pp. 439–461). New York: Alan R. Liss.

Moran, T. H. (1986). Environmental and neural determinants of behavior in development. In E. M. Blass (Ed.), *Handbook of behavioral neurobiology: Developmental psychobiology and developmental neurobiology* (pp. 99–128). New York: Plenum Press.

Moran, G., Fentress, J. C., & Golani, I. (1981). A description of relational patterns during "ritualized fighting" in wolves. *Animal Behaviour, 29,* 1146–1165.

Murphey, R. K. (1986). The myth of the inflexible invertebrate: Competitive and synaptic remodelling in the development of invertebrate nervous systems. *Journal of Neurobiology 17,* 585–591.

Narayanan, C. H., Fox, M. W., & Hamburger, V. (1971). Prenatal development spontaneous and evoked activity in the rat *(Rattus norvegicus albinus). Behaviour, 40,* 100–134.

Oppenheim, R. W. (1981). Ontogenetic adaptations and retrogressive processes in the development of the nervous system and behavior. In K. Connolly & H. Prechtl (Eds.), *Maturation and behavior development* (pp. 73–109). London: Spastics Society Publications.

Oyama, S. (1985). *The ontogeny of information: Developmental systems and evolution.* Cambridge, England: Cambridge University Press.

Posner, M.I., & Presti, D. E. (1987). Selective attention and cognitive control. *Trends in Neuroscience, 10,* 13–17.

Prechtl, H. F. R. (1986). Prenatal motor development. In M. G. Wade & H. T. A. Whiting (Eds.), *Motor development in children: Aspects of coordination and control* (pp. 53–64). Dordrecht: Martinus Nijhoff.

Premack, D. (1986). *Gavigai!: Or the future history of the animal language controversy.* Cambridge: The MIT Press.

Provine, R. R. (1986). Behavioral neuroembryology: Motor perspectives. In W. T. Greenough & J. M. Juraska (Eds.), *Developmental neuropsychobiology* (pp. 213–239). New York: Academic Press.

Rauschecker, J. P. (1984). Neuronal mechanisms of developmental plasticity in the cat's visual system. *Human Neurobiology, 3,* 109–114.

Rummelhart, D. E., McClelland, J. L., and PDP Research Group (Eds.). (1986). *Parallel distributed processing: Vol. 1, Foundations.* Cambridge: The MIT Press.

Singer, W. (1986). Neuronal activity as a shaping factor in postnatal development of visual cortex. In W. T. Greenough & J. M. Juraska (Eds.), *Developmental neuropsychobiology* (pp. 271–293). Orlando, FL: Academic Press.

Smotherman, W. P., & Robinson, S. R. (1987). Psychobiology of fetal experience in the rat. In N. A. Krasnegor, E. M. Blass, M. A. Hofer, & W. P. Smotherman (Eds.), *Perinatal development: A psychobiological perspective* (pp. 39–60). New York: Academic Press.

Stent, G. S. (1981). Strength and weakness of the genetic approach to the development of the nervous system. *Annual Review of Neuroscience, 4,* 163–194.

Tees, R. C. (1986). Experience and visual development: Behavioral evidence. In W. T. Greenough & J. M. Juraska (Eds.), *Developmental neuropsychobiology* (pp. 317–361). Orlando, FL: Academic Press.

Teitelbaum, P. (1977). Levels of integration of the operant. In W. K. Honig & J. E. R. Staddon (Eds.), *Handbook of operant behavior.* Englewood Cliffs, NJ: Prentice-Hall.

Thelen, E. (1986). Development of coordinated movement: Implications for early human development. In M. G. Wade & H. T. A. Whiting (Eds.), *Motor development in children:*

*Aspects of coordination and control.* Dordrecht: Martinus Nijhoff.

Whitehead, A. N. (1978). *Process and reality.* New York: The Free Press.

Willshaw, D. J., & C. von der Malsburg (1976). How patterned neural connections can be set up by self-organization. *Proceedings Royal Society of London, B194,* 431–445.

Windle, W. F. (1940). *Physiology of the fetus.* Philadelphia: Saunders.

Wolgin, D. L. (1982). Motivation, activation, and behavioral integration. In R.L. Isaacson & N. E. Spear (Eds.), *The expression of knowledge* (pp. 243–290). New York: Plenum Press.

# 3

# Self-Organization in Developmental Processes: Can Systems Approaches Work?

Esther Thelen
*Indiana University*

*the induction of novel behavioral forms may be the single most important unresolved problem for all the developmental and cognitive sciences.*
—Wolff, 1987, p. 240

What does behavior come from? As modest observers of humans and other animals in their early times of life, we must ask this question every day. It is the most profound of questions. Nearly every field of human inquiry— philosophy, theology, cosmology, physics, geology, history, biology, anthropology—asks in some way about the origins of new forms. How can we start with a state that is somehow less and get more? What is the ultimate source of the "more"?

Traditionally, developmentalists have sought the source of the "more" either in the organism or in the environment. In one case, new structures and functions arise as a result of instructions stored beforehand, encoded in the genes or in the nervous system (and ultimately in the genes) and read out during ontogeny like the program on a computer tape. Alternatively, the organism gains in form by absorbing the structure and patterning of its physical or social environment through its interactions with that environment.

Of course, no contemporary developmentalist would advocate either pole in the nature–nurture dichotomy. Everyone now is an interactionist or a transactionalist or a systems theorist. We have example after example in both human and other animal research of the reciprocal effects of organism and environment in effecting developmental change. We would likely find

77

no cases that would show anything else. Why then, can Wolff claim that the induction of new forms remains a great unsolved problem?

At one level, it seems clear that no current developmental models — whether they invoke interactional, transactional, or systems concepts, have been especially successful in accounting for a wide range of empirical data. That is, we lack general principles of development that apply across species or across domains in one species, and that can account for both the exquisite regularities and the often frustrating nonlinearities, regressions, and variabilities that characterize the emergence of new forms.

Recently, several authors have criticized current developmental theorizing on perhaps an even deeper level. Oyama (1985), for example, cogently argued that by assigning the sources of ontogenetic change to either instructions from within the organism or information in the environment we have never come to grips with the ultimate origins of new forms. We seek to find the plans pre-existing somewhere that impose structure on the organism. Nativism and empiricism thus both share the assumption that "information can preexist the processes that give rise to it" (p. 13). This assumption of prior design located inside or "out there," leads to an inevitable logical trap — who or what "turns on" the genes, who or what decides what information out there is "good." However elaborate our story of regulator genes, feedback loops, comparators, and schema, Oyama claimed that we finally require a cause — and the old homunculus rears its head, although in more sophisticated guise. *Postulating an interaction of genes and environment in no way removes this logical impasse.* It merely assigns the pre-existing plans to two sources instead of one.

In a similar vein, Haroutunian (1983) criticized Piaget — surely our most thorough-going interactionist — for failing to acknowledge the logical consequences of equilibration through accommodation and assimilation. Piaget's logical nemesis is also infinite regress: How can equilibration produce new forms through accommodation and assimilation that are not properties of these functions themselves? How does the organism know to differentiate schema in the right direction? If the organism is testing hypotheses about the world, against what standards are those hypotheses tested? Piaget's solution, Haroutunian claimed, was an implicit genetic nativism.

Are there, then, any candidates for general developmental principles that will avoid the logical pitfalls of dualistic theories and yet provide more than just rhetoric, principles that will provide structure to guide empirical research, formulate testable hypotheses, and integrate data within and across species and domains?

For many years, developmentalists have recognized that systems principles of biological organization offer a conceptually elegant solution to the problem of new forms. Systems principles are well-known: wholeness and order, adaptive self-stabilization, adaptive self-organization, hierarchical structuring (Laszlo, 1972). In addition to the classic statements of Von Bertalanffy (1968), Laszlo (1972), Waddington (1972), and Weiss (1969), a number of recent excellent essays and reviews detail the application of systems theory to development (e.g., Brent, 1978, 1984; Kitchener, 1982; Lerner, 1978; Overton, 1975; Sameroff, 1983; Wolff, 1987).

It is specifically the principle of *self-organization* that rescues developmentalists from the logical hole of infinite regress. That is, in biological systems, *pattern and order can emerge from the process of the interactions of the components of a complex system* without the need for explicit instructions. In Oyama's (1985) terminology:

> Form emerges in successive interactions. Far from being imposed on matter by some agent, it is a function of the reactivity of matter at many hierarchical levels, and of the responsiveness of those interactions to each other. . . . Organismic form . . . is constructed in developmental processes.

Systems formulations are intuitively attractive for many developmental issues, in addition to the question of the origins of novel forms. Despite this, systems remain more of an abstraction for most working developmentalists than a coherent guide to investigation or synthesis. I believe there are a number of reasons why systems have not "worked."

Oyama (this volume) suggested that the resistance to concepts like emergent order stems both from the prevailing reductionist and mechanistic approaches in biology and from a long tradition of belief in causation by design. Invoking emergent order seems like a retreat into vitalism. Equally important, I believe, is that we have had no accessible translation of systems principles to empirical design, methodology, and interpretation. By their very nature, systems are complex, multicausal, nonlinear, nonstationary, and contingent. The inherent nonlinearity and nonstationarity poses a real challenge to our needs for prescription and predictability. As a result, workers will often resort to a systems explanation only after their more direct main-effect or interactional models fail to explain a body of data. Systems views are often relegated to the discussion sections of papers: If everything affects every else in a complicated way, then it must be a system (Woodson, 1988). Such post hoc incantation can dilute systems concepts to the point of vacuousness. Thus, although we need complexity and multicausality in our models because we have complexity and multicausality in our organisms, systems views seemingly lead to insurmountable obstacles for empirical analysis.

Certain contemporary work in physics, chemistry, biology, and psychology may now weaken the traditional resistance to the idea that organisms can produce pattern without prescription. The active fields of synergetics and nonlinear dynamics in physics, chemistry, and mathematics, for example, show in mathematically precise ways, how complex systems may produce emergent order, that is, without a prescription for the pattern existing beforehand (see, for example, Haken, 1983, 1985; Madore & Freedman, 1987; Prigogine, 1980; Prigogine & Stengers, 1984). Where is the "design" that allows aggregations of molecules to form laser lights, flow patterns in fluids, crystals, cloud formations, and other nonrandom collectives of simple subunits? In biology, field theories of morphogenesis in plants and animals allow for the highly complex differentiation of structural and functional elements from more simple, nongenetic factors such as gradients, nearest neighbor calculations, cell-packing patterns, and so on (e.g., French, Bryant, & Bryant, 1976; Gierer, 1981; Meakin, 1986; Mittenthal, 1981). Developmental neurophysiologists are using terms such as *self-assembly* to describe the establishment and refinement of neural networks as a dynamic and contingent process (e.g., Barnes, 1986; Dammasch, Wagner, & Wolff, 1986; Singer, 1986).

There is a growing trend toward viewing adult nervous system function also as a dynamic and self-organizing process; that is, modeling function as the emergent property of the assembly of elemental units, none of which contains the prescription or command center (Skarda & Freeman, 1987; Szentagothai, 1984). This work ranges from mathematical formulations of simple behaviors in relatively primitive organisms—locomotion in the lamprey eel, for example (Cohen, Holmes, & Rand, 1982), to computational models of the highest human brain functions such as memory and language (e.g., Hopfield & Tank, 1986; Rumelhart & McClelland, 1986; Shrager, Hogg, & Huberman, 1987). I rely especially on the theoretical and empirical studies of human motor behavior of Kelso and his colleagues (Kelso, Holt, Kugler, & Turvey, 1980; Kelso & Tuller, 1984; Kugler, Kelso, & Turvey, 1980) based on dynamic principles, and in which the details of coordinated movement are seen to arise from the synergetic assembly of muscle collectives.

What these diverse formulations share—and what offers the empirical challenge to students of behavioral development—is the assumption that a higher order complexity can result from the cooperativity of simpler components. Vitalistic forces need not be invoked; it is the unique utilization of energy that can create "order out of chaos." Thus, the order and regularity observed in living organisms is a fundamental consequence of their thermodynamics; that they are open systems that use energy flow to organize and maintain stability. This means that unlike machines, biological systems can actively evolve toward a state of higher organization (Von Bertalanffy, 1968).

But will systems work for developmentalists? In the remainder of this chapter, I outline a number of principles derived from the field of synergetics (the physics of complex systems) that have special relevance for the study of developing systems. I then suggest that these principles may be useful in two ways. First, on a metaphoric or heuristic level, I offer a characterization of developing systems that may serve as a guide for examining and understanding multicausal and nonlinear phenomena in ontogeny. I apply the systems metaphor to several domains of early sensorimotor development in humans and other animals, and I suggest how synergetic principles may lead to testable systems hypotheses about the origins of new forms. Finally, I present examples from an ongoing study of infant motor coordination designed to use synergetic principles. Please note that I invoke these concepts with great caution and in the spirit of exploration. When the principles of complex systems have been applied to biological systems (e.g., Kelso & Schöner, in press), the phenomena modeled have been relatively simple and many variables could be rigorously controlled. We normally do not have that level of control over naturally developing organisms, nor can we be confident of the stationarity of our behavior over the measurement interval.

My introduction to synergetic principles came through my interest in early motor development. A fundamental question for understanding motor behavior is how a system composed of many, many "degrees of freedom"—muscle groups, joints, neuronal elements, and so on—"compressed" these degrees of freedom into coordinated movement with precise spatial and temporal patterning. The traditional theories invoking either "motor programs" or feedback-based machine models were beset with the same logical problem that faces developmental theories: the origins of new forms. Kelso and his colleagues have used synergetic principles to show how the neuromuscular system can be "self-organizing"; that is, how trajectories and coordinative modes can emerge without the need for prescriptive solutions (see Kelso & Tuller, 1984). A basic assumption is that synergetic principles of organization are so general that they may be applied across systems and time spans; that new forms arise in development by the same processes by which they arise in "real-time" action (see Fogel & Thelen, 1987; Kugler, Kelso, & Turvey, 1982; Thelen, 1986b; Thelen & Fogel, in press; Thelen, Kelso, & Fogel, 1987).

## PATTERN FORMATION IN COMPLEX AND DEVELOPING SYSTEMS

### Compression of the Degrees of Freedom and Self-Organization

Complex systems are systems with many elements or subsystems. These elements can combine with each other in a potentially very large number of ways; the system has an enormous number of "degrees of freedom" (Fig. 3.1). Under certain thermodynamic conditions—thermodynamic non-equilibrium (a directed flow of energy)—these elements can self-organize to generate patterned behavior that has much fewer dimensions than the original elements. That is, when the participating elements or subsystems interact, the original degrees of freedom are compressed to produce spatial and temporal order. The multiple variables can then be expressed as one or a few *collective variables*.

At any point in time, the behavior of the complex system is dynamically assembled as a product of the interactions of the elements in a particular context. At the same time that information is compressed, the resulting lower dimensional behavior can be highly complex and patterned. Behavioral complexity may be manifest in patterns evolving in space and time, in multiple patterns and stable states, and in remarkable adaptability to perturbations. Note that there is no prescription for this order existing prior

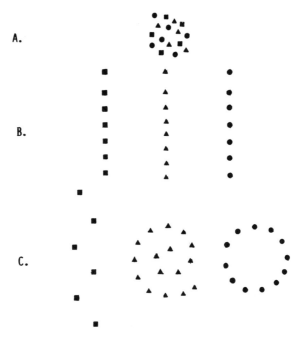

FIG. 3.1. Schematic depiction of self-organization in a complex system. (A) A complex system consists of a very large number of noisy elements or subsystems with very many degrees of freedom. (B) Under certain thermodynamic conditions, such systems can self-organize to produce lower dimensional dynamics; the degrees of freedom are reduced. (C) The dynamical system, in turn, exhibits behavioral complexity; it can have multiple patterns, multiple stable states, and adaptable configurations.

to the dynamic assembly, either in the individual elements or in the context; the order grows out of the relations.

These phenomena are best illustrated by a dramatic, nonbiological example: the now-famous Belousov–Zhabotinskii autocatalytic chemical reaction. When simple chemicals — bromate ions in highly acidic medium — are placed in a shallow glass dish, a remarkable series of events begins (see Fig. 3.2):

A dish, thinly spread with a lightly colored liquid, sits quietly for a moment after its preparation. The liquid is then suddenly swept by a spontaneous burst of colored centers of chemical activity. Each newly formed region creates expanding patterns of concentric, circular rings. These collide with neighboring waves but never penetrate. In some rare cases, rotating one-, two- or three-armed spirals may emerge. Each pattern grows, impinging on its neighboring patterns, winning on some fronts and losing on others, organiz-

FIG. 3.2. Evolving forms in the Belousov–Zhabotinkii reaction. The spontaneous development of structure can be seen in a sequence of photographs (left panels in each pair) that shows waves of chemical activity propagating through a receptive liquid medium. These complex forms can be remarkably well modeled by a simple computer simulation (right panels). (From Madore & Freedman, 1987.) Reprinted with permission.

ing the entire surface into a unique pattern. Finally, the patterns decay and the system dies, as secondary reactions drain the flow of the primary reaction. (Madore & Freedman, 1987, p. 253)

It would, of course, be impossible to describe the Belousov–Zhabotinskii reaction in terms of the behavior of the individual ions. There are too many of them and a nearly infinite number of degrees of freedom. The dramatic patterns, however, represent a much more compressed description. Whereas the behavior of the individual atoms is random and chaotic, the patterns show order in both space and time. Although they compress the original degrees of freedom, these patterns are themselves complex.

Where do these beautiful patterns and elaborate designs come from? No pattern generator or schema can be found. The order is truly emergent from the initial conditions: the mix of the chemicals and the constraints of the container, the room temperature, and so on. Scientists can simulate these self-organizing properties by a computer program that sets up very simple initial conditions. When the program runs, the sequence of pattern emerges, but a program for the pattern itself was never written.

The parallel between the Belousov–Zhabotinskii reaction and the events of early biological morphogenesis is striking. From the fertilized egg, a seeming homogeneous bag of chemicals, the embryo divides, cleaves, invaginates, becomes polarized and lateralized, develops layers, and so on. Models of early morphogenesis have much in common with those used to simulate the Belousov–Zhabotinskii reaction as they call on gradient fields, states of excitation, nearest neighbor effects, and simple rules of interaction.

But unlike the chemical reaction, which decays as the elements reach thermodynamic equilibrium, the embryo is supplied with a continual supply of energy through metabolic processes. It remains in this thermodynamic nonequilibrium, and as it utilizes energy, its emergent forms not only remain, but become more elaborated, each pattern generating its own subpatterns and so on until a great number of functional structures have been generated. Of course the process is not random as species quite precisely reproduce themselves. In this case however, the genome may be thought to greatly underspecify the resultant product. Much evidence exists that genetic information sets the initial conditions, so to speak, but does not encode the topology that enfolds.

On a different level, behavior in developing organisms is likewise a result of the unique cooperativity of the subsystems in a context. Because of the thermodynamic status of living organisms, complexity in behavior may be an emergent property. No iconic representations of the behavior, either in the form of genetic codes, maturational timetables, reflexes, or cognitive schemes need exist a priori. As such, behavior is never hard-wired, but flexibly assembled within certain organismic constraints and the demands of the context or task. Order, therefore, is a product of *process,* not instruction. It is noteworthy that contemporary parallel models of neuronal and higher brain function are predicated on the processing of many individual subunits, none of which contains the icon or command of the resultant memory unit, perceptual trace, or word representation.

This formulation allows us to make another important claim. Because biological systems are openly exchanging energy with their surrounds, the state of the organism and the context for action (the task demands) are formally equivalent in the assembly of the cooperative interaction. Therefore, there is no dichotomy between organism and environment. Neither has privileged status in effecting change. It is as meaningless to talk of a decontextualized organism as of an environment without biological meaning to the animal. However, we may identify parameters either within or without the organism which act as agents of change, without being prescriptives for change.

## Dynamic Stability

Self-assembled behavior of complex systems is dynamically stable in any given context. Given a particular biological organization, and a particular context, we can say that the system prefers a certain range of behavioral outputs (characterized in dynamic terminology as an abstract *attractor* state; Abraham & Shaw, 1982). The system will "settle into" this dynamic stability from a number of initial states and will tend to return to its attractor regimes when perturbed. In Fig. 3.3, I have illustrated a hypothetical state space, the "fitness space" of an individual. The two axes of this state space are defined as the possible states of two measured variables of fitness, body temperature, and heart rate. Normal adult humans occupy a certain preferred part of this space. Illness or exercise may shift you temporarily to one portion of the space, but your system "wants" to return to the dark central spot and will do so after the perturbation of illness or exercise. This is a dynamic stability because the system is not rigidly fixed to a confined region of the state space, but tends to stay in and return to a constrained region.

Dynamic systems theory identifies a number of such attractor regimes (Fig. 3.4). Behavior that tends to converge around a single or several output states are called *point attractor* systems, whereas repetitive or cyclical behavior is characterized as a *limit cycle attractor.* A special attractor regime currently of great biological interest is the *chaotic* or strange attractor. Chaotic systems are globally deterministic, but locally nondeterministic. They look noisy by conventional statistical tests, but they are not. Their behavior can be captured by certain sets of equations, thus,

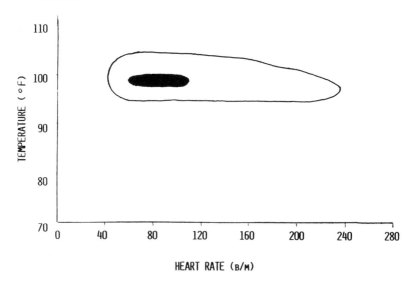

FIG. 3.3. Hypothetical "fitness space" of a normal human individual showing dynamic range of heart rate and temperature. Individual "prefers" to spend time in the dark center portion, but is not limited to it. When perturbed, the system normally returns to the center oval.

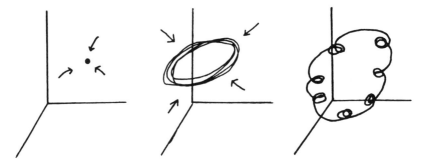

FIG. 3.4. Three hypothetical attractors plotted in three-dimensional state space. (A) Point attractor. (B) Limit cycle attractor. (C) Chaotic attractor. Arrows indicate that dynamic trajectories tend to converge on these behavior patterns of the collective variable.

they have fewer degrees of freedom than truly random noise (Skarda & Freeman, 1987).

The attractor concept helps to understand how behavior can be both stable and variable. Developing organisms are neither stereotyped and "hard-wired" nor are they random. Behavior fluctuates, but within limits. That is, organisms tend to show a delimited number of behavioral patterns, which within certain boundary conditions, will act like dynamic attractors.

These states will be the preferred configuration from a number of initial conditions, and they will be relatively resistant to perturbation. As a consequence of this dynamic assembly, developing organisms remain flexible in the face of tasks, but only within the constraints of their energetically stable possible states.

## Attractors Stabilize and Destabilize During Ontogeny

Because the components of developing systems are always in flux, the attractor states themselves have dynamic trajectories. Some behavior becomes more stable, more tightly constrained, more skilled, and less subject to perturbations. New walkers, like new drivers, must focus all their attention to the task and are easily distracted and dislodged. With experience, the skill becomes so stable that conversation, even chewing gum, is possible, and the walker can compensate for all manner of obstacles. Increasing skill can be conceptualized as an increasingly stable attractor.

Likewise, many ontogenetic phenemona require attractors to destabilize; behavior becomes less reliable, more disruptable, and more variable. For example, in infant mammals, sucking is a highly stable attractor state. All intact infant mammals must suckle in a skilled and reliable manner at birth. However, with weaning, suckling becomes more context dependent, less obligatory, more variable, and more likely to be interrupted. Eventually, the motor pattern itself disappears, as adults cannot reproduce the behavior.

I have characterized the continual and gradual changes during development as the stabilization and destablization of preferred attractor states. What about the notorious discontinuities in development? As I discuss in the following sections, discontinuous changes also require the disruption of stable states.

## Discontinuous Phase Shifts

Complex systems may exhibit multiple behavioral patterns. An important characteristic of such complex systems is that they switch between patterns *in a discontinuous manner,* by exhibiting discrete phase transitions. That is, the shift from one stable behavioral mode (attractor regime) to another behavioral regime occurs without stable intermediate states (Haken, 1983). *Bifurcations* are phase shifts where the collective variable jumps into to two or more discrete, stable modes. Complex systems may undergo multiple bifurcations (Fig. 3.5), resulting in increasing behavioral complexity. Phase shifts and bifurcations give rise, therefore, to new forms and multiple states.

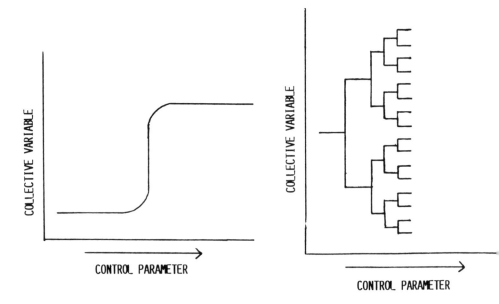

FIG. 3.5. The appearance of new forms through discontinuous phase shift. (A) Scaling on a control parameter shifts the system into a new state without a stable intermediate. (B) Scaling on a control parameter induces multiple stable behavioral states.

Developing organisms are well known to display qualitatively discrete phases during ontogeny. Sometimes, the animal seems even to lose behavioral forms or regress to less mature performance. The premier developmental question is, of course, the nature of the transition from one developmental stage to another — the emergence of new forms. How does a system retain continuity and yet produce discontinuous mainfestations?

## Control Parameters

Developmental theorists may well look to synergetic principles for help with the perennial puzzle of continuity-within-discontinuity. In complex systems, behavior that is ordered results from the cooperativity of the subsystems. But at points of change — phase shifts — not all of the elements drive the system into a new phase. An important synergetic principle is that at a phase transition, scaling on only one or a few *control parameters* shifts the entire system. Because of the holistic nature of cooperative systems, this change in a crucial variable beyond a critical point reverberates to a system-wide reorganization (Kelso & Schöner, in press). Again, because organismic and contextual variables are equally important in the dynamic assembly of behavior, there is no formal difference between exogenous and endogenous sources of change. The control parameter must in no way be envisioned as a prescription for change. Control parameters do not themselves encode or represent change. They may be rather unspecific, like physical parameters of pressure, temperature, or energy to the system, but they act to reorganize the system in specific ways. Continuity is maintained because most of the components of the system have not materially changed; discontinuity is manifest because the components relate to one another in a different fashion, and their low-dimensional, collective behavior has undergone a qualitatively shift.

Here I would like to illustrate such a nonequilibrium phase shift and the role of the control parameter with a compelling real-time example from the human motor system, which has been elegantly modeled by Kelso and his colleagues using synergetic principles (Haken, Kelso, & Bunz, 1985; Kelso, Scholz, & Schöner, 1986; Schöner, Haken, & Kelso, 1986). Kelso asked human subjects to flex and extend their index fingers in time to a metronome, beginning at a slow pace and with the fingers moving out-of-phase, that is, with one finger flexing while the other was extending. As the experimenter increased the metronome pacing, subjects spontaneously and instantaneously shifted their coordination pattern from out-of-phase to in-phase at repeatable critical points in the speed scalar. (No such shift occurs if subjects begin with in-phase movements.) The degrees of freedom contributing to finger-flexing movements were compressed by the motor system such that the behavior could be described by much fewer variables — in this case the relative phasing between fingers. Although out-of-phase movements were stable at lower speeds, at a critical point the system assumed a new, and presumably more stable regime. No prescription for this phase shift is assumed; the new coordinative pattern arose from the task demands and the thermodynamics of the combined elements that produced it. In this case, a single control parameter — the energy delivered to the system to increase the speed, appeared to drive the phase shift. The anatomical and physiological elements participating in the ensemble were reorganized to produce a different output while themselves remaining stable.

## Control Parameters in Developing Systems

We have proposed that at developmental transitions, one or several components of the complex system may act as control parameters, including variables in the context or in the environment (Fogel & Thelen, 1987; Thelen, 1988). Although all of the elements or subsystems are essential for the systems output, only one or a few of the subsystems will trigger transitions, which, in turn, will lead to system-wide reorganization.

This principle helps explain the heterochronic, asynchronous, and often nonlinear character of behavioral ontogeny. We commonly observe "pieces" of a functional behavior long before the performance of the mature behavior. These pieces seem to be used out of sequence, in inappropriate or different functional contexts, only under certain experimental conditions, or otherwise not properly "connected" with the other elements needed for goal-directed activity.

Theories that assume that developmental change is driven by a unified timetable in the form of maturational plans, neurological reorganizations, or cognitive structures have had difficulty accounting for both the anticipations of function and regressions. In this systems approach, we strongly emphasize that contributing components may mature at different rates. The component processes are thus developing in parallel, but not synchronously or symmetrically. Figure 3.6 depicts a developing system composed of many component profiles in a heterarchical, rather than a hierarchical assembly. At any point in time, behavior is a compression of these components within a specific task context. This means that some elements of functional actions may be in place long before the performance but may not be manifest until

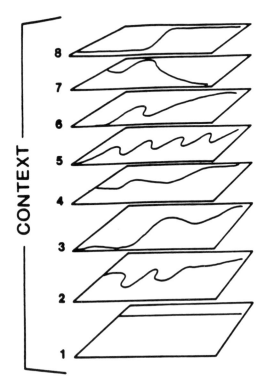

FIG. 3.6. Developing systems pictured as a layered ensemble of subsystems, each with its own developmental trajectory. The low-dimensional behavior (collective variable) is assembled only within a contextual frame. No subsystem has hierarchical priority.

the slowest component allows the system to dynamically assemble in a new form (the *rate-limiting* component).

Because it is the task, not instructions that exist prior to the task, which assembles the components, these subsystems may be opportunistically appropriated for different actions for different ontogenetic goals. The component is continuously available, but as it is only manifest in a task, its expression is task specific. For example, leg kicks may be used by young infants as expressive or exploratory behaviors, although these coordinated activities may be later recruited for locomotor systems. Fogel and Thelen (1987) and Thelen (1981) give other examples of coordinative patterns transiently recruited for tasks quite unrelated to their mature forms.

## How Control Parameters Drive Developmental Change

*Scalar Changes in a Single Control Parameter.* In particular, we have proposed that control parameters can act to trigger developmental transitions in two ways. First, there may be scalar changes in one or more existing components that reach the critical values that initiate a phase shift. These may be identified at many levels of analysis: incremental growth in anatomical systems, increase (or decrease) of neural elements or concentrations of neurotransmitters, changing perceptual, cognitive or motor abilities or memory capacity, or change of attentional mechanisms.

Contextual factors may, however, be equally potent in effecting the appearance of new forms. We have especially stressed the role of the social partners of young animals in promoting developmental change (Fogel & Thelen, 1987). Social conspecifics often create contexts that support or facilitate the organization of systems by substituting for organismic elements that are later developing. Human parents, for example, continually provide access to objects, appropriate "frames" for social dialogue, correctly scaled language opportunities, and so on, which provide a task context within which the child's organismic capabilities may coalesce. Without these supportive contexts, the infant performs at a less mature level.

I offer the phenomenon of the newborn stepping response as an illustration of how, in a systems approach, a scalar change in a crucial control parameter can lead to the emergence (or in this case, the disappearance!) of ontogenetic forms. The regression of the coordinated stepping seen in normal newborns has conventionally been interpreted as the result of maturing cortical inhibitory centers. Donna Fisher and I (Thelen & Fisher, 1982) found, however, that a simple contextual manipulation — placing the infant supine — "restored" the patterned behavior even in infants who performed no steps when held upright. We proposed that the developmental transition from stepping to no-stepping was triggered by a simple, nonneural scaling of a body composition parameter, the increase of nonmuscular or fat tissue, which made the legs comparatively heavy and weak and prevented the infant from lifting the leg upright, but only when the infant was in the biomechanically demanding upright posture (Thelen & Fisher, 1982). My colleagues and I have shown that stepping in young infants can be elicited or supressed by a number of contextual manipulations that systematically change the biomechanical demands on the legs, including postural changes, submerging in water, adding weights, and placing infants on motorized treadmills (Thelen, 1986a; Thelen, Fisher, & Ridley-Johnson 1984; Thelen, Fisher, Ridley-Johnson, & Griffin, 1982).

In dynamic systems terminology, then, the low-dimensional behavior of stepping, characterized by a definable relation between the excursions of the joints of each limb and between the two legs, is not a product of some abstract "program" for stepping that exists before the performance. Rather, it is the interaction of the contributing components, including the biomechanical elements in relation to a specific task context, which determines whether the infant steps or does not step. The body composition control parameter effects a developmental shift in one context, but perhaps not in other contexts. In other words, under certain conditions, the stepping topography represents a preferred and stable output of the system. Changing the internal or external conditions causes the system to reassemble in another attractor state. We therefore cannot define the system removed from the context.

*The Control Parameters Themselves Change During Ontogeny.* Conventional single-causal models of developmental change assume that the control parameter in any one domain remains stationary over long periods of developmental time (i.e., that cognitive reorganizations or cortical growth organize diverse aspects of behavior over a long time span). Our systems view, however, proposes that the control parameters themselves shift as the contributing components grow and differentiate and as the physical and social contexts of the organism change as a result of its development. This is the second source of transitions. The process of development itself is nonlinear, and as the systems regroup and coalesce, these nonlinearities serve as a continuing wellspring for new forms. In Fig. 3.7, I represent these changing control parameters as the migration of a surface in three-dimensional state space.

Control parameters for developmental shifts at different ages and in different domains cannot be identified *a priori.* Identifying the sources of change remains an empirical exercise at every level of analysis. This is important because sometimes it is the nonobvious contributions to the system that drive the shift, as I illustrated with the newborn stepping

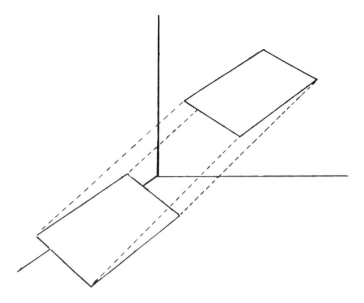

FIG. 3.7. Developing system depicted as a surface in three-dimensional state space. With time, the surface itself migrates in the space, resulting in changing control parameters.

system. Although, for example, the onset of verbal language appears to reflect a major cognitive reorganization, it is at least an open possibility that what in fact delimits the appearance of words is articulatory control over the vocal apparatus. Thus, although brain development may be a necessary condition for the appearance of new behavioral modes, it may not be sufficient, because we can never assume a one-to-one mapping of the structural basis of behavior and its performance in any individual or at any time. We can find many other instances of developing systems where only careful experimental analysis can dissect the interacting systems to reveal the driving subsystems.

For example, coordinated stepping behavior while upright reappears in the repertoire of normal infants at about 10 months. I have proposed elsewhere that the control parameter driving this developmental shift (from no-stepping to stepping) is different from the one responsible for the earlier transition (Thelen, 1984). In particular, voluntary walking emerges when elements of both balance and extensor muscle strength reach values critical for allowing infants to support their weight on one leg in a stable manner while the other is lifted for the step. When we support newly stepping infants by holding their hands, or by providing then with walkers, we augment these control parameters and allow the system to display its more mature patterns (i.e., infants can successfully step).

## Adaptive Behavior Emerges
## From Successive Bifurcations

Ontogenetic systems thus increase in complexity by a cascade of successive bifurcations or phase shifts. As the system reorganizes through the scalar change in a component, the newly emergent forms themselves act as control parameters. Changes in any one domain therefore may become amplified and have system-wide reverberations. What may appear to be a small change or acquisition may trigger a succession of major developmental landmarks—I provide examples here. I emphasize, however, that the track of successive bifurcations is a stochastic rather than a deterministic process. Ontogenetic outcomes are similar in the members of a species because certain attractor regimes are dynamically stable and certain configurations are more likely than others. Individual differences are possible because the fluctuations of the internal and external millieu provide elements of uncertainty and because the collective variable is exquisitely sensitive to the task. That is, the system may find alternative configurations to meet task constraints. For example, the task of moving toward a goal may be accomplished by young infants by a variety of locomotor modes—rolling, crawling, creeping, scooting, propelling in a wheeled device, and so on. The precise configuration is a function of the maturational and motivational state of the infant and the constraints of the support surface, provision of the wheeled device and so on.

## Phase Transitions Result
## From the Amplification of Fluctuations

By what processes do control parameters induce changes of form? In complex systems, change results from the amplification of naturally occurring fluctuations or instabilities as the control parameter is scaled passed a critical value (Kelso, Scholz, & Schöner, 1986).

As a result of their complexity and multiple degrees of freedom, biological systems are *dynamically* stable. This means that they exist within a range of possible states and fluctuate among those states. As one component is gradually changed, there exists a point where the coalition of elements is no longer stable. Normal fluctuations become amplified until this noise disrupts the dynamic stability and the system autonomously reorganizes into a new stable state. Note again that fluctuations may become amplified from such control parameters acting outside as well as within the organism (Fig. 3.8).

Stability can be measured in complex systems in two ways. First, if the system is driven by a small perturbation away from its stationary state, it will tend to return to that stationary state. The time it takes to return to

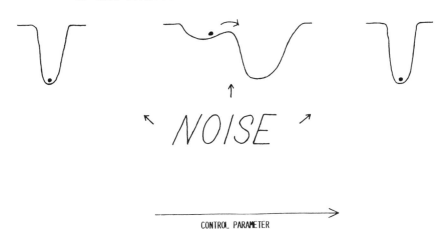

FIG. 3.8. Phase shifts result from the amplification of normally occurring fluctuations or noise. The stability of a complex system is depicted in the steepness of a potential well; stable systems have steep wells. It is difficult to dislodge the ball from the steep well. At certain values of a control parameter, the internal fluctuations overwhelm the system stability and the system seeks new stable modes.

stationarity is a function of the stability of the system, and surprisingly, independent of the size of the perturbation, if it is small. Second, the inherent noise in any system acts as perturbations on the behavior. If the system is stable, the noise produces few variations from the stable state. At points of instability, however, the noise drives the collective behavior into more variable manifestations (Fig. 3.8).

From these considerations, we can make two powerful predictions about nonequilibrium systems at the point of phase transitions. First, that we should be able to detect the essential enhanced fluctuations at phase transitions in the form of increased variability in our behavioral measure. (This assumes we have chosen the correct collective variable to describe the behavior of interest, a nontrivial problem and one I discuss further later.) Second, because the system is inherently less stable at these transitions, it should be more sensitive to perturbations and thus restore itself to its stable attractor more slowly when perturbed.

These predictions were rigorously confirmed in the bilateral rhythmical finger movement experiments by Kelso and colleagues previously mentioned. These investigators found clear evidence of enhanced fluctuations in the relative phase measure just before and during the spontaneous phase shift from out-of-phase to in-phase coordination (Kelso, Scholz, & Schöner, 1986). In addition, when they mechanically perturbed the movements, they observed a slower return to an equilibrium state at or near the phase transition (Scholz, Kelso, & Schöner, 1987).

What does this mean for developing organisms? That ontogenic change results from a dialetic process of equilibrium arising from disequilibrium has long been a feature of developmental theories, including those of Piaget, Vygotsky, Lerner, Langer, Riegel, Overton, and Werner. However, the empirical instantiation of equilibration has been of little concern. Certainly, contemporary Piagetian research has centered more on the validity of a structural approach and the validation of invariant sequences than on Piaget's actual process of change.

If phase shifts through amplification of fluctuations are characteristic of systems in general, we should, by using the appropriate empirical strategy, be able to detect these phenomona. Indeed, such a demonstration would offer strong support to the autonomous or self-organizing abilities of developing systems.

## USING DYNAMICAL SYSTEMS PRINCIPLES TO UNDERSTAND DEVELOPMENT: SOME EXAMPLES

Thelen, Kelso, and Fogel (1987) and Fogel and Thelen (1987) show how dynamic principles can help explain persistent puzzling aspects of early motor and expressive-communicative development. Here I present some additional examples.

### Behavioral States in the Newborn Period: Self-Organization and Phase Shifts

Thelen, Kelso, and Fogel (1987) suggested that the clustering of discrete variables seen in newborn state behavior was an important illustration of phase shifts or discontinuities in behavioral organization. Wolff (1987) has recently written an eloquent analysis of state behavior from a dynamic systems perspective.

In this treatment, Wolff emphasized the nonlinearity of state as a behavioral organizer in the newborn period. This nonlinearity means that there is no one-to-one correspondence between the input to the system and its response. Newborns are indeed very nonlinear: Their motor patterns form discrete clusters, and a stimulus presented in one cluster (such as sleep) may lead to a very different response than when the identical stimulus is presented during another cluster (such as alert wakefulness). Transitions from one behavioral state to another usually occur relatively abruptly, with unstable intermediate conditions.

Wolff explicitly rejected the traditional conceptualization of infant state as points along a continuum of behavioral arousal or activation. The traditional view assumes that one central agency such as the brainstem drives the discrete motor patterns, but is extrinsic to them. Rather, the cluster of behaviors we identify as state, Wolff argued, represent self-organizing aggregates of movement patterns, which are stable and resist perturbation. No outside executive assembles these clusters; states "fall out" because the system can exist only in one of several stable attractor regimes. These attractor regimes may themselves be different as development progresses; that is, the ensemble of interactive motor patterns may change with age.

Presumably, a number of control parameters can disrupt the dynamic stability of one state and lead to a qualitative shift to a new state. If a sleeping infant is tickled very gently, he or she may remain asleep. however, if we increase the tactile stimulation, there will likely be a point where the stability of the sleep state is disrupted, and the infant awakens. If he or she immediately falls asleep again, we would judge the infants sleep state to be very deep; that is, the attractor regime is very stable. If the infant stays awake, we could assume that she was close to the transition point to wakefulness and the tickling acted as a control parameter driving the phase shift. Likewise, nonnutritive sucking may be the control parameter to shift the fussy infant into a more quiet state (see also Fogel & Thelen, 1987).

Evidence from the early development of sleep states supports this self-assembly view. In premature infants, differentiation of active and quiet sleep states occurs progressively with age from a more indeterminate sleep type. Curzi-Dascalova, Peirano, and Morel-Kahn (1988) showed that this differentiation could be characterized by the association of increasing numbers of state criteria behaviors from 31 to 41 weeks of gestational age. They recorded EEG, eye movements, tonic chin EMG, gross limb movements, and respiration. In the youngest premature infants, only the EEG and eye movement patterns "hung together" to distinguish active and quiet states from indeterminate sleep. By 41 weeks, states were reliably characterized by larger constellations of variables. As sleep states entrap more components, they also become more stable, in terms of well-defined and regular cycles. State development looks not so much like the maturation of a single controlling structure as the progressive strengthening of stable attractor states that serve, in turn, as major organizers of behavior.

## Variability and Instability at Phase Shifts: Three Examples

The three examples I offer — two recent human studies and the well-studied weaning period in rat pups — fulfill dynamic predictions: that increased variability and more sensitivity to perturbation will accompany ontogenetic transitions.

*Postural Stability.*   Shumway-Cook and Woollacott (1985) studied the development of postural stability in three groups of children aged 15–31 months, 4–6 years, and 7–10 years. The children stood on a moveable platform that provided a rapid forward or backward displacement of a few centimeters to which subjects respond by an appropriate postural compensation. The experimenters measured the onset latency of the contraction of the stabilizing muscle groups in the lower leg and the delay between the onset of the activation of the lower leg and thigh muscles over a number of trials. The oldest group of children and adults showed consistent responses that rapidly adapted over succeeding trials; that is, the subjects damped their responses to minimize overcompensation to the perturbation. The youngest children also showed consistent, rather longer latency responses, but they did not habituate to the destabilizing trials—a less mature strategy. In the transition group of 4- to 6-year-olds, the response latencies were not only significantly longer than in the younger and older groups, but also the variability was greatly increased, both within and between subjects (Fig. 3.9). Postural compensation, like stepping, is a dynamic product of the neurological mechanisms detecting the perturbation and producing the corrective response and biomechanical considerations, in this case, the natural sway frequency of the body. (Children have a faster sway rate than adults, Forssberg & Nashner, 1982.) These authors speculated that the rapid change of body proportion seen in the 4–6 age range may have disrupted the stable, but less adaptable, earlier stage. In dynamic terminology, the body proportion may have acted as one (although likely not the only) control parameter. In addition, the 4- to 6-year-old group performed more poorly when they were given discrepant information about their postural stability from two sensory modalities, vision and ankle and foot proprioception. Younger infants apparently rely largely on visual input, whereas older subjects are able to rapidly integrate the two sources. In the transition group, however, the perturbation proved to be much more disruptive.

*Piagetian Conservation.*   Church and Goldin-Meadow (1986) presented a compelling measure of instability in transitions in a classic Piagetian conservation task. When these authors asked 5- to 8-year-old children to explain their conservation judgments nearly all children gestured spontaneously as they spoke. Some children, however, conveyed information in their gestures about the task that did not match the information of their spoken explanation. These "discordant" children were far less consistent in the nature of their explanations of the various conservation tasks and in matching the actual judgment of conservation with their explanation. These authors suggested that the discordant children "appeared to have pieces of information that they had not yet consolidated into a coherent explanatory system" (p. 59). In dynamic terms, the tasks did not elicit a

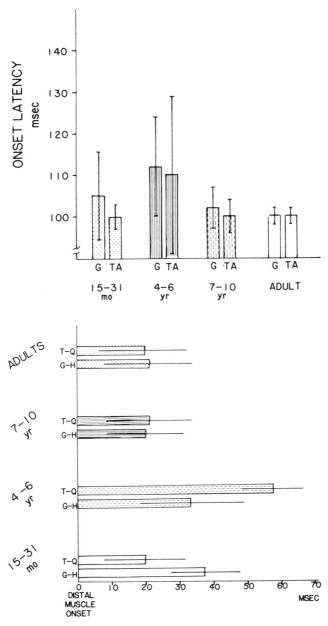

FIG. 3.9. (A) Average onset latency (+ *SD*) in the appropriate distal muscle in response to a forward sway translation (G) or backward sway translation (TA) as a function of age. Response latencies are slower and more variable in children 4–6. (B) Temporal delay between distal and proximal muscle activation as a function of age. Children ages 4–6 demonstrate greatest temporal delay in activation of proximal muscles suggesting diminished synergic coupling between distal and proximal muscles. (From Shumway-Cook & Woollacott, 1985.) Reprinted with permission.

stable attractor state—either conservation or nonconservation. If we consider verbal production as one compression of the degrees of freedom and gestural production as yet another way that the system can reduce the dimensionality for a lower dimensional output, we have a dramatic example of the fluid assembly of the components, especially at a time when system has not settled in to a more stable regime.

Indeed, the children in the discordant group proved to be much more sensitive to environmental perturbations. When the experimenters explicitly trained these children on conservation principles or even just allowed them practice with the materials, the children improved both on their judgments and on their explanations. Concordant children did not benefit from training. This intervention, therefore, acted as the crucial control parameter that pushed the unstable system into new forms. The stable systems of the concordant children could not be disrupted. It is consistent with a Piagetian interpretation to conclude that naturally occurring experience with conservation-like tasks would eventually shift the system into the conserving mode.

*Weaning in Rat Pups.* In the rat pup, the shift from suckling to independent ingestion of food is a well-defined behavioral transition. In the first 2 weeks of life, rats meet their nutritional needs exclusively by suckling and after 28 days they only eat and drink independently. The shift in feeding modes is most pronounced between days 21 and 24 (Hall & Williams, 1983).

Although under natural conditions the transition is relatively discrete, experimental manipulations have revealed that the process is a complex one, reflecting the synergetic and symbiotic relationship between the behavior and physiology of both the mother and the pup. Noteworthy from the present systems view is the mobility of the component subsystems and their ability to coalesce in particular task-specific configurations that can be relatively independent of age.

For example, although the rat pups do not normally eat and drink independently for several weeks after birth, Hall and Bryan (1980) have shown that even newborn rat pups will ingest liquid or semisolid food from the floor of a test chamber. In young pups, this oral activity was activated only when the ambient temperature was high. The presence of food and external warmth served as control parameters to shift the rat pups into an ontogenetically more mature performance, independent ingestion.

Equally intriguing is the demonstration by Pfister, Cramer, and Blass (1986) of a context-determined prolongation of suckling. These experimenters provided weaning-aged rat pups with a succession of nursing dams and their 16- to 21-day-old litters. Under these conditions, rats continued to nurse until as much as 70 days of age, long beyond the time they were eating independently, but they attached to the nipple and withdrew milk only when the younger littermates had attached. A combination of the social facilitation of nursing littermates, a dam who allowed continued nursing, and the continuation of the suckling experience here coalesced to maintain the animal in a stable state characteristic of an earlier ontogenetic stage.

It is noteworthy that during the natural weaning transition, ingestive behavior in a choice situation was highly variable and subject to disruption. The youngest rat pups in Stoloff and Blass' (1983) forced choice experiment consistently chose to suckle and the over 28-day group never chose suckling over eating. However, the 21–24 day transition group exhibited highly unstable and variable responses, and their choice behavior was described as "markedly affected by each manipulation undertaken in this experiment" (p. 451).

These results make it unlikely that there is a "weaning clock" somewhere in the rat pup, ticking off time or metering out some "weaning substance." Rather, weaning may be a phenomena emergent from this confluence of ongoing systems, each with constraints and demands. In recently completed work, Thiels (1987) has shown that at the weaning transition, rat pups show increases not only in independent eating and drinking, *but also in many other actions as well* (see Fig. 3.10). The increased locomotor ability of the pup, its increased size and energy demands, its abilities to move away from the mother to seek food, and so on, are all contributions to the weaning transition and potential control parameters. No specific weaning instructions need be invoked. Weaning falls out, so to speak, from an ensemble of dynamic processes.

## The Development of Early Lateral Preferences: Phase Shifts and Attractors

By the age of 2, human children show lateral preferences for hand use almost as consistently as adults. Developmentalists have long been intrigued with the developmental origins of laterality, especially because hemispheric specialization for manual behavior may be related to specialization for speech. Nonetheless, it is not easy to determine when and how this preference is manifested in infancy. Lateral preferences often appear to wax and wane, making prediction from infant hand use to adult handedness very difficult.

The strong, predominantly rightward, asymmetrical head posture seen in the newborn period makes it likely that the central nervous system is laterally biased from birth. Indeed, neonatal head preference is a good predictor of hand-use preference in the second year (Michel & Harkins, 1986). There is considerable debate over whether the asymmetries of head posture are manifestations of the same lateralities that are later expressed in

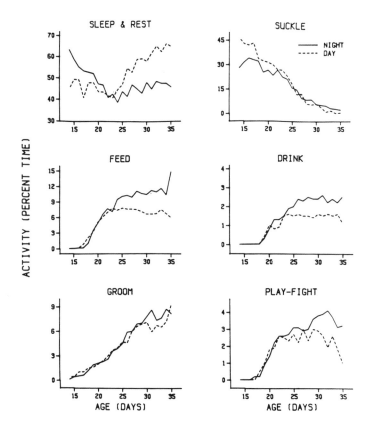

FIG. 3.10. Percent time rat pups spend in various activities as a function of age. Note increase of many independent functions between ages 20–25 days. (From Thiels, 1987.) Reprinted with permission.

handedness, or whether these head postures induce handedness through biasing hand-eye contact and arm movements (see Young, Segalowitz, Corter, & Trehub, 1983, for further elaboration of this debate and several models of laterality development).

In a recent review, Michel (in press) offered a plausible scenario by which the initial head biasing has cascading effects leading to eventual laterality in handedness. Head orientation leads to an asymmetry of visual regard of the hand and arm movement, which in turn, may induce asymmetrical reaching, and later manipulation. Thus, the infant's own experiences generate laterality in progressively developing skills.

If, however, the system is inherently biased, why is infant handedness so shifting and unstable? Michel suggested that the actual manifestation of the preferred hand is a function of both the infant's level of manual skill and the particular task. For example, Michel, Ovrut, and Harkins (1986) tested 6- to 13-month-old infants for lateral preference in three manual skills: reaching for objects, manipulating objects, and coordinating complementary bimanual actions. Infants generally showed consistent hand-use preferences among the tasks (and about 75% were right handed). However, there were some surprising shifts. Although all of the 12-month-old infants preferred the same hand for reaching and bimanual manipulation, 56% of the 13-month-olds chose the opposite hand for bimanual manipulations from the hand they used for reaching. It is important to note that bimanual manipulation becomes a common skill for infants only in about the 12th month. Michel speculated that many of the reaches of the 13-month-old infants were with the nonpreferred hand so that the preferred hand could be left free to begin bimanual manipulation. When bimanual manipulation becomes practiced, presumably infants could both reach and manipulate with the preferred hand. Lateral preference is a useful metric only when combined with a task analysis.

This account of lateral preference is consistent with a dynamic systems view. Let us depict strong, adult-like lateral preferences for hand use as two point attractors whose stability is represented by the steepness of the well seen at the bottom left of Fig. 3.11. The attractor for the right hand is very strong; the ball "prefers" to roll to the bottom of the well and will return there very quickly when perturbed. Right-handed people may be able to use the left hand for some tasks, but they prefer not to under ordinary circumstances. However, if their right arms were in a cast and sling, they would recruit the left hand to do tasks not ordinarily undertaken. That is,

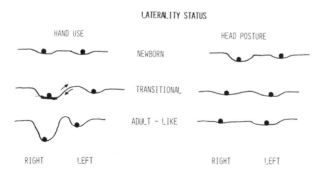

FIG. 3.11. Lateral preference depicted as a series of point attractor states. Hand use attractors are the left-hand panel; head posture attractors on the right hand panel. Transitional states are bistable and are especially sensitive to task context.

given a strong perturbation (broken arm), the ball can be shaken out of the deep well into another attractor state (left hand use), as a qualitative phase shift.

We can characterize newborn head posture as a relatively strong attractor, which entrains the arm and hand system to become progressively more laterally differentiated. However, in the transitional period, the attractor basins are shallow. Even rather small perturbations will drive the ball out of the well, up over the wall, and into the opposite hand attractor. The system is especially sensitive to the task and skill-level interaction because each new demand acts as a perturbation. Thus, the onset of bimanual manipulation acts as a control parameter and disrupts the stability of the reaching laterality, leading to a phase shift.

How does this account differ from a model of development as simply increasing hemispheric laterality? Here I emphasize the systems nature of lateral preference, which is always assembled "softly" in relation to the task and action patterns available to the infant. The system prefers certain places in the state space, but it is not restricted to them. Accomplishing the task is always a higher priority than the particular means by which the infant executes the action, so that the attractors are shallow enough to allow for flexibility in the face of obstacles. Likewise, the system becomes lateralized only as it supports adaptive actions. At the same time, the hand use attractors are becoming lateralized and stable, the head posture attractors are becoming progressively weaker. It is not adaptive for action to have an obligatory, or even strongly preferred head posture. Similarly, spontaneous leg movements develop from an initial strong asymmetry to symmetrical activity, reflecting the demands of locomotion and postural support for bilateral symmetry (Thelen, Fisher, & Ridley-Johnson, 1983).

Although hand use preference may indeed reflect an increasing hemispheric specialization, this explanation alone misses the richness and complexity of the process of change over time. We sometimes view the nonlinearity and nonstationary of behavior over time as noise in the smooth trajectory toward maturity. The lesson from nonlinear dynamical systems is that these aberrations are the very stuff of ontogenetic change. It is at these transitions that the system reveals what holds it together and what drives it to new forms. A synergetic strategy of development will exploit these nonlinearities for a deeper understanding of process.

## AN EMPIRICAL STRATEGY BASED ON SYSTEMS PRINCIPLES

We know that self-organizing phenomena in physics, chemistry, and some biological systems may be modeled with precision and elegance. This goal may not be attainable with behaving and developing organisms. Can principles of complex systems help developmentalists in our everyday unraveling of real life behavior? Do we have just another set of agreeable postulates which are neither objectionable nor useful?

I believe the lessons from complex systems analysis can serve developmentalists well, not only as a conceptual framework, but as an empirical strategy that is independent of level and content domain. Nothing I propose here for operationalizing systems is, in itself, new. Developmentalists have been using these methods — observational, longitudinal, experimental — since the adoption of scientific methods for studying ontogeny. What may be new, however, is the systematic linking of these strategies to synergetic principles:

1. The focus is on process not just outcome measures.
2. No component or subsystem has ontological priority.
3. Task and context, not instructions, assemble behavior.
4. Control parameters are not stationary. (The state space itself evolves through time.)

The first requirement for a systems approach is to identify the essential collective variables and their behavior. What is the best way to describe, for any particular organism and set of developmental questions, how the system compresses the degrees of freedom? Note that this description of the collective states can be done in many domains and at many levels of analysis. For infant animals, this may be a measure of perceptual performance or motor output, a psychophysiological measure, or variables indexing social interaction. The dynamical description is level-independent. However, the choice of an appropriate collective variable is neither a trivial nor a simple matter because ontogeny is so often nonlinear. Because we are interested in the processes of developmental change, it is likely that our first approach would be longitudinal. For animals like humans, where significant individual variability often renders group means meaningless, the analysis may require a case-study design.

Because we assume in this perspective that the task or context, not pre-existing instructions, assembles the system into a measurable collective variable, it is essential that our developmental descriptions also contain a task analysis. This also may be difficult, especially in long-term longitudinal studies, because the meaning of the task or context itself changes with the development of the infant. For example, grasping a 1-inch cube is not the same task for a 3-month-old as for a 12-month-old simply because of the body scale changes in the dimensions of the hand relative to the object (Newell, 1986). Nonetheless, it is a mistake to assume that sources of developmental shifts are organismic when they may indeed be in the match between the organism and the task.

The second step in this analysis is to identify the developmental transitions or where the organism shifts from one stable mode of performance to a new mode. Again, if there is variability in the age-dependent onset of new behaviors, or if complex contextual eliciting factors are involved, such shifts may be best discovered in the course of individual developmental profiles. Synergetic theory predicts that at such transitions, the system will show enhanced fluctuations and loss of stability. In developmental data we would expect an increase in the variability of our collective variable—that is, an increase in the deviations from the mean performance when compared to either the earlier stable performance or the new behavioral mode.

Experimentally induced perturbations or facilitations at the point of transitions can test the stability of the system. Developmentalists may probe a transition by experimentally perturbing the infant with an appropriate contextual manipulation (or, in nonhuman species, a surgical or pharmacological intervention). Systems near phase transitions are predicted to recover more slowly than those in more stable states.

The third, and crucial, step is to try to identify the control parameters: the one or few variables in the complex system that drives the shift. How can this be done? First, we would expect that a component or subsystem acting as a control parameter would itself show scalar changes in the time period of the phase transition. One clue to identifying control parameters is to look for variables that themselves change rapidly prior to or during the phase shift. This is not foolproof, however! In dynamic systems even small changes in crucial scalars can amplify fluctuations and lead to new equilibrium states.

If we understand our developing organism fairly well, we can make reasonable guesses about which components may drive developmental systems. Nonetheless, it may be a mistake to assume a control parameter a priori. A more fruitful strategy would be to map several likely control parameters so that they may be tested individually.

Once candidates for control parameters are identified, we can perform experimental manipulations or exploit the natural variability among individuals to confirm whether changes in the single parameter drive the system reorganization. The former tactic is more easily employed if we can discover a contextual manipulation that will serve as a substitute for a natural control parameter. In humans, neural or organismic variables may need correlational methods or observation of nonnormal populations.

The final step in a synergetic strategy would be the integration of the different levels of description. In the abstract, the dynamics at the neural level should be coupled to the dynamics at the behavioral level, and so on, regardless of the level used. For example, Kelso and Scholz (1985) have related amplifications in fluctuations at phase transitions seen in the kinematics of finger movements to similar phenomena measured at the level of muscle contractions. Such elegant mappings may be quite difficult over developmental time.

## A SYNERGETIC APPROACH TO LOCOMOTOR DEVELOPMENT

The onset of independent, upright locomotion—learning to walk—can be viewed as a dramatic phase shift in motor development. One day, the infant cannot walk alone, and the next day he or she toddles by herself. Traditional explanations attribute this milestone to maturational changes in an executive function as increasing cortical or cognitive control of movement. My colleagues and I have suggested that walking alone is not so much commanded as emergent. No "walking" schema per se need exist; the behavior is rather the stable compression of many variables in an organism with a particular neural, anatomical, and biomechanical configuration, with certain motivations and goals, and supported on a permissive substrate. The benefit of viewing walking as a multicomponent emergent phenomena is to open a window on how the skill is actually constructed during development.

For a synergetic strategy we must first ask: By what collective variable can we capture the compression of the degrees of freedom involved when people walk? A number of kinematic and kinetic variables might suffice. We focus on one essential characteristic of human bipedal walking: the regular, 180 degrees out-of-phase alternation of the legs needed to maintain both upright stability and forward progress. (Humans could use other symmetrical gait patterns such as hopping or galloping, but presumably they are less efficient.) When infants begin to locomote in the upright position, they use an alternating gait, although they are more variable in their phasing than in older toddlers and children (Clark, Whitall, & Phillips, 1988). How do they acquire this ability? Is this a pattern that emerges with independent locomotion? What component skills do infants need to step? How does the environment support this skill?

Infants are capable of regularly alternating movements of their legs long before the onset of upright locomotion. Even in the newborn period, supine leg kicks may alternate, but the limbs appear loosely coupled. Throughout the first year, leg kicks seem to be like a weak, cyclic attractor. Alternation is a preferred, but not very stable state (Thelen, 1985).

This stability greatly increased, however, with a simple contextual manipulation. When I supported 7-month-old infants, who normally do not step, over a motorized treadmill, I saw dramatic increases not only in their step rate, but in the strictly alternating excursions of their limbs (Thelen, 1986). These treadmill steps were not simple reflexes, but dynamic and adaptive motor coordinations. Infants not only adjusted their step rate in accord with the speed of the treadmill in a manner identical to independent walkers, but also were able to compensate for extreme perturbations—one leg driven at twice the speed of the opposite leg—to maintain the right-left alternation (Thelen, Ulrich, & Niles, 1987). It is unlikely that, at 7 months, either the onset of stepping or the continual compensations were mediated by conscious or voluntary processes.

Figure 3.12 illustrates such leg alternation in a single 8-month-old infant girl (CH). CH's leg excursions were tracked by means of an optico-electronic motion detection system through a series of trials beginning with the treadmill belts turned off and continuing through seven more trials where the speed of the belts was gradually scaled up. The speed adjustment was made after 5 seconds in each trial except the first moving belt trial. It is easy to see where the 5-second perturbation occurred and CH's subsequent adjustment to maintain alternation. After the eighth trial, the belt was again turned off. In this second no-movement trial, CH performed some leg movements, but they were poorly coordinated. Finally, we perturbed coordination by moving one belt twice as fast as the other, but the infant still kept on walking!

Thus, the collective variable of interest is a measure of interlimb phasing—the relative coordination of one limb to another. These patterned movements represent the low-dimensional output of a system composed of many components—neurological networks, bones, joints, muscles with characteristic strength and tone, and motivational and attentional elements, including the infant's state, physiological parameters, and so on.

We may ask about the developmental course of this coordinative ability, and especially about two transitions. First, at what point in ontogeny does this neuromotor ability develop? Second, what allows coordinated upright stepping to become manifest during the last few months of the first year? Our ultimate question is, which of the essential elements in the system will serve as control parameters in effecting the development shifts?

Beverly Ulrich, my collaborator in this work, and I began our synergetic strategy with an effort to understand the dynamics of our collective variable over developmental time. We used a multiple case-study, longitudinal design by observing nine infants each month from age 1 month until they walked independently or refused the treadmill (usually between 7 and 9 months). Each infant participated in two identical experimental sessions each month to assess within-age variability and to elicit optimal performance. The treadmill task is identical to the series of trials just described for infant CH, one of the subjects in the study. In addition, we obtained Bayley scales of motor development, behavioral state assessments, and anthro-

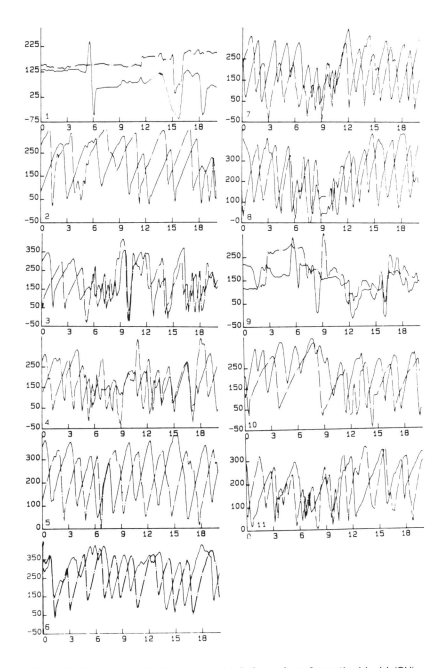

FIG. 3.12. Excursions of the right and left foot of an 8-month-old girl (CH) as a function of treadmill speed condition. Trials 1 and 9 are with the belt turned off. In trials 2–8 the speed is gradually increased; the increase occurs after 5 seconds of the trial. Note CH's adjustment. Trials 10 and 11 are "split-belt" trials, where one belt is moving at twice the speed of the opposite belt. Note the continuation of alternation.

pometric measurements because previous research suggested that these variables affected stepping performance.

I present here some preliminary results in the single infant, CH, to illustrate the paradigm. In Fig. 3.13, we plot the cycle durations of alternating steps taken by infant CH as a function of age and treadmill speed trial. (Remember that trials 1 and 9 are on stationary belts and that the belt speed was gradually increased in trials 2–8). In general, cycle duration was inversely related to belt speed, but in months 1–3, CH's performance was erratic. By month 4, however, she adjusted her steps to the belt speed, and she continued to do so, although the very fastest belt speeds sometimes appeared to inhibit performance. (We do not know whether this reflected an inability of the legs to cycle at such a high frequency or a fatigue effect, but other infants also showed this decrement at the highest speeds.)

We can also look at a more precise index of bilateral coordination, the relative phasing between the movements of each leg. In mature stepping, the step of cycle of one leg is initiated at 50% of the cycle duration of the opposite leg (the limbs are precisely 180 degrees out-of-phase). In Fig. 3.14, we can see that in the early months, CH's interlimb phasing is very variable, but that it approaches the adult-like 50% value more consistently in the second half of the year. The coupling between the limbs becomes tighter. The other infants in our sample showed remarkably similar developmental trends.

These descriptive data give us a picture of the dynamics of change of the abililty to coordinate the two legs. Some ability, albeit rather primitive, is manifest at the first month. In CH, we saw no abrupt transitions from no stepping to fully articulated stepping on the treadmill, but rather a gradual increase in steps with age. This suggested that the basic mechanism whereby limbs respond to a backward stretch by alternating swings is in place at a very early age, but that the system is not very stable. The attractor becomes progressively stronger with age.

These results are only the first step in a synergetic strategy; an understanding of the dynamics of our collective variable over developmental time. It is an essential (but often laborious) step to identify the points of transition when the system is unstable and when the control parameter dynamics can be explored. In the case of treadmill-elicited stepping, this analysis points to the first 3–4 months as the period of most rapid change, reflected in instability and variability. We have some indication of a relative decrement in treadmill performance at months 1 and 2 and then a more rapid improvement. What, then; are the control parameters shifting the system at these transition times?

One source of clues is to look at the other elements of the system indexed by the anthropometric, state, and motor maturity measures. In Fig. 3.15, for example, we show CH's stepping performance plotted with several other

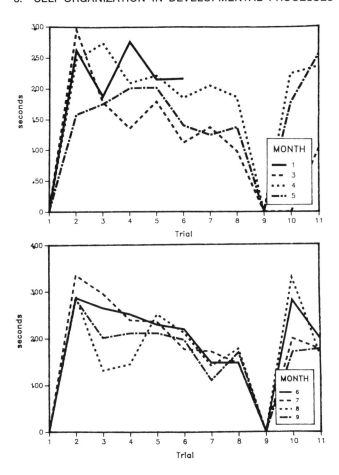

FIG. 3.13. Cycle durations of alternating steps performed by CH as a function of treadmill speed. Each trace represents the "better" day of each month's testing. Trials as in Fig. 3.12. Note decrease in cycle durations as belt speed increases and increased sensitivity to treadmill speed in especially in months 5–8. CH did not step at all in month 2.

anthropometric indices. The first few months are a time of especially rapid changes in the rate of weight gain, and in measures of chubbiness and leg volume. Do these other system variables act as control parameters for treadmill stepping? Clearly, we cannot answer this question on the basis of correlational and case-study data. Many other things change very rapidly in the first few months of life that may affect this behavior. Nonetheless, this method does allow us to dissect our system to see what components are in place and what components are rapidly changing and may be candidates for

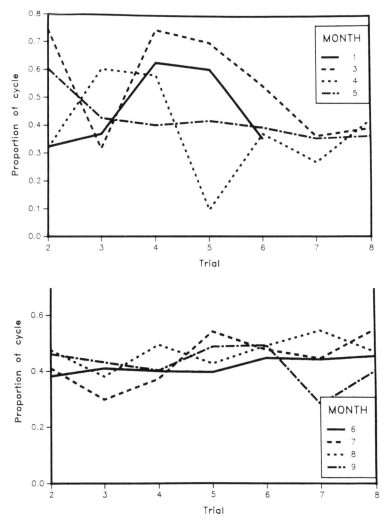

FIG. 3.14. Relative phase lags between left and right foot steps in infant CH as a function of age and treadmill speed. Lags are expressed as the proportion of the step cycle of one leg when step in the opposite leg was initiated.

control parameters. This then suggests possible experimental manipulations to test causal hypotheses.

## CONCLUSION

In this view, ontogenetic change is the reorganization of components to meet adaptive tasks. It assigns the sources of new forms to the self-

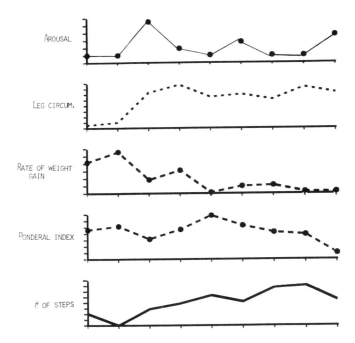

AROUSAL

LEG CIRCUM.

RATE OF WEIGHT GAIN

PONDERAL INDEX

# OF STEPS

FIG. 3.15. Anthropometric measures, "arousal" scale, and number of treadmill steps of infant CH from months 1 through 10. Anthropometric indices include *rate* of weight gain, summed circumferences of the thigh and calf, and Ponderal Index, weight/length$^3$. Note that there are rapid changes in the first four months on all variables.

organizing properties of systems that use energy in a particular configuration. Pattern and complexity can emerge from the cooperativity of more simple elements. It says that developing systems are stable and predictable where their adaptive demands have constrained, through phylogenetic mechanisms, their range of solutions. (All mammals must suckle; at birth, the architecture of the suckling system leads to a very stable periodic attractor.) But this view also accounts for the variability and flexibility of these same systems when the task demands are not strict, or when experimental manipulations challenge the developing organisms with unique circumstances. (Suckling can also be curtailed, or prolonged, or the action patterns used for other goals, such as exploration.) Because prescriptions for action do not exist outside of the context that elicits action, components are free to assemble and reassemble within the constraints of the organism and the task. The physical and social context of the developing animal is more than just a supportive frame; it is an essential component of the assembled system. In such systems, new forms arise when the stability of the system is disrupted when random fluctuations are amplified by the scaling of a critical component. The process of developmental change is thus normally accompanied by a period of instability, where the system is exploring, so to speak, another level of stability.

A dynamic systems perspective may require new empirical strategies in which variability is the substance rather than the noise. By identifying developmental transitions, where the system may be "fooled" into progressions and regressions, we can then test the limits of the organism and the context in eliciting new forms. In reality, many developmentalists have implicitly adopted such an empirical strategy; this perspective provides a rationale consistent with pattern-formation processes in other physical and biological systems.

## ACKNOWLEDGMENTS

I thank Scott Kelso and Alan Fogel for their important contributions to the ideas presented here and Beverly Ulrich and David Niles for their invaluable collaboration on the research. This chapter was supported by National Science Foundation Grant BNS 85 09793, National Institutes of Health Grant RO1 HD 22830, and a Research Career Development Award from the National Institutes of Health.

## REFERENCES

Abraham, R. H., & Shaw, C. D. (1982). *Dynamics—The geometry of behavior.* Santa Cruz, CA: Aerial Press.

Barnes, D. M. (1986). Brain architecture: Beyond genes. *Science, 233,* 155–156.

Brent, S. B. (1978). Prigogine's model for self-organization in nonequilibrium systems: Its relevance for developmental psychology. *Human Development, 21,* 374–387.

Brent, S. B. (1984). *Psychological and social structures.* Hillsdale, NJ: Lawrence Erlbaum Associates.

Church, R. B., & Goldin-Meadow, S. (1986). The mismatch between gesture and speech as an index of transitional knowledge. *Cognition, 23,* 43–71.

Clark, J. E., Whitall, J., & Phillips, S. J. (1988). Human interlimb coordination: The first 6 months of independent walking. *Developmental Psychobiology, 21,* 445–456.

Cohen, A. H., Holmes, P. J., & Rand, R. H. (1982). The nature of coupling between segmental oscillators of the lamprey spinal generator for locomotion: A mathematical model. *Journal of Mathematical Biology, 13,* 345–369.

Curzi-Dascalova, L., Peirano, P., & Morel-Kahn, F. (1988). Development of sleep states in normal premature and full-term newborns. *Developmental Psychobiology, 21,* 431–444.

Dammasch, I. E., Wagner, G. P., & Wolff, J. R. (1986). Self-stabilization of neural networks, I: The compensation algorithm for synaptogenesis. *Biological Cybernetics, 54,* 211–222.

Fogel, A., & Thelen, E. (1987). The development of expressive and communicative action in the first year: Reinterpreting the evidence from a dynamic systems perspective. *Developmental Psychology, 23,* 747–761.

Forssberg, H., & Nashner, L. M. (1982). Ontogenetic development of postural control in man: Adaptation to altered support and visual conditions during stance. *The Journal of Neuroscience, 2,* 545–552.

French, V., Bryant, P. J., & Bryant, S. V. (1976). Pattern regulation in epimorphic fields. *Science, 193,* 969–981.

Gierer, A. (1981). Generation of biological patterns and form: Some physical, mathematical, and logical aspects. *Progress in Biophysics and Molecular Biology, 37,* 1–47.

Haken, H. (1983). *Synergetics: An introduction* (3rd ed.). Heidelberg, Berlin: Springer-Verlag.

Haken, H. (Ed.). (1985). *Complex systems: Operational approaches in neurobiology, physics, and computers.* Heidelberg, Berlin: Springer.

Haken, H., Kelso, J. A. S., & Bunz, H. (1985). A theoretical model of phase transitions in human hand movements. *Biological Cybernetics, 51,* 347–356.

Hall, W. G., & Bryan, T. E. (1980). The ontogeny of feeding in rats. II. Independent ingestive behavior. *Journal of Comparative and Physiological Psychology, 93,* 746–756.

Hall, W. G., & Williams, C. L. (1983). Suckling isn't feeding, or is it? A search for developmental continuities. *Advances in the Study of Behavior, 13,* 219–254.

Haroutunian, S. (1983). *Equilibrium in the balance: A study of psychological explanation.* New York: Springer-Verlag.

Hopfield, J. J., & Tank, D. W. (1986). Computing with neural circuits: A model. *Science, 233,* 625–633.

Kelso, J. A. S., Holt, K. G., Kugler, P. N., & Turvey, M. T. (1980). On the concept of coordinative structures as dissipative structures: II. Empirical lines of convergence. In G. E. Stelmach & J. Requin (Eds.), *Tutorials in motor behavior* (pp. 49–70). New York: North-Holland.

Kelso, J. A. S., & Scholz, J. P. (1985). Cooperative phenomena in biological motion. In H. Haken (Ed.), *Complex systems: Operational approaches in neurobiology, physical systems, and computers* (pp.124–149). Berlin: Springer.

Kelso, J. A. S., Scholz, J. P., & Schöner, G. (1986). Non-equilibrium phase transitions in coordinated biological motion: Critical fluctuations. *Physics Letters A, 118,* 279–284.

Kelso, J. A. S., & Schöner, G. (in press). Toward a physical (synergetic) theory of biological coordination. In R. Graham (Ed.), *Lasers and synergetics.* Heidelberg, Berlin: Springer.

Kelso, J. A. S., & Tuller, B. (1984). A dynamical basis for action systems. In M. S. Gazzaniga (Ed.), *Handbook of cognitive neuroscience* (pp. 321–356). New York: Plenum Press.

Kitchener, R. F. (1982). Holism and the organismic model in developmental psychology. *Human Development, 25,* 233–249.

Kugler, P. N., Kelso, J. A. S., & Turvey, M. T. (1980). On the concept of coordinative structures as dissipative structures: I. Theoretical lines of convergence. In G. E. Stelmach & J. Requin (Eds.), *Tutorials in motor behavior* (pp. 3–47). New York: North Holland.

Kugler, P. N., Kelso, J. A. S., & Turvey, M. T. (1982). On the control and co-ordination of naturally developing systems. In J. A. S. Kelso & J. E. Clark (Eds.), *The development of movement control and co-ordination* (pp. 5–78). New York: Wiley.

Laszlo, E. (1972). *Introduction to systems philosophy.* New York: Harper & Row.

Lerner, R. M. (1978). Nature, nurture, and dynamic interaction. *Human Development, 21,* 1–20.

Madore, B. F., & Freedman, W. L. (1987). Self-organizing structures. *American Scientist, 75,* 252–259.

Meakin, P. (1986). A new model for biological pattern formation. *Journal of Theoretical Biology, 118,* 101–113.

Michel, G. F. (in press). Self-generated experience and the development of lateralized neurobehavioral organization in infants. In J. S. Rosenblatt (Ed.), *Advances in the study of behavior* (Vol. 17). New York: Academic Press.

Michel, G. F., & Harkins, D. A., (1986). Postural and lateral asymmetries in the ontogeny of handedness during infancy. *Developmental Psychobiology, 19,* 247–258.

Michel, G. F., Ovrut, M. R., & Harkins, D. A. (1986). Hand-use preference for reaching and object manipulation in 6- through 13-month-old infants. *Genetic, Social, and General Psychology Monographs, 111,* 409–427.

Mittenthal, J. E. (1981). The rule of normal neighbors: a hypothesis for morphogenetic pattern regulation. *Developmental Biology, 88,* 15–26.

Newell, K. M. (1986). Constraints on the development of coordination. In M. G. Wade & H. T. A. Whiting (Eds.), *Motor development in children: Aspects of coordination and control* (pp. 341–360). Dordrecht, Netherlands: Martinus Nijhoff Publishers.

Overton, W. F. (1975). General systems, structure, and development. In K. F. Riegel & G. C. Rosenwald (Eds.), *Structure and transformation: Developmental and historical aspects* (pp. 61–81). New York: Wiley.

Oyama, S. (1985). *The ontogeny of information: Developmental systems and evolution.* Cambridge: Cambridge University Press.

Pfister, J. F., Cramer, C. P., & Blass, E. M. (1986). Suckling in rats extended by continuous living with dams and their preweanling litters. *Animal Behaviour, 34,* 415–420.

Prigogine, I. (1980). *From being to becoming.* San Francisco: W. H. Freeman.

Prigogine, I., & Stengers, I. (1984). *Order out of chaos: Man's new dialogue with nature.* New York: Bantam.

Rumelhart, D. E., & McClelland, J. L. (Eds.). (1986). *Parallel distributed processing: Explorations in the microstructure of cognition. Vol. I: Foundations.* Cambridge, MA: Bradford Books /MIT Press.

Sameroff, A. J. (1983). Developmental systems: Contexts and evolution. In P. H. Mussen (Ed.), *Handbook of child psychology. 4th ed., Vol. I. History, theory, and methods* (pp. 237–294). New York: Wiley.

Scholz, J. P., Kelso, J. A. S., & Schöner, G. (1987). *Nonequilibrium phase transitions in coordinated biological motion: Critical slowing down and switching time.* Manuscript submitted for publication.

Schöner, G., Haken, H., & Kelso, J. A. S. (1986). A stochastic theory of phase transitions in human hand movement. *Biological Cybernetics, 53,* 1–11.

Shrager, J., Hogg, T., & Huberman, B. A. (1987). Observation of phase transitions in spreading activation networks. *Science, 236,* 1092–1094.

Shumway-Cook, A., & Woollacott, M. H. (1985). The growth of stability: Postural control from a developmental perspective. *Journal of Motor Behavior, 17,* 131–147.

Singer, W. (1986). The brain as a self-organizing system. *European Archives of Psychiatry and Neurological Sciences, 236,* 4–9.

Skarda, C. A., & Freeman, W. J. (1987). How brains make chaos in order to make sense of the world. *Behavioral and Brain Sciences, 10,* 161–195.

Stoloff, M. L., & Blass, E. M. (1983). Changes in appetitive behavior in weanling-age rats: Transitions from suckling to feeding behavior. *Developmental Psychobiology, 16,* 439–453.

Szentagothai, J. (1984). Downward causation? *Annual Review of Neuroscience, 7,* 1–11.

Thelen, E. (1981). Kicking, rocking, and waving: Contextual analysis of rhythmical stereotypes in normal human infants. *Animal Behaviour, 29,* 3–11.

Thelen, E. (1984). Learning to walk: Ecological demands and phylogenetic constraints. In L. P. Lipsitt (Ed.), *Advances in infancy research* (Vol. 3, pp. 213–250). Norwood, NJ: Ablex.

Thelen, E. (1985). Developmental origins of motor coordination: Leg movements in human infants. *Developmental Psychobiology, 18,* 1–22.

Thelen, E. (1986a). Treadmill-elicited stepping in seven-month-old infants. *Child Development, 57,* 1498–1506.

Thelen, E. (1986b). Development of coordinated movement: Implications for early development. In H. T. A. Whiting & M. G. Wade (Eds.), *Motor skill acquisition in children* (pp. 107–124). Dordrecht, Netherlands: Martinus Nijhoff.

Thelen, E. (1988). Dynamical approaches to the development of behavior. In J. A. S. Kelso, A. J. Mandell, & M. R. Shlesinger (Eds.), *Dynamic patterns in complex systems* (pp. 348–369). Singapore: World Scientific Publishers.

Thelen, E., & Fisher, D. M. (1982). Newborn stepping: An explanation for a "disappearing reflex." *Developmental Psychology, 18,* 760–775.

Thelen, E., Fisher, D. M., & Ridley-Johnson, R. (1983). Shifting patterns of bilateral coordination and lateral dominance in the leg movements of young infants. *Developmental Psychobiology, 16,* 29–46.

Thelen, E., Fisher, D. M., & Ridley-Johnson, R. (1984). The relationship between physical growth and a newborn reflex. *Infant Behavior and Development, 7,* 479–493.

Thelen, E., Fisher, D. M., Ridley-Johnson, R., & Griffin, N. (1982). The effects of body build and arousal on newborn infant stepping. *Developmental Psychobiology, 15,* 447–453.

Thelen, E., & Fogel, A. (in press). Toward an action-based theory of infant development. In J. Lockman & N. Hazen (Eds.), *Action in social context.* New York: Plenum.

Thelen, E., Kelso, J. A. S., & Fogel, A. (1987). Self-organizing systems and infant motor development. *Developmental Review, 7,* 39–65.

Thelen, E., Ulrich, B., & Niles, D. (1987). Bilateral coordination in human infants: Stepping on a split-belt treadmill. *Journal of Experimental Psychology: Human Perception and Performance, 13,* 405–410.

Thiels, E. (1987). *Behavioral and energetic factors in weaning in Norway rats.* Unpublished doctoral dissertation, Indiana University.

Von Bertalanffy, L. (1968). *General system theory.* New York: George Braziller.

Waddington, C. H. (1972). Form and information. In C. H. Waddington (Ed.), *Towards a theoretical biology* (Vol. 4, pp. 109–145). Edinburgh: Edinburgh University Press.

Weiss, P. A. (1969). The living system: determinism stratified. In A. Koestler & J. R.Smithies (Eds.), *Beyond reductionism: New perspectives in the life sciences* (pp. 3–55). Boston: Beacon Press.

Wolff, P. H. (1987). *The development of behavioral states and the expression of emotions in early infancy: New proposals for investigation.* Chicago: University of Chicago Press.

Woodson, R. H. (1988). Individual, development, and ontogeny. Manuscript in preparation. Dept. of Psychology. University of Texas at Austin.

Young, G., Segalowitz, S. J., Corter, C. M., & Trehub, S. E. (Eds.). (1983). *Manual specialization and the developing brain.* New York: Academic Press.

# 4 The Developing Family System

Jay Belsky
Michael Rovine
Margaret Fish
*The Pennsylvania State University*

## INTRODUCTION

There is no shortage of reasons to study the period of individual and family development surrounding the birth and rearing of the first child. Perspectives such as life-course sociology (Elder, 1981), life-span developmental psychology (Baltes, Reese, & Lipsitt, 1980), and the ecology of human development (Bronfenbrenner, 1979) all draw attention to the developmnent significance and potential of major life transitions of which the transition to parenthood certainly qualifies. Not only does the addition of the first child to the family have implications for the quality and functioning of the marital relationship, but it also brings with its new roles and challenges for each parent while simultaneously marking the beginning of the postnatal development of a new human being.

In view of the confluence of events and processes that take place during this period of family formation, it should come as little surprise to learn that this developmental period has figured prominently in the studies of scientists from diverse disciplines. Sociologists were among the first to recognize the significance of the transition to parenthood, alerted in part by Simmel's assertion that the transformation of the two-person marital dyad to a three-person system would disrupt the intimacy that had been established between husbands and wives. As a consequence of this orientation, much of the initial sociological inquiry in this area was devoted to determining whether, indeed, the transition to parenthood represents a "crisis" for the family and, in particular, how the marital relationship is affected once the role of parent, with its attendant responsibilities, is added to that of spouse.

Developmental psychologists have been drawn to the first year of parenthood in their quest to understand the nature of infant development and the extent to which individual differences in child functioning discerned in the opening years of life forecast the future functioning of the child. In addition, a great deal of attention has been paid to the social experiences that infants have with their parents and the extent to which variation in these interactional exchanges influence and are influenced by individual differences in children. Although the initial work on these latter topics focused almost exclusively on the mother–infant relationship, the past 15 years has witnessed an explosion of interest in the young child's relationship with his or her father.

One major consequence of this focus on father has been the increased awareness that children develop not merely in mother–infant or even father–infant dyads, but rather in family systems (Belsky, 1981). There would seem to be grounds for arguing, then, at least in terms of developmental psychology and particularly with respect to the study of infancy, that consideration of fathers literally brought the family together. The addition of the father to the child's world created, for researchers, another relationship—a relationship between mother and father: (i.e., marital relationship). It was at this juncture that the foundation was set for integrating, across the disciplines of developmental psychology and family sociology, the study of individual and family development during the childbearing and early childrearing years. By tradition, these two fields of study had generally divided up the family in such a manner that it was the sociologists who studied marriages and developmental psychologists who studied parent–child relationships (Aldous, 1977). There were many costs to this division of labor, not the least of which were that sociologists paid too little attention to how differences among children might affect differences in marital functioning whereas developmentalists failed to consider how marriages influenced parent–child relationships and child development.

It is of interest to note that the field of study where this latter concern figured centrally was that of child clinical psychology (Emery, 1982). Repeatedly it had been demonstrated that behavior problems in preschool and school-age children frequently emerged in the context of marital discord. What this clinical literature neglected was the developmental origins of children's behavior problems and the family processes linking marital discord to child behavior problems. To summarize, what existed until relatively recently then was a situation in which one set of specialists studied marriages (sociologists), another studied parent–infant relationships and infant development (developmental psychologists), and still a third studied discordant marriages and problem children (clinical psychologists).

Reflection upon this state of affairs suggests that what was lacking in the rigorous empirical study of the family was a systems perspective; that is, a frame of reference drawing attention to the multiple elements of the family system, the subsystems that these elements formed, and the interrelation of these subsystems. Unfortunately, much of the writings on systems in general and family systems in particular is so abstract and general that it leaves the researcher without clear insight into how systems concepts should be translated into the research process (Bateson, 1979; Miller, 1978; Minuchin, 1985; Sameroff, 1982; Walsh, 1981). Tending to confirm this impression is the fact that the language, or better yet, the rhetoric, of systems theory when applied to the family has all too often been used by clinical practitioners and investigators in ways that call into question its scientific utility. Indeed, it seems all too often that systems language is called on when the complex nature of the phenomenon is not well understood — or has not been empirically substantiated. With a few rare exceptions (e.g., Christensen & Margolin, 1988; Sroufe, Jacobvitz, Mangelsdorf, DeAngelo, & Ward, 1985), the authors of this chapter have found writings about family systems confusing if not obfuscatory, providing few tangible leads as to how to go about investigating the developing family system.

When stripped of much of its rhetoric, however, the notion of a system or a systemic perspective does seem to have at least one important lesson to teach those interested in the developing family during the period of the transition to parenthood. The family must be conceived in terms of multiple levels of analysis, consisting of elements that together constitute subsystems, and that like the elements are reciprocally interrelated, comprising an entity that is not reducible to the sum of its parts. Thus, in terms of the family, attention must be paid to individuals as the basic elements of the family, to relationships as the core subsystems that the individuals in the family create as interacting elements, and to the interrelation of individuals (i.e., elements) and relationships (i.e., subsystems). More concretely, such a perspective demands that attention be paid to adults as well as to children, to marital as well as to parent–child relationships, and to the triadic family system in addition to parent–infant and spousal dyads.

In this chapter we apply this perspective in considering the family system from the period before the birth of the first child through the infant's first year. In addition to drawing together related, but all too often distinct literatures, we report findings from our own research on the early childbearing and childrearing years of the family life cycle. Following a description of our own database, we turn attention to the elements of the family and consider infant and adult development during the child's opening year of life. The second substantive section deals with relationship development, focusing on mother–infant, father–infant, and husband–wife relationships. The third section examines the interrelation of relationship subsystems by considering, within and across time, the relation of mothering and fathering and of marriage and parenting. Finally, attention is turned to the mother/wife–husband/father–infant triad in an effort to consider all dyads simultaneously.

## THE PENNSYLVANIA INFANT
## AND FAMILY DEVELOPMENT PROJECT

The Pennsylvania Infant and Family Development Project is a three-cohort longitudinal study of maritally intact, working- and middle-class families bearing and rearing their first child. The purpose of the project is to enhance understanding of marriage, parenting, and infant development during the child's first year of life. Some 250 families have been enrolled in the study during the last trimester of pregnancy; 173 of the 184 families participating in the second and third cohorts of the project are the subjects of this report. (The remaining 11 families terminated participation in the research project in its earliest stages.)

Families were recruited into the project with the help of the largest obstetrical practice in the semirural central Pennsylvania community in which The Pennsylvania State University is located. Of those families that qualified for participation (bearing first child and expecting to live in local area for at least 1 year), approximately 50% of those contacted agreed to participate. With two important exceptions, families in each of the two cohorts were treated identically. Those participating in the second cohort were observed at home three times during the infant's first year (1, 3, and 9 months) whereas those participating in the third cohort were observed only twice (3 and 9 months). In addition, families in the second cohort were randomly assigned to treatment conditions varying in terms of parental exposure to a newborn behavioral assessment; because no effects of this intervention were discerned (Belsky, 1985), cohort two was combined with cohort three for purposes of all following analyses.

The study design involved an initial home contact with husband and wife during the beginning of the last trimester of pregnancy; during this visit the nature of the investigation was detailed, informed consent was obtained, the couple was interviewed, and lengthy questionnaires were left for spouses to complete individually. The infant was tested within the first 10 days of life to obtain information on behavioral capabilities. When infants were 1 (second cohort only), 3, and 9 months of age, two 1-hour home observations were conducted, one at a time when only mother was home with the infant and another when both parents were home. Only the two-parent observations are discussed in this chapter.

At the completion of the 3- and 9-month observations, couples were again interviewed and lengthy questionnaires much like those administered prenatally were left with the parents. Finally, when infants were 12 and 13 months of age they were brought to the University laboratory for the Strange Situation, an assessment of infant–parent attachment security.

## Subjects

The subjects of this study are 173 maritally intact, working- and middle-class Caucasian families. Two-thirds of the fathers were college graduates; 16% had less than a high school education. The respective figures for mothers were 58% and 24%. At the time of the prenatal enrollment, approximately 33% of fathers and 21% of mothers held professional positions; 22% of the fathers and 25% of mothers had unskilled jobs. Families' average annual income in the year prior to their infants' birth was $24,000; 14% of the households earned more than $40,000 per year and 46% earned under $20,000 per year. Husbands averaged 28.6 years of age and wives, 26.6 years. Couples had been married an average of 3.9 years. Fifty-eight percent of the infants were male; all infants were healthy at birth.

## Methods

### Individual Functioning

*Parents' Personality.*    Included as part of the lengthy prenatal questionnaire were three personality scales. The ego strength subscale from Cattell, Eber, and Tatsuoka's (1970) 16 PF Questionnaire was selected to assess emotional stability and maturity. The self-esteem and interpersonal affect scales from the Jackson (1976) Personality Inventory were selected to assess, respectively, positive feelings about self and the nature and extent of an individual's empathic feelings towards others. Parents in the second cohort were asked to respond (by mail) to these questionnaires again when their infants were 15 months of age. They also completed a semantic differential measure of their personal opinion of themselves prenatally and at 3 and 9 months; this involved responding to a series of 10 bipolar adjectives (e.g., boring–interesting, friendly–lonely, useless–worthwhile), with seven points separating the two extremes. Respondents' scores were calculated by summing their ratings across the 10 items.

*Neonatal Functioning.*   When the infants were born, Brazelton (1973) Neonatal Behavioral Assessments were administered by a specially trained examiner, either in the hospital within the infant's first 3 days of life (second cohort) or at home when the infant was between 7 and 10 days of age (third cohort). Behavior was scored by means of conventions developed by Jacobson, Jacobson, Fein, and Schwartz (1984) that generate six subscales, five of which were employed in the study: orientation, range of state, motor, autonomic stability, and regulation of state (for details see Belsky & Rovine, 1987).

*Infant Temperament.*   Three months after the infant's birth, mothers completed the Infant Characteristics Questionnaire (Bates, Freeland, & Lounsbury, 1979), a 24-item instrument designed to yield four subscores pertaining to perceived infant temperament: fussy/difficult, unadaptable, dull, and unpredictable.

## Family Relationships

*Marital Relationship.*   Prenatally, and again when infants were 3 and 9 months of age, spouses individually completed the Braiker and Kelly (1979) four-factor scale of intimate relations that assesses two marital activities, maintenance or problem-solving communication and conflict, and two marital sentiments, love for the spouse and ambivalence about the relationship (internal consistency reliabilities > .65). For some analyses these four intercorrelated measures are composited. Positive Marriage was created by summing the Love and Maintenance scores and Negative Marriage was created by summing Conflict and Ambivalence scores. A ratio of Negative to Positive aspects of the marriage was also created by standardizing the Negative and Positive composite variables, dividing the negative by the positive, and then multiplying the resultant ratio by 100. Scores below 100 indicate relationships in which positive features outweigh negative features; scores above 100 indicate the reverse.

In addition to these individual reports of the marital relationship, spouses jointly responded to questions about their household division of labor and the time they spent in joint leisure activities during the prenatal interview and again when infants were 3 and 9 months of age. The former construct was assessed through couple's reports of who was responsible for four traditionally female tasks (cooking dinner, doing laundry, grocery shopping, house cleaning) using a 5-point response scale ranging from almost always husband (1) to almost always wife (5); internal consistency exceeded .65 at all times of measurement. Joint leisure was assessed by asking couples how regularly they engaged in a series of recreational activities together (e.g., watching television, taking a walk, going to a movie, playing sports together) using a 6-point response scale ranging from once a month or less (1) to more than once a day (6); internal consistency exceeded .55 at all times of measurement.

Finally, as part of the observations of the mother/wife–husband/father–infant triad, naturally occurring marital interaction was coded (see later) in terms of whether, during each 15-second sampling interval, spousal communication focused upon baby-related and/or nonbaby-related matters; whether both members of the couple were jointly attending to the infant and/or sharing pleasure (e.g., smiling at one another, laughing together) because of the baby's activities; and whether nonbaby-related interactions between husband and wife were positively affectionate (e.g., spouses kiss, hug, or praise one another, laugh together, smile at each other, affectionately touch each other). At the completion of each sampling interval, overall spousal engagement was rated on a 4-point scale (for details see the following section and Belsky, Lang, & Rovine, 1985).

*Parent–Infant Relationships.* When infants were 1, 3, and 9 months of age naturalistic, 1-hour home observations were conducted at a time when both parents were at home and the infant was expected to be awake and alert. During these late afternoon and early evening observations parents were instructed to go about their everyday household routine and ignore as much as possible the presence of the observer; emphasis was placed by the observer on his or her interest in recording the behavior of the infant. Using a procedure described more fully elsewhere (Belsky, Gilstrap, & Rovine, 1984), five behavioral functions (not mutually exclusive) were coded for each parent–infant dyad; these included contingently responding to some aspect of the infant's behavior (Respond); focusing the infant's attention on some object or event in the environment and/or arousing the attentional state of the infant as in dyadic play (Stimulate/Arouse); diapering, wiping, washing, or grooming the baby or engaging in some other activity focused on basic physical care (Caregiving); expressing positive emotional feelings toward the baby by hugging, kissing, smiling at or verbalizing endearments (Positive Affection); and engaging in personal leisure activities involving reading or watching television (Read/Watch TV). Infant behavior was coded whenever the infant showed distress vocalizations, be they whimpers or full-blown cries (Fuss/Cry); evidenced positive affect by smiling, laughing, or displaying excitement or exuberance in some manner (Smile/Excite); and/or vocalized (Vocalize).

At the end of every 15-second observation interval, each dyad (mother–infant, father–infant, husband–wife) was rated on a 4-point reciprocal engagement scale that assessed the extent and the intensity of interaction ranging from no interaction (0) and minimal interpersonal exchange (1), as when a parent merely held or looked at the baby, to intense reciprocal engagement (3), as when a parent–infant interaction was extended, involving high levels of focused parent and infant attention (as frequently evident in face-to-face play or other social or object-mediated games). Ratings and scores for all measures were summed across the hour observation.

All observers were trained intensively over a period lasting no less than 2 months and consisting of practice coding of videotaped and live interactions. During the course of the study more than 50 reliability checks were made. Intercorrelation of total frequency scores for each of the discrete behaviors and for the engagement ratings ranged from .74 to .97, with a mean of .92.

When infants were 12 and 13 months of age mother and father, respectively, were observed with their infant at the University in the Ainsworth and Wittig (1969) Strange Situation in order to assess the security of infant–parent attachment. All sessions were videotaped and coded in terms of conventions outlined by Ainsworth, Blehar, Waters, and Wall (1978) by individuals trained by personnel from the University of Minnesota (B. Vauhgn, M. Ward). Ninety percent interrater reliability was established with regard to major security classifications (A, B, C) and all tapes were coded by no fewer than two independent raters; all major discrepancies were resolved by conference.

## INDIVIDUAL DEVELOPMENT

This first section is comprised of two parts. First, we focus on adult development and then on infant development, with a special focus on stability and change in temperament.

### Adult Development Across the Transition to Parenthood

Anyone who has become a parent can attest to the changes that take place in one's life with the assumption of the parental role. It is for this reason that parenthood is frequently viewed as the key to adulthood, as the bearing of a child not only makes one a mother or father but, in so doing, an adult (Fawcett, 1978; Hoffman, 1978). Adults themselves list the bearing of children and the establishment of a family as a major turning point in their lives (Lowenthal, Thurnher, & Chiriboda, 1976).

What this suggests, of course, is that the transition to parenthood should be a time of adult development: This possibility has long been acknowledged (Benedek, 1970; Bibring, Dwyer, Huntington, & Valenstein, 1961). Psychoanalytic theorists have often conceptualized pregnancy and early parenthood as a series of development tasks that, by inducing stress and conflict, have the potential of stimulating psychological maturation (Benedek, 1970; Bibring et al., 1961; Deutsch, 1945). Gutmann (1975) observed that new fathers in several cultures became less selfish and more responsible (see also Lewis, 1986); Shereshefsky and Yarrow (1973) found that women's "psychological integration" increased following the birth of a child; and Hoffman (1978) reported a decrease in egocentrism and an increase in responsibility associated with early motherhood.

Implicit in the psychoanalytic formulation of pregnancy and parenthood as developmental tasks is the recognition that the opportunity for increased maturity is not always realized (Rossi, 1968). Shainness (1963) sounded this theme by referring to the transition to parenthood as a "crucible tempering of the self" and noting that the tempering process could go awry, resulting in damage to the individual and to the individual's relationships. Indeed, the results of one detailed study of some 17 middle-class women led its author to conclude that "while most women experienced pregnancy and early parenthood as a period of psychological stress, only part of the sample concomitantly experienced a growing sense of adulthood and the personality integration suggestive of a new development stage" (Leifer, 1977, p. 89).

Perhaps the strongest support for the notion that the transition to parenthood represents an opportunity for development comes from life-span developmental psychology and life-course sociology (Baltes, et al., 1980; Brim & Wheeler, 1966; Havighurst, 1973; Neugarten, 1968). The core assumption of the life-span perspective is that development and growth are not restricted to childhood and adolescence. Further, individual development after childhood is stimulated by new situations, new role partners, and new demands that elicit different behaviors while providing new rewards and negative sanctions (Antonucci & Mikus, in press). It is assumed that along with the emergence of new behaviors, as demanded by new roles and responsibilities, will come changes in the person (Lidz, 1976; Sarbin & Allen, 1968). Turner (1978) argued that roles that become deeply merged with the person have an impact on personality formation. Certainly, parenthood would seem to qualify as such a development-inducing role.

Despite the widespread view that parenthood offers developmental opportunities, rigorous, and particularly longitudinal empirical inquiry into the nature and process of normative development across the transition to parenthood, is quite limited. Although some work has touched on topics like personal efficacy (McLaughlin & Micklin, 1983; Sirigano & Lachman, 1985) and masculinity and femininity (Feldman, Biringer, & Nash, 1981; Peterson, Peterson, Redman, Nicholls, & Blasenak, 1986), most of the research has focused narrowly on emotional well-being, broadley defined.

This is especially true of the clinical research (Fedele, Goldberg, Grossman, & Pollack, in press), where attention has been further restricted to clinical disturbances such as psychosis and nonpsychotic postpartum depression. Although the former syndrome is estimated to affect less than .02% of the population (Cutrona, 1982; Kaij & Nilsson, 1972), incidence rates of the latter condition, for which no formal diagnostic criteria yet exist, ranged between 3 and 33% in 11 studies reviewed by Cutrona (1982). Using data from more recent investigations with more rigorous assessment strategies, Hopkins, Marcus, and Campbell (1984) estimated that approximately one in five women experience a clinical depression in the postpartum period.

Longitudinal studies in which depression, anxiety, or self-esteem have been measured, both during pregnancy and afterward, present an inconsistent picture of the changes in mood that accompany transition to parenthood. Feldman and Nash (1984), for example, found that negative mood (measured by items like hurt feelings, sad, tense, overwhelmed) declined across an 8-month period from the last trimester of pregnancy through 6 months postpartum in their sample of 21 middle-class, Caucasian women bearing and rearing firstborns. Similarly, Grossman, Eichler, and Winickoff (1980), in their larger study of demographically similar women bearing both first and laterborns, reported that by the time of the infant's first birthday anxiety and depression had declined, anxiety from a peak at 2 months postpartum and depression from a peak at 8 months pregnancy (see also O'Hara, Neunaber, and Zekoski, 1984). In an English investigation, Elliot, Rugg, Watson, and Brough (1983) also discovered that anxiety and depression declined from pregnancy through the infant's first year (see also Cox, Connor, & Kendell, 1982).

In contrast to these results are those from Leifer (1977) who intensively studied a small sample of highly educated, White women from the first trimester of pregnancy through 7 months postpartum. By 2 months postpartum feelings of depression had increased and "this predominantly negative mood tone persisted for a majority of women at seven months postpartum suggesting that these changes were not transient reactions to stress accompanying delivery and adaptation to the new infant, but a more permanent aspect of the first postpartum year" (p. 89). Consistent with these findings are those of Curtis-Boles (1983) indicating that self-esteem, indexed by the discrepancy between descriptions of self and the ideal self on eight subscales of The Adjective Checklist (Gough & Heilbrun, 1980), decreased significantly from the last trimester of pregnancy through 18 months postpartum in her sample of middle-class, first-time mothers. Analyses of responses by women participating in our second longitudinal study to a similar bi-polar adjective checklist (i.e., personal opinion questionnaire) also revealed a modest but significant change in mothers' (but not fathers', see later) personal opinions of themselves from the last trimester of pregnancy through 9 months postpartum. Other personality instruments assessing interpersonal affect, ego strength, and self-esteem, however, which were completed by only a (motivated) subset of these women prenatally and again 15 months after their babies' births, revealed no change (see Table 4.1).

Women are not the only ones whom clinical research suggests may suffer emotionally following the transition to parenthood, as early clinical studies reported psychopathological responses of men upon becoming parents (for summary, see Fedele et al., in press). When prospective, longitudinal data are examined, however, investigations, including our own (see Table 4.1), are quite uniform in discerning no change in men's positive and negative moods following the transition to parenthood (Feldman & Nash, 1984; Grossman, Pollack, Golding, & Fedele, 1987; Sirigano & Lachman, 1985). It must be noted that the men studied in the investigations just cited were all middle class and well educated, so it remains quite possible that under more stressful socioeconomic conditions anxiety and depression might increase following parenthood with a concomitant decline in self-esteem.

Although it is clear, at least in the case of women, that some change in self-related feelings may coincide with the transition to parenthood, it is by no means certain that the changes chronicled in mood states and feelings about self would qualify as evidence of adult development. Indeed, the data seem consistent with Rossi's (1968) assertion that the stress that parents often experience should not be equated with maturation. Moreover, when

TABLE 4.1
Stability and Change in Parent Personality

| | Pre | 15 Mos | F | Cross-time Stability (r) | | |
|---|---|---|---|---|---|---|
| *Mother (n = 33)* | | | | | | |
| Interpersonal affect | 27.1 | 26.8 | NS | .83*** | | |
| Ego strength | 25.4 | 24.9 | NS | .64*** | | |
| Self-esteem | 29.6 | 30.0 | NS | .87*** | | |
| *Father (n = 32)* | | | | | | |
| Interpersonal affect | 29.1 | 29.4 | NS | .69*** | | |
| Ego strength | 24.0 | 24.4 | NS | .49** | | |
| Self-esteem | 26.7 | 26.6 | NS | .88*** | | |
| | Pre | 3 | 9 | F(2,112) | P:3 | 3:9 | 8:9 |
| *Personal Opinion (n = 57)* | | | | | | |
| Mother | 58.5 | 60.3 | 56.9 | 2.90* | .41*** | .43*** | .39** |
| Father | 57.8 | 58.1 | 56.1 | NS | .50*** | .50*** | .64*** |

NS = Nonsignificant
*p < .05
**p < .01
***p < .001

personality is viewed from the perspective of individual differences, rather than changes in average levels of functioning or stages of development, consistent evidence exists that individuals remain strikingly stable from the period before to after the transition to parenthood (Leifer, 1977). Grossman et al. (1980) in their study which followed a large number of women from the second trimester through the infant's first year reported that "previously well functioning women tended to continue to function well and those who were anxious and depressed at the initial contact, late in pregnancy, and at two months postpartum were still more distressed at one year" (p. 117). The same was true of fathers in their study. Feldman and Nash (1984) reported similar findings based on correlations between last trimester and 6-month postpartum measures of positive mood and measures of being emotionally and physically drained. Across roughly the same developmental period Boles (1981) also found that the ranking of men and women on measures of self-esteem remained very stable. Finally, a picture of stability also emerges very clearly from our own data. As the correlation coefficients presented in Table 4.1 indicate, both men and women who felt good about themselves prenatally felt good about themselves 1 year later (9 months postpartum), whereas those who scored poorly on self-esteem, ego strength, and interpersonal affect prior to the baby's arrival scored similarly when their infants were 15 months of age.

In summary, despite the fact that parenthood is often viewed as an opportunity for adult development, the available evidence provides little support for the contention that this developmental transition fosters fundamental change in personality and the self-system. Although changes in mood from pregnancy to parenthood have been chronicled in some studies, research on individual differences suggests that personality remains quite stable over time. Perhaps the problem has been that the wrong measures have been taken, or that it is not clear how to measure maturity. Perhaps, too, research designs have been limited in terms of the time between assessments, as 1 year is too short a period to expect fundamental changes to take place. Finally, there would seem to be greater need to heed Rossi's (1968) dictum that the developmental opportunity offered by the life-course transition of parenthood is realized by some and not by others. Only in the arena of personal efficacy has much effort been made in addressing this possibility (McLaughlin & Micklin, 1983; Sirigano & Lachman, 1985).

## Infant Development: The Case of Temperament

Although it is by no means clear to what extent adults change across the transition to parenthood, it is incontestable that during the first postpartum year dramatic change takes place in the developing infant. Despite this fact, one thing does not change—from the start infants are active contributors to their own development. It is now a truism in developmental psychology that parents not only influence children but that individual characteristics of children affect the manner in which parents behave toward them and the impact that such parental care has on them. When it comes to examining characteristics of infants that play a central role in their own development, none has figured more prominently in developmental research than those referred to under the general rubric of temperament.

Although definitions of temperament vary (Bates, 1987; Goldsmith et al., 1987), there appears to be general agreement that biologically based individual differences in infant characteristics and behavioral tendencies have developmental relevance. Where disagreement still exists, even among so-called temperament researchers, is in the dimensions of variation that make up temperament. In addition to the original nine dimensions offered by Thomas, Chess, and Birch (1968; Thomas & Chess, 1977), currently popular in the empirical literature are Rothbart's (1981) four dimensions (negative reactivity, positive reactivity, behavioral inhibition, capacity to focus and switch attention), Buss and Plomin's (1984) three dimensions (negative emotionality, sociability, activity), and Bates' (Bates et al., 1979) four dimensions (fussiness, adapatbility, social responsiveness, predictability). Perhaps the dimension most common to all schemes is that of negative emotionality, the dimension at the core of the notion of "difficult temperament."

The issue of stability and change has been a major focus of research on infant temperament. Across the first 12 to 18 months of life, parent report measures such as the Infant Behavior Questionnaire (Rothbart, 1981) and Infant Characteristics Questionnaire (Bates et al., 1979) have revealed low to moderate stability for most dimensions, with greater stability emerging after 6 months of age (Bates, 1987; Pettit & Bates, 1984; Rothbart, 1981, 1986). Perceived difficultness has shown moderate stability from 6 to 24 months (Bates, 1987), and fear or distress to limitations also has shown stability after 6 months (Rothbart, 1981).

Matheny and his associates have presented perhaps the strongest empirical evidence that objective behavioral assessments of temperament during the newborn period forecast individual differences in objectively measured behavioral functioning into the second year of life (Matheny, Riese, & Wilson, 1985; Riese, 1987). Their findings, based on detailed assessment of neonatal behavior related to temperament and periodic standardized laboratory procedures, suggest that the aggregation of multiple ratings into summary scores increases predictive power. Stability from early assessment to 9 months centered principally on emotional tone, with infants who were irritable and difficult to soothe neonatally continuing to show more distress at 9 months as well as 24 months and to be less attentive and less socially responsive at the later assessment.

In our own work we have examined stability and change in temperament-related aspects of behavioral functioning in a variety of ways, using both behavioral indicators and maternal reports. Some evidence of stability consistent with the findings of Matheny et al. (1985) emerges from an analysis linking neonatal behavior with affect expression in the Strange Situation at 12 months of age (Belsky & Rovine, 1987). Infants likely to become distressed upon separation from mother, as indexed by security classifications B3–C2, performed differently on the Brazelton Newborn Behavioral Assessment than did infants who were less likely to become distressed upon separation (as indexed by A1–B2 classifications). In two separate samples (cohorts two and three) the former group displayed significantly less autonomic stability, and in one of the two samples these infants also evinced significantly less alertness and orienting capacity. Moreover, infants who were more prone to distress at 1 year of age were viewed by their mothers, as 3 month olds, as having more difficult temperaments. The fact that newborn behavior and maternal reports of temperament were more strongly and consistently associated with the A1–B2 versus B3–C2 arrangement of Strange Situation classifications than they were with the more traditional security arrangement (A . B vs. C; A + Cvs B), led us to conclude that temperament affects not so much whether an infant develops a secure attachment with his or her mother as it does the manner in which security or insecurity is expressed in the Strange Situation. (See Gunnar, Mangelsdorf, Kestenbaum, Lang, & Larson, 1987, for an alternative interpretation of the nature of differences between infants classified A1–B2 and B3–C2.)

Consistent with the evidence linking neonatal behavior with that of Strange Situation classifications in highlighting continuity over time in temperament-related behavior are the stability coefficients produced from correlating maternal temperament reports obtained at three and nine months. All four dimensions of temperament assessed using the Infant Characteristics Questionnaire, and a cumulative difficulty index created by summing the four, are highly stable across this 6-month period (see Table 4.2). The same is true, although to a far lesser extent, of the behavioral measure of fussiness obtained from the 1-hour home observations of the family triad at each time of measurement. Thus, it appears that infants who are more fussy, difficult, unadaptable, dull, or unpredictable at 3 months of age tend to look similarly (to their mothers) 6 months later.

This evidence of stability should not blind us to the fact that change takes place over time as well. Such change is evident not only in the fact that mean levels of infant fussiness (reported and observed) decline from 3 to 9

TABLE 4.2
Stability and Change in Infant Temperament

|  | Mean Scores | | F | Cross-age |
|---|---|---|---|---|
|  | 3 mos | 9 mos | (1,168) | r |
| *Maternal Report* |  |  |  |  |
| Fussy/difficult | 18.24 | 17.51 | 4.41* | .49*** |
| Unadaptable | 8.48 | 9.41 | 9.36** | .29*** |
| Dull | 5.60 | 5.82 | NS | .34*** |
| Unpredictable | 9.19 | 8.84 | NS | .48*** |
| Cumulative difficulty | 41.46 | 41.58 | NS | .41*** |
| *Observation* |  |  | *(1,161)* |  |
| Fussiness | 33.75 | 17.94 | 63.36*** | 17* |

*p < .05
**p < .01
***p < .001

months, whereas perceived unpredictability increases (see Table 4.2), but also in the instability of individual differences apparent in even the highly significant stability coefficients presented in Table 4.2. Comparable instability is evident in the aforementioned studies of Matheny and Riese that present perhaps the best evidence to date pertaining to the stability of temperament from the newborn period onward. To further explore this instability we identified at 3 and 9 months, using our observational measure of infant fussiness, a group of frequently and infrequently distressed infants by splitting the distribution of cry scores into thirds and taking the top and bottom thirds of the distribution. What we observed upon cross-tabulating membership in each of these extreme groups at 3 and 9 months was that of 57 infants who were frequently distressed at 3 months, 37% of them were classified as frequent criers at 9 months (high–tide) and 44% of them were classified as infrequent criers at this age (high–low). Similarly, of those 56 infants classified as infrequently distressed at 3 months, 41% of them cried relatively little 6 months later (low–low), and 34% cried a great deal (low–high). Clearly, the expression of negative emotionality in some infants is stable over time, but for others this is decidedly not the case.

Although it is likely that we have underestimated the degree of stability by relying, at each time of measurement, upon a single behavioral assessment to assess negative emotionality, evidence linking attachment security to change in temperament convinces us that the instability we have documented is real. When we examined the security of infant–mother and infant–father attachment of the four groups of infants, it turned out that the subgroup that changed from low to high levels of distress from 3 to 9 months were significantly more likely to be insecure in their relations to one or both parents than were all other infants ($\chi^2[1]$ = 3.92, $p$ < .05); 43% of their infant–parent relationships were insecure in contrast to a 26% rate for other infants.

These data as well as those presented by others suggests that even though there is a significant degree of stability in infant temperament over time, particularly with respect to negative emotionality, there is also a good deal of change—and that at least some of this change may be a result of experience in interpersonal relationships. This suggests, as Thomas (1984, p. 105) noted some time ago, that "rather than the simple question of whether temperament is or is not consistent over time, the more significant issue would appear to be the identification of the factors which may influence continuity or discontinuity." As it turns out, this important concern has been relatively neglected in the empirical literature. Nevertheless, three investigations provide fairly consistent evidence that patterns of maternal care and other family processes play a role in whether or not infants become more or less difficult to care for over time.

The most revealing research is that of Matheny (1986), which indicates that even though prior temperament proved to be the best predictor of subsequent temperament between 12 and 24 months, changes were associated with maternal expressiveness and involvement, family cohesiveness, and adequacy of the home environment. More specifically, infants who became less negative in terms of emotional tone, more attentive, and more socially oriented (i.e., more tractable) had mothers who were more expressive and involved with them and came from families that were more emotionally cohesive. Consistent with these findings is evidence from Washington, Minde, and Goldberg's (1986) investigation of preterm infants indicating that babies whose temperaments were seen to become more difficult over time had mothers who evinced less sensitivity in caregiving, whereas those seen (by their mothers) to become easier to care for over time had more sensitive and competent mothers. Although these findings are generally replicable of those of Matheny (1986), highlighting the importance of maternal care, Engfer's (1986) finding that German mothers who perceived their infants to become more difficult from 4 to 18 months experienced more marital difficulty are consistent with Matheny's (1986) data concerning family cohesiveness. Presumably, under conditions of general family stress, the quality of maternal care deteriorates (Belsky, 1984) and, as a result, so does the infant's capacity to regulate his or her negative emotionality. Conversely, when marital and general family processes promote maternal sensitivity, this serves to facilitate the self-regulatory capacity of the infant and leads to positive change in negative emotionality.

When we sought to identify the conditions of continuity and discontinuity in infant temperament by comparing the four cry groups identified on the basis of 3- and 9-month behavioral data on a variety of infant, parent, and family measures, evidence emerged consistent with the results of prior research. Most noteworthy, perhaps, were the findings that those infants who changed from being highly distressed to rarely distressed had mothers who felt most positive about themselves (high self-esteem) before their babies were born [$F(1,83) = 6.74$, $p < .01$], whereas those who changed from least to most distressed had fathers who tended to be the least interpersonally sensitive before the baby's birth [$F(1,83) = 2.88$, $p < .10$]. The importance of women's self-esteem, it turns out, is most evident in the case of infants who, as newborns, were especially irritable; seven of the eight infants who were high on range of state on the Brazelton exam and frequent criers when observed at 3 months but still ended up in the low crying group at 9 months had mothers who scored above the median on self-esteem. Evidence also emerged from our analyses that characteristics of infants played a role in the stability of negative emotionality over time. In comparison to all other infants, those identified as frequently distressed at both 3 and 9 months were most irritable and had the highest range of state as newborns [$F(1,77) = 9.84$, $p < .01$], whereas those who cried least frequently at both ages tended to be most skilled in soothing themselves as newborns [as indexed by regulation of state: $F(1,79) = 2.80$, $p < .10$].

Although these data suggest that characteristics of the infant are responsible for some of the continuity in temperament whereas it is characteristics of partners (mediated presumably by the care they provide) that are responsible for discontinuity in temperament, it is evident that a good deal more empirical work is needed with respect to the conditions of continuity and discontinuity in infant temperament before any firm conclusions can be drawn. From what is currently available in the empirical literature, the most accurate statement we can make is that although possible explanations abound as to why some infants tend to cry, others do not tend to cry, and still others change, we simply do not know why some infants remain the same relative to others, whereas others change. It may simply be that some infants are more impervious to experiential input when it comes to negative emotionality, so they will remain high or low criers, whereas others are more susceptible to experience and so may become more or less negative in their affective expression.

## RELATIONSHIP DEVELOPMENT

Studying relationship development in the family triad during the infant's first year of life requires consideration of three dyadic relationships: mother–infant, father–infant, and husband–wife. In this section, then, we consider first how marriages change across the transition to parenthood and then focus upon the parent–infant interaction.

## Marital Change Across the Transition to Parenthood

Prior to the transition to parenthood the nuclear family is synonymous with the marital dyad. With the addition of another individual, however, the family system increases in complexity; as one new, relatively helpless individual (i.e., the infant) is added to the pre-existing marriage, the number of interpersonal relationships in the family triples. Presumably, this dramatic change in family structure alters the functioning of the husband–wife relationship.

Investigation of such change, as well as that which more generally accompanies the transition to parenthood, has changed dramatically in the last decade, as implied by the oft repeated criticisms of the early, pioneering work of Hobbs (1965, 1968). Contemporary research on this period of family formation has totally — and wisely — forsaken past concerns with crisis and, in so doing, has abandoned methodologically flawed, cross-sectional and retrospective designs in favor of prospective, longitudinal ones.

Before proceeding to review what has emerged from such recent investigations, it must be noted that there are a variety of ways to conceptualize marriages and, as a result, a myriad of ways to measure them. In this brief summary of the current state of our knowledge about how marriages change across the transition to parenthood, we follow Huston and Robins (1982) in distinguishing marital behavior, interactions, and activities from more subjective feelings and attitudes about one's spouse and the marital relationship. We recognize, of course, the interdependence of these analytically convenient units, as behavioral events and subjective feelings are inevitably reciprocally and causally related.

### Activities and Interactions

Studies of marital change across the transition to parenthood address three distinct, yet interrelated aspects of the marital relationship as considered from a behavioral perspective: division of labor, leisure activities, and affectively toned interactions.

*Division of Labor.* It is commonly assumed that one effect of having a baby is the traditionalization of the household division of labor, with wives/mothers coming to assume more responsibility for those chores that have, by tradition, been considered the woman's responsibility in the home (e.g., laundry, shopping, meal preparation, cleaning). Although some evidence calls into question this belief (Goldberg, Michaels, & Lamb, 1985; White & Booth, 1985), there does exist a good deal of evidence that supports the proposition (Belsky et al., 1985; Cowan, Cowan, Coie, & Coie, 1978; Cowan et al., 1985; LaRossa & LaRossa, 1981; McHale & Huston, 1985; for summary, see Belsky & Pensky, in press). This should not be read to imply, however, that prior to the baby's birth husbands perform more tasks like cooking and cleaning than wives or that responsibilities are roughly equivalent, only that the absolute burden on women in the household seems to increase across the transition.

*Leisure Activities.* Less attention has been paid to the ways in which couples spend time together than to who does what in the household, but the research that does exist seems to indicate what the extensive needs of the young baby and the additional costs incurred in rearing a child affect the time spouses spend in recreational activities together or alter how they spend their time with one another. In our first study of the transition to parenthood, for example, we found a significant decline from the last trimester of pregnancy through 9 months postpartum in the frequency with which couples did things together, such as going out to dinner, to the movies, or watching television (Belsky, Spanier, & Rovine, 1983). Complementing these results are those of McHale and Huston (1985) whose investigation of newlywed parents indicated that the transition to parenthood speeds the decline in recreational time spent together.

*Affectively Toned Interactions.* In view of the changes that seem to occur following the transition to parenthood in household division of labor and leisure activities, it stands to reason that the behavioral interactions that take place between spouses would also change with the onset of parenthood. And several studies do indicate that the frequency, nature, and/or quality of positively toned interactions between husband and wife declines over time (Belsky et al., 1985; Belsky et al., 1983; McHale & Huston, 1985); this pattern has been discerned observationally as well as with self-report instruments that assess frequency with which interchanges occur with sufficient frequency to be satisfying to spouses.

There is also some evidence that the incidence of negative interchanges increases across the transition at the same time that positive interactions are declining. Cowan et al. (1985), for example, found that although frequency of conflict increased for those experiencing the transition to parenthood, frequency of conflict actually decreased for a control group of couples that did not become parents.

## Subjective Feelings and Attitudes

In view of the changes that we have considered in marital activities and interactions, it seems reasonable to expect that the feelings that husband and wife have for each other and for their marital relationship should also be affected by the experience of becoming parents. And much of the evidence that is available points to the decline in marital satisfaction across the transition to parenthood (Belsky et al., 1983; Cowan et al., 1985; Moss, Boland, Roxman, & Owen, 1986; Ryder, 1973), although even this result has not been universally documented (McHale & Huston, 1985; White & Booth, 1985; see Belsky & Pensky, in press, for discussion of inconsistencies). When deterioration of marital quality is detected, it is more often than not the case that the negative change is greater for wives than for husbands (e.g., Belsky et al., 1983; Hobbs, 1965; Hobbs & Wimbish, 1979; Russell, 1974; Waldron & Routh, 1981). The work of Cowan et al. (1985), however, suggests that men and women differ in their "journeys into parenthood," such that "the impact of becoming a parent is felt first by women" and "only later do men feel the negative effects" (p. 469).

In large measure, the changes just summarized, many of which were discerned in our first investigation of the transition to parenthood (Belsky et al., 1983), are replicated in findings pertaining to families participating in our second two cohorts. Analysis of questionnaire data indicate that feelings of love for the spouse declined as did positive marital communications (maintenance), and that feelings of ambivalence and experience of conflict increased (see Table 4.3). This negative change was more pronounced for wives than for husbands, as reflected by significant statistical interactions between time and spouse in the case of love [$F(1,162) = 4.59$, $p < .05$] and maintenance [$F(1,162) = 10.15$, $p < .01$]; Fig. 4.1 depicts the differential pattern of change using the sum of the love and maintenance scores (i.e., Positive Marriage). Examination of the data in Table 4.3 pertaining to marital interaction observed during the course of our home observations also reveals that overall couple engagement declined from 3 to 9 months postpartum, most likely because the frequency of baby-related communication decreased (though joint attention showed the opposite pattern). No evidence was found in this two-cohort database, however, of any changes in positively affectionate spousal behavior during the 1-hour observations, conceivably because base rates were so low to begin with. Finally, it is noteworthy that the household division of labor became more traditional over time and frequency of joint leisure activities declined.

Although it is clear that negative changes in marital functioning took place across the transition to parenthood, two things must be noted. First, in all cases the magnitude of the change was modest rather than dramatic. Second, although mean levels of marital functioning changed, and typically

TABLE 4.3
Marital Change Across the Transition to Parenthood: Central Tendencies and
Individual Differences

| | Time[a] | | | F Ratios |
| --- | --- | --- | --- | --- |
| | Pre | 3 Mos | 9 Mos | (2,161) |
| Self-Report[b] | | | | |
| Love | 78.9 | 76.8 | 75.1 | 38.20*** |
| Maintenance | 31.1 | 29.6 | 28.6 | 35.05*** |
| Conflict | 19.8 | 20.0 | 21.1 | 10.46*** |
| Ambivalence | 11.2 | 11.8 | 12.9 | 15.76*** |
| Couple Interview[c] | | | | |
| Division of labor | 25.1 | 25.7 | 26.3 | 9.93*** |
| Joint leisure | 16.4 | 15.2 | 14.7 | 31.82*** |

| | | | | F Ratios | |
| --- | --- | --- | --- | --- | --- |
| | | | | 1 vs 3 | 3 vs 9 |
| | 1 Mos. | 3 Mos. | 9 Mos. | (1,57) | (1,165) |
| Observation[d] | | | | | |
| Total engagement | 118.8 | 108.6 | 89.9 | NS | 18.53*** |
| Baby-related | 31.6 | 28.9 | 24.6 | NS | 8.02*** |
| Joint attention | 25.4 | 33.4 | 40.2 | NS | 6.73* |
| Share pleasure | 2.9 | 3.9 | 3.5 | NS | NS |
| Nonbaby-related | 34.9 | 35.0 | 31.6 | NS | NS |
| Positive | 2.2 | 2.9 | 3.2 | NS | NS |

*$p < .05$
***$p < .005$
[a]Main effect means of spouse factor from 2(Spouse: Husband, Wife) ×
3(Time: Prenatal, 3 mons, 9 mons)
ANOVAs
[b]$n = 169$
[c]$n = 171$
[d]$n = 59$ (1–3 mons); 167 (3–9 mons)

in a negative direction, individual differences remained remarkably stable across this period of family transition. As the stability coefficients depicted in Table 4.4 indicate, the relationships that seemed to be functioning best prior to the infant's birth were, in large measure, still functioning best nine months afterward; and this pattern was evident whether one looked at husbands' or wives' reports which, it should be noted, were highly related at all times of measurement ($p < .001$).

In summary, then, the arrival of a first child seems to be associated with small to modest declines in overall marital quality, with positive feelings and interactions decreasing and negative feelings and interactions increasing. It is by no means the case, however, that having a baby rejuvenates a poor relationship or seriously impairs a strong relationship. Indeed, it must

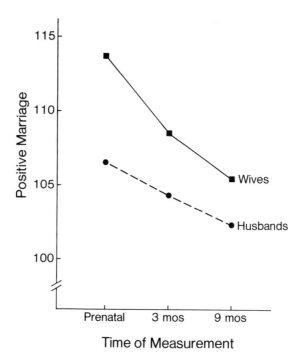

Time of Measurement

FIG. 4.1. Changes in positive aspects of the marriage of husbands and wives.

TABLE 4.4
Stability of Individual Differences in Marriage

| | Wife | | | Husband | | |
|---|---|---|---|---|---|---|
| | P–3 mos. (n = 165) | 3–9 mos. (162) | P–9 mos. (162) | P–3 mos. (165) | 3–9 mos. (162) | P–9 mos. (162) |
| *Individual Self-Report* | | | | | | |
| Positive marriage | .70*** | .76*** | .70*** | .80*** | .68*** | .66*** |
| Negative marriage | .73*** | .65*** | .62*** | .72*** | .78*** | .66*** |
| | (n = 172) | (n = 171) | (n = 172) | | | |
| *Couple Interview* | | | | | | |
| Division of labor | .63*** | .73*** | .67*** | | | |
| Leisure activities | .44*** | .64*** | .51*** | | | |

***p < .001

140

be noted in closing this subsection of the chapter that some have argued that the changes associated with the transition to parenthood tend to occur in marriages over time anyway, irrespective of whether or not spouses become parents (White & Booth, 1985). Our own reading of the evidence suggests to us, however, that the transition to parenthood tends to accelerate and accentuate these more normative patterns of marital change (Belsky & Pensky, in press; Cowan et al., 1985).

## Mother–Infant and Father–Infant Interaction in the Triad

One of the major changes that has taken place in the study of the early childbearing and childrearing years of the family life cycle has been the inclusion of fathers in studies of parent–infant interaction and child development more generally. Exactly why fathers and fathering were "discovered" by developmental psychologists some 10–15 years ago is by no means clear, but presumably it had something to do with changes taking place in American society, particularly with regard to the roles of men and women. No doubt as a result, the initial investigations of the father–infant relationship were designed to show that infants formed emotional bonds with the men in their lives and that fathers were as capable and sensitive as mothers in caring for their babies.

The earliest work by Lamb (1977a) did in fact demonstrate that infants become attached to their fathers by the time they are 12–18 months of age, but further indicated that, when stressed, most infants prefer contact with their mothers (Lamb, 1977b). Although mothers appeared to be the infant's primary source of security, fathers filled the role of playmate. Not only is a disproportionate amount of father's involvement with the infant spent in play relative to that of mother (e.g., Kotelchuck, 1976; Richards, Dunn, & Antonis, 1977), but it is also the case that infants and older children tend to react more positively to the playful antics of their fathers (e.g., Clarke-Stewart, 1978; Lamb, 1976). The major reason for this seems to be the distinct styles with which mothers and fathers (on average) play with their infants: Mothers tend to engage in object-oriented or toy-mediated play, or in conventional social games like peek-a-boo and patty-cake, and fathers' play tends to be far more physical or rough and tumble in style and idiosyncratic in nature (Clarke-Stewart, 1978; Lamb, 1977b; Power & Parke, 1982; Yogman, 1983; Yogman, Dixon, Tronick, Als, & Brazelton, 1977). Of interest, however is the fact that these differences in parental style are not seen as routinely in other countries (e.g., Sweden: Lamb, Frodi, Hwang, & Frodi, 1982) or in rearing arrangements that depart from the traditional nuclear family (e.g., Israeli Kibbutz: Sagi, Lamb, Shoham, Duir, & Lewkowicz, 1985).

Besides documenting distinct styles of play, early investigations also revealed that fathers could be just as interested, nurturant, and stimulating interactive partners with their infants as were mothers. In particular, the work of Parke and his colleagues revealed not only that fathers could skillfully feed their newborns and sensitively respond to their distress cues (Parke & Sawin, 1975), but also that men modified their speech when addressing infants in much the same way as did mothers (Phillips & Parke, 1981). That is, they used shorter phrases, repeated sounds, and raised the pitch of their voices, recreating the style of talking that appears to match the attentional and perceptual capacities of the young infant and has come to be known, apparently erroneously, as "motherese."

The fact that fathers "could" be as skilled as mothers and as involved with their infants as mothers does not mean, however, that on a day-to-day basis the roles and behaviors of men and women in the family are interchangeable. The fact of the matter is that despite shifts in cultural attitudes regarding male and female roles in the family, practice has not kept pace with ideology. Several naturalistic, observational studies underscore this point most clearly. In our first longitudinal investigation of mother–father–infant interaction, we observed in a sample of working and middle-class families that mothers were significantly more involved with their infants than were fathers–even when observations were conducted in the late afternoon/early evening, a time when men were often newcomers to the family and many mothers had been home all day with their infants (Belsky et al., 1984). Exactly the same findings emerge when the data obtained during the mother–father–infant observation sessions of the families that are the subject of this report are subjected to analysis (see Table 4.5). At 1, 3, and 9 months postpartum, mothers responded to, stimulated, expressed positive affection toward, and provided more basic care for their infants than did fathers. Just like in our earlier study, the only thing that men did more of than women was engage in personal leisure activity (i.e., read/watch television)!

It is especially noteworthy that these systematic differences between parents, reflective as they are of rather traditional family roles, emerge from investigations of families in other countries. In Israel, for example, Greenbaum and Landau (1982) observed 96 middle and lower class households and found that across the first year of he infants' lives mothers greatly exceeded fathers in verbal interaction. When Sagi et al. (1985) observed Israeli parents whose children were cared for during the day by nonparental caretakers on the kibbutz (metapelet) interacting in the parents' living quarters at 8 and 16 months postpartum, they found that mothers were more likely than fathers to laugh, vocalize, display affection, hold, and engage in routine caregiving. And finally, but perhaps most noteworthy, a study of Swedish fathers who had taken advantage of the country's

TABLE 4.5
Mother–Father–Infant Interaction in the Triad

| Parent Behavior | Mother | | | Father | | | 1-3 Mos (n = 56) | | | 1-9 Mos (n = 162) | | |
|---|---|---|---|---|---|---|---|---|---|---|---|---|
| | 1 | 3 | 9 | 1 | 3 | 9 | T[a] (1,55) | P[b] (1,55) | T × P (1,55) | T (1,161) | P (1,161) | T × P (1,161) |
| Engage total | 166.5 | 177.3 | 143.1 | 103.9 | 121.6 | 109.6 | 5.02* | 21.37*** | NS | 30.72*** | 46.80*** | 4.07* |
| Respond | 17.4 | 16.7 | 20.0 | 10.9 | 12.3 | 14.4 | NS | 12.94*** | NS | 7.29* | 21.26*** | NS |
| Stimulate | 47.6 | 58.7 | 55.5 | 35.5 | 45.9 | 47.3 | 7.17** | 6.24* | NS | NS | 17.48 | NS |
| Caregive | 64.1 | 45.4 | 26.2 | 23.1 | 20.3 | 12.9 | 8.28** | 59.26*** | NS | 75.21*** | 86.13*** | 12.71*** |
| Pos. aff. | 6.0 | 9.6 | 6.6 | 3.3 | 5.7 | 3.6 | 11.65** | 23.22*** | NS | 26.51*** | 44.19*** | NS |
| Read/TV | 35.6 | 27.5 | 23.8 | 60.6 | 46.7 | 40.2 | 4.34* | 15.17*** | NS | NS | 55.51*** | NS |

| Infant Behavior | 1 | 3 | 9 | 1-3 Mos (1,55) | 3-9 Mos (1,161) |
|---|---|---|---|---|---|
| Vocalize | 14.6 | 47.4 | 76.2 | 87.87*** | 122.60*** |
| Fuss/cry | 24.9 | 16.7 | 11.2 | 8.81** | 18.39*** |
| Smile | 1.1 | 15.4 | 27.8 | 69.00*** | 78.14*** |

[a]T = Time effect
[b]P = Parent effect
*p < .05
**p < .01
***p < .001
NS: Nonsignificant

143

*parental* leave policy and remained at home to care for their inflants for 1 or more months, revealed that these "nontraditional" men were no more involved with their infants when observed at 8 and 16 months postpartum than were more traditional men — and less interactively involved than the women in both family types (Lamb, Frodi, Hwang, & Frodi, 1982; Lamb, Frodi, Hwang, & Steinberg, 1982).

The evidence just summarized from our own research, and particularly that from nontraditional families, highlights the need to distinguish parental competence and performance (Belsky & Volling, 1987; Parke & Tinsley, 1987); although it is clear that fathers are capable of being involved parents, particularly when situations are structured to afford them little else to do, it is just as clear that during the course of routine activities in the home that the role of parent remains primary for most mothers and secondary for most fathers, a pattern also discerned in studies of preschool and school-age children (Baumrind, 1982; Russell & Russell, 1987).

Despite this reality and the differences it underscores in the nature of the mother–infant and father–infant subsystems of the family, it is noteworthy that some basic similarities characterize mother–infant and father–infant interaction patterns in the infants' first 9 months of life. The first of these is reflected in the comparable treatment of sons and daughters by mothers and fathers and in the comparable developmental changes that take place in the frequency with which particular parenting behaviors are displayed. The similar developmental profiles in the case of mothering and fathering result, no doubt, in response to the changing demands of the developing infant whose smiling and vocalizing is increasing from 1–3–9 months at the same time his or her fussiness is decreasing (see Table 4.5).

Further evidence of the similarity of mother–infant and father–infant interaction patterns emerges from a series of principal component analyses of mothering and fathering behavior at 1, 3, and 9 months postpartum (see Table 4.6). In the case of both parents, the first principal component at 1 month reflects high positive loadings on respond, stimulate, and express positive affection, with low negative loadings on stimulate and read. For both parents, principal component loadings are virtually identical at 3 and 9 months as well, with an important change taking place in the magnitude and direction of the loading for the variable stimulate, which has become strong and positive for each parent. As important as these comparable factor structures are, they are less noteworthy than the similarity in the associations generated when composite scores based on these principal components are correlated with contemporaneous measures of infant behavior (see Table 4.7).

For mothers and fathers alike, frequent smiling and attentive alertness on the part of the 1-month-old infant is related to low levels of maternal and paternal involvement, raising the possibility that busy parents of a newborn

TABLE 4.6
Mothering and Fathering: First Principal Components*

| Parent Behavior | 1 Month | | 3 Months | | 9 Months | |
|---|---|---|---|---|---|---|
| | Mother | Father | Mother | Father | Mother | Father |
| Respond | .85 | .82 | .82 | .75 | .74 | .78 |
| Stimulate | −.14 | −.10 | .77 | .74 | .79 | .78 |
| Caregive | .56 | .71 | .44 | .54 | .60 | .32 |
| Positive Affection | .68 | .73 | .64 | .66 | .59 | .46 |
| Read/Watch TV | −.47 | −.13 | −.31 | −.22 | −.41 | −.34 |
| Eigenvalue | 1.66 | 1.74 | 1.97 | 1.87 | 2.04 | 1.65 |
| Variance | 33% | 35% | 39% | 37% | 41% | 33% |

*Principal axis analysis with oblique rotation to produce promas solution consisting of no more than two factors; first factor displayed.

TABLE 4.7
Contemporaneous Association Between Parental Involvement
and Infant Behavior

| | Parental Involvement+ | | | | | |
|---|---|---|---|---|---|---|
| | 1 Mos. | | 3 Mos. | | 9 Mos. | |
| Infant Behavior | Mother | Father | Mother | Father | Mother | Father |
| Fuss | .19 | −.02 | .27*** | −.04 | .13 | −.03 |
| Vocalize | −.29* | −.27* | .17* | .19** | .09 | .02 |
| Smile | .17 | .00 | .12 | .24** | .14 | .08 |
| Alert/explore | −.33** | −.44*** | −.02 | .09 | −.02 | .06 |
| | (n = 59) | | (n = 175) | | (n = 167) | |

*p < .05
**p < .01
***p < .001
+Based on composite scored using weighting from principal components analysis.

are inclined not to intrude on an apparently contented baby, whereas at 3 months frequent vocalizations and even smiling on the part of the infant coincide with high levels of maternal and paternal involvement, thereby suggesting patterns of parent–infant play. By 9 months, and again in the case of both parents, infant behavior is generally unrelated to measured parental involvement. Where a difference does emerge in the interrelation of parental and infant behavior in the case of mothers and fathers—and consistently so at all three ages—is in the association between infant fussiness and parental involvement. Although high levels of infant crying are associated with higher levels of maternal involvement, and significantly so at three months, they are virtually unrelated to fathering at all three times of measurement. Such findings are consistent with the notion that although father's principal role might be that of playmate, a primary component of the mother role remains comforter and basic-care provider.

The reporting of this last set of analyses should make it evident that there exist both basic similarities and differences in mother–infant and father–infant relationships, at least as revealed by patterns of interaction in the family triad. The similarities we suspect are basic to the behavior of any partner interacting with the developing infant. The differences, on the other hand, undoubtedly reflect core differences in the experiences of men and women in the family and thereby highlight the distinct nature of the mother–infant and father–infant relationship subsystems.

## INTERDEPENDENCE OF RELATIONSHIPS

Through this point we have considered individual development and relationship development in our analyses of the developing family system. The next issue addressed in this attempt to apply basic principles of a system's perspective to our data involves the interrelation of relationships. A basic proposition of system's theory, when applied to the family, is that boundaries between subsystems are likely to be somewhat open so that some degree of influence among relationship subsystems is to be expected. In considering the mutual influences among relationship subsystems in three-person families, there are two basic sets of interdependencies to be considered, one pertaining to the relation between the two parent–infant relationships and the other to the relation between marital and parent–infant relationships.

### Parent–Infant Relationships

Consideration of research conducted to date, particularly during the infancy period, reveals that far more attention has been paid to the interrelation of marital and parent–infant relationships than to that between mother–infant and father–infant relationships, at least insofar as the interrelation of individual differences in relationships is concerned. Although a good deal of work has been conducted documenting basic similarities and differences in patterns of mother–infant and father–infant interaction, and thus in highlighting the different roles that men (the playmate) and women (the caregiver) tend to play in the nuclear family, less effort has been made to determine how the functioning of one parent–infant relationship might affect the other. This does not mean, however, that no thought has been given to processes that could link the two parent–infant relationship subsystems. Parke and Sawin (1980), for example, have suggested that mutual modeling effects exist between mother and father whereby partners adopt one another's behaviors during early infancy.

In an attempt to explore whether such processes might take place, two sets of correlational analyses were conducted using the composite measures of mothering and fathering that emerged from our principal components analyses of mother–infant and father–infant interaction in the triad. The first analysis consisted of simply correlating, within time, the composite measures of mothering and fathering. The second, based on the results of the first, consisted of a path analysis designed to determine whether, over time, earlier patterns of mothering and fathering influenced the later behavior of mothers and fathers in the triad.

Results of the first analysis revealed that the nature of the statistical interdependence between mothering and fathering changed over time. Although it was marginally the case when the infant was 1 month of age that in families in which mother was highly involved with the infant so was the father [$r(59) = .23, p < .10$], by 3 and 9 months postpartum the reverse was true, with maternal and paternal involvement being inversely correlated [$r(175) = -.21, p < .01; r(167) = -.19, p < .05$, respectively]; in households in which mothers were highly involved with the infant, fathers tended were less involved.

Consideration of these contemporaneous correlations suggests several possible processes of influence. In the baby's first month, periods of awake and alert activity may draw the attention and involvement of both parents, or it may be that each parent is drawn to the baby on the basis of the activity of the other parent. Just a few months later, once the infant is more frequently awake and demanding, parents may adopt a simple division of labor, such that the participation of one parent with the infant permits the other parent to be involved in other household activities; alternatively, the involvement of one parent may simply limit the participation of the other parent.

Given the fact that these speculations are based on contemporaneous correlations, it is impossible to determine whether any actual cross-parent influence process was, in fact, operating. In hopes of shedding more empirical light on such processes, the aforementioned path analysis was conducted to see whether either parent's activity influenced the other parent at a subsequent point in time. Although a simple cross-lagged correlational analysis suggested that high levels of maternal involvement at three months led to less father involvement 6 months later [$r(167) = -.21, p < .01$], the results of the path analysis, which controlled for the stability of maternal and paternal involvement over time (via standardized coefficients), revealed no apparent influence of one parent on the other over time (see Fig. 4.2) Thus, we could find no evidence within this data set that what transpired

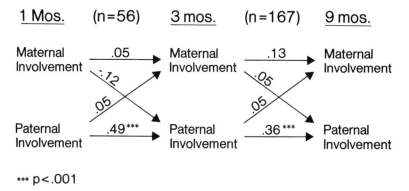

FIG. 4.2. Path analysis linking maternal and paternal involvement over time/coefficients are standardized (betas).

between mother and infant at one point in time influenced or was influenced by what transpired between father and infant at another point in time. Although it is possible that the relative independence of the two relationships was an artifact of the measures available to us, it is noteworthy that in our study (Belsky & Rovine, 1987), as well as in others (Grossman, Grossman, Huber, & Wartner, 1981; Main & Weston, 1981), this independence of the two relationships also emerges when the security of infant–parent attachment is the means of measuring the two parent–child relationships.

## Marital and Parent-Infant Relationships

Very early in their attempts to conceptualize the role of the father in the family, developmentalists came to recognize that much of his influence on the child might be indirect (Belsky, 1981; Lewis & Weinraub, 1976; Parke, 1978; Pedersen, Yarrow, Anderson, & Cain, 1978). By calling attention to the father's potential for influencing the child by affecting the quality of care that mothers provide, the significance of the relationship between mother and father, that is, between husband and wife, was underscored. As it turns out, a good deal of evidence exists indicating that sensitive, supporting parenting and harmonious marriages go together, and this seems to be true in the case of both men and women (e.g., Durrett, Richards, Otaki, Pennebaker, & Nyquist, 1986; Feldman, Nash, & Aschenbrenner, 1983; Goldberg & Easterbrooks, 1984; Meyer, in press). To be noted, however, is the fact that some investigators have found what appear to be compensatory processes whereby higher levels of parental involvement are associated with less satisfied marriages (Brody, Pillegrini, & Sigel, 1986; Easterbrooks & Emde, 1986; Engfer, in press). The work of Engfer (in press) in Germany appears to reconcile these two sets of findings as it suggests that the quality of maternal care is compromised, even in the face of increasing involvement, when problems exist in the marital relationship (see also Christensen & Margolin, 1988).

In our own work we have sought to illuminate the interrelation of marital and parent–infant relationships in a number of ways. First, we have examined relations between measures of marriage obtained prenatally and the observational measures of mothering and fathering. Second, we have examined, both within and across time, relations between the observational measures of marital and parent–infant interaction. Finally, we have examined the interrelation of changes in marriage across the transition to parenthood and security of infant–parent attachment.

Results of the first two sets of analyses provide evidence that variation in the quality and functioning of the marital relationship is more systematically related to fathering than it is to mothering. This can be seen in the simple correlations presented in Table 4.8, the top two rows of which depict the extent to which the ratio of negative to positive aspects of the marriage measured prenatally predicts mother–infant and father–infant interaction in the family triad at 1, 3, and 9 months, and the bottom row that displays the contemporaneous associations between the composite measures of parental involvement and marital interaction at each time of measurement. Rather consistently, these results indicate that fathers are more involved with their infants when marital relationships are viewed by both husbands and wives as less negative and more positive before the child is born and when interaction between spouses is frequent. To determine whether this simple correlational pattern might actually reflect the influence of the marriage on the father, a path analysis was conducted linking marital

TABLE 4.8
Interrelation of Marriage and Parenting

|  | Mothering | | | Fathering | | |
|---|---|---|---|---|---|---|
| Prenatal Quest. | 1 Mos (n = 58) | 3 Mos (n = 175) | 9 Mos (n = 167) | 1 Mos (n = 48) | 3 Mos (n = 175) | 9 Mos (n = 167) |
| Neg Wife — Marr. Pos | −.25* |  |  | −.31* | −.17* | −.18* |
| Neg Husb — Marr. Pos |  |  |  |  | −.20** | −.17* |
| Marital Interaction | .30* |  | .16* | .18 | .44*** | .35*** |

*p < .05
**p < .01
***p < .001

interaction with maternal and paternal involvement. Inspection of Figure 4.3 reveals that high levels of marital interaction do indeed lead to high levels of father involvement, at least from 1 to 3 months, and that fathers who were highly involved with their infants at 3 months tend to remain highly involved with their infants 6 months later. It is also noteworthy that no evidence of parental involvement influencing the marital relationship emerges from this analysis, or of mothering being affected by the marriage.

These data clearly suggest, as have findings from our first cohort (Belsky et al., 1984), that the roles of mother and wife are more independent than those of father and husband. Fathers who are involved with their infants tend to come from families in which marital interaction is frequent and husbands and wives are satisfied with their relationships with one another. It further appears that the more consistent association between marriage and fathering in this sample of nondistressed families results from the fact that fathers are more susceptible to being influenced by their marriages than are mothers. Quite conceivably, this is a function of the fact that the role of father is less well defined than that of mother so that the father is more subject to the influence process. The care that mothers offer babies may be too highly canalized — by biological imperatives such as breastfeeding, by a lifetime of anticipatory socialization for motherhood and, of course, by contemporary expectations.

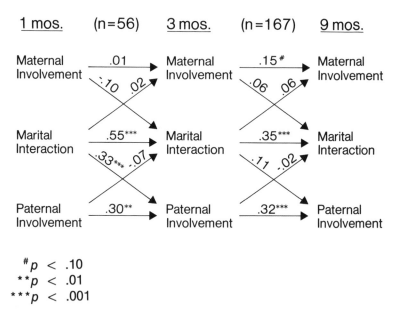

FIG. 4.3. Path analysis linking marital interaction and parental involvement; coefficients are standardized (betas).

Despite the results of the preceding analyses we cannot conclude that individual differences in the mother–infant relationship are unrelated to the quality of the marriage. Not only is some of the correlational evidence consistent with the findings of other studies linking mothering and marital quality, but additional evidence consistent with this notion emerges when changes in marriage across the transition to parenthood are examined as a function of attachment security. Results of a 3 (Time: prenatal, 3 mos., 9 mos.) ×2 (Attachment: Secure vs. Insecure) repeated measures analysis of variance, using the ratio of negative to positive aspects of the marriage as the index of marital quality, revealed that mothers of secure infants viewed their marriages less negatively and more positively than those of insecure infants [$F(1,158) = 4.08$, $p < .05$], and that beyond this main effect for attachment group the quality of the marriage, as appraised by the mother, deteriorated more over time for mothers of insecure infants than for mothers of secure infants [Time × Attachment interaction: $F(2,316) = 3.80$, $p < .05$]. Figure 4.4 displays the developmental profiles of mothers of the two groups of infants; recall that the higher the score on the ratio measure, the more negative the marriage.

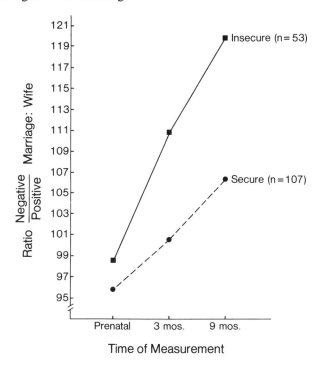

FIG. 4.4. Changing ratio of negative to positive aspects of the marriage reported by wife as a function of infant–mother attachment security.

In considering the findings depicted in Fig. 4.4 there are several important things to keep in mind. The first is that the association between
marriage and attachment security is consistent with cross-sectional findings
reported by several other investigators indicating that insecure
infant–mother attachment relationships are associated with less satisfactory
marital relationships (Durrett, Otaki, & Richards, 1984; Goldberg &
Easterbrooks, 1984; Soloman, 1982). Although such results undoubtedly
reflect the fact that the seeds of insecurity are being sown prior to its
measurement at 1 year of age, it would be mistaken to conclude that, in any
simple sense, it is marital quality that unidirectionally affects the developing
infant–mother relationship. Not only are there theoretical reasons to expect
a bidirectional process of influence to characterize the dynamics of the
association between marriage and attachment discerned in this investigation, but it must be noted that attachment security empirically covaries with
personality which itself covaries with marriage: Mothers of secure infants
evinced significantly greater interpersonal sensitivity prenatally on the
measure of interpersonal affect from the Jackson Personality Questionnaire
than did mothers of insecure infants [$F(1,157) = 6.39$, $p < .01$] and tended
to express higher personal opinion of themselves when measures of personal
opinion obtained at three different times of measurement (prenatal, 3 mos.,
9 mos.) were summed together [$F(1,50) = 3.14$ $p < .10$]. Moreover, when
the personal opinion data were subjected to longitudinal analysis as a
function of attachment security strikingly different developmental profiles
emerged in the case of mothers of secure and insecure infants [$F(2,102)
= 6.02$, $p < .01$]: Although mothers of insecure infants evinced a marked
decline in their personal opinions of themselves, particularly from 3 to 9
months postpartum, those of secure infants evinced no such decline, and
even displayed some hint of increasingly positive feelings about themselves
from the last trimester of pregnancy to three months postpartum (see Fig.
4.5). What makes such findings particularly noteworthy is that these very
indices of personality and psychological functioning were themselves related to measures of marriage. For example, wives who had a higher
personal opinion of themselves prenatally scored better on the negative-to-
positive ratio index of marriage before the infant was born ($r = .49$, $p
< .001$) as well as at 3- and 9-months postpartum (both $rs = .16$, $p < .05$).

The network of interconnections between marital change and attachment
security, attachment security and personality, and between personality and
marriage revealed by this set of findings highlight as well as any others from
this investigation the systemic nature of the family system. It is not just the
case that marital change affects the developing infant–mother attachment
relationship or that this relation between relationship subsystems in the
family is reciprocal and bidirectional. Rather it appears that the interde-
pendency that emerged from our analysis of attachment and marriage takes

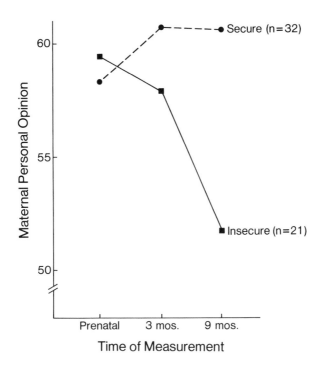

FIG. 4.5. Maternal personal opinion across time as a function of inflant-mother attachment security.

place in the context of linkages between mother's personality and psychological well-being and the family relationships in which she participates.

The fact that no relation between attachment security and marital quality emerged when the infant-father relationship was the focus of inquiry leads us to wonder whether the particular measures that we employed in our analyses are differentially sensitive to variation in the two parent-infant relationships. The fact that our indice of father involvement covaries more consistently with measures of the marriage than does that of maternal involvement, whereas the measure of infant-mother attachment covaries with marriage more than that of infant-father attachment alerts us to the possibility that the two measurement contexts — the family triad and the Strange Situation — may be differentially effective for assessing each parent-child relationship. Consistent with this line of reasoning is evidence that indices of father's personality significantly covaried with the observational measures of fathering in a manner consistent with those previously reported between infant-mother attachment and maternal personality.

What all these findings indicate, of course, is that the marital and parent-infant relationship subsystem are interdependent as a system's framework would suggest and, moreover, that they are more systematically interrelated, at least insofar as we can determine, than are the two parent–infant relationships. The evidence linking personality and marriage and personality and parent–infant relationships indicates, further, that complete understanding of the family system rests not simply on knowledge of the interdependence of relationship subsystems but also requires consideration of the individuals who participate in those relationships.

## THE FAMILY TRIAD

One of the greatest challenges of trying to apply a system's perspective to the family involves the precept "that the whole is greater than the sum of its parts." How, in particular, is one to characterize the family as an entity beyond its simple structural properties (e.g., two-parent, single-parent, extended, etc.)? It is by no means clear that family researchers have yet succeeded in surmounting this challenge, although the clinical literature is replete with general characterizations of family systems as enmeshed, chaotic, and conflicted.

With the data available to us on mother–infant, father–infant, and husband–wife interaction in the triad we explored several strategies of creating family types before settling on the rather simple and straightforward procedure of splitting each of our composite indices (based on principal components analysis) of mothering, fathering, and marital interaction at the median and then generating profiles of each family at each time of measurement using this information from all three dyads. This resulted in some families being characterized by high levels of mother–infant, father–infant, and marital interaction (M + F + HW +), some being characterized by low levels of interaction in each of the three dyads (M − F-HW-), and the remainder being characterized by some combination of high and low levels of involvement in the three dyads (e.g., M + F + HW- M-F + HW + , M-F-HW + ).

To determine whether or not this configurational strategy was in any way useful we initiated our analysis of the family triad by comparing family types that evinced high or low levels of involvement across all three dyads comprising the triad. At 1-month postpartum, 14 families qualified as interactively uninvolved, that is, as having scores below the median on all three relationship subsystems, and 12 qualified as interactively very involved, that is, as having scores above the median on all three dyads. In comparing these families on a series of demographic, parental, and family measures, noteworthy differences that anteceded the infant's birth emerged. Although the two types of families did not differ from each other demographically or in terms of the child's gender, in families in which all three dyads were relatively disengaged both wives and husbands viewed their marital relationship as more negative and less positive (on the ratio measure) in the last trimester of pregnancy [$F(4,24) = 4.78$, $p < .05$; 3.64, $p < .10$, for wives and husbands, respectively] than did spouses from households in which all three dyads were highly engaged. Moreover, mothers from the disengaged families scored lower on self-esteem [$F(1,24) = 4.53$, $p < .05$] and evinced less interpersonal sensitivity [$F(1,24) = 8.38$, $p < .01$] on the prenatal personality measures. When families identified as falling into one of these two types at either 3 or 9 monthes ($ns = 47$ and 49) were compared on the same measures, the prenatal marital differences emerged once more [$F(1,94) = 3.94$, 5.99, both p $< .05$ for wives and husbands, respectively]. In other words, there was rather consistent evidence that in highly engaged and in very disengaged family triads, marital relationships differed prior to the child's birth, with further evidence, at least at the time of the 1-month observation, that mothers in these two extreme family types differed in terms of their psychological functioning as well.

The discovery that families that were highly engaged (M + F + HW + ) or disengaged (M-F-HW-) at 1 month and at 3 or 9 months consistently differed in terms of their marital relationships (prenatally) raised the possibility that this replicated finding was a function of the fact that families that were very interactive or not very interactive across all three dyads at one point in time tended to remain that way at subsequent points in time. As a first step in exploring this issue of the stability of the family system, the distribution of the eight family types generated by our median split procedure was examined at each time of measurement (see Table 4.9). This revealed a rather interesting developmental pattern: Although 45% of the families at 1 month of age could be characterized as highly engaged

TABLE 4.9
Relative Frequence of Eight Family Types at Three Times of Measurement

| Family Type* | 1 Mos. | 3 Mos. | 9 Mos. |
|---|---|---|---|
| M – F – HW – | 19.6% | 15.4% | 17.2% |
| M + F – HW – | 8.9% | 18.5% | 17.3% |
| M – F + HW – | 12.5% | 11.7% | 9.8% |
| M – F – HW + | 12.5% | 8.0% | 6.2% |
| M + F + HW – | 7.1% | 3.7% | 4.9% |
| M + F – HW + | 7.1% | 9.3% | 9.3% |
| M – F + HW + | 7.1% | 15.4% | 16.7% |
| M + F + HW + | 25.0% | 17.9% | 18.5% |

*M = Mother-infant dyad; F = Father-infant dyad; HW = Husband-wife dyad; + reflects dyad score above the median and – reflects dyad score below the median.

(M + F + HW +) or highly disengaged (M-F-HW-), by 3 and 9 months postpartum two additional family types emerged as particularly frequent; these involved households in which only the mother–infant dyad was highly engaged (M + F-HW-) and in which only the mother–infant dyad was relatively disengaged (M-F + HW +). At both 3 and 9 months these four family subtypes, representing 50% of those which our median split strategy configured, characterized more than two-thirds of the family systems.

Reflection on these four family subtypes suggested that what we might have identified were two variants of two distinct family systems. In one, there was only limited interaction in all three dyads or if there was much in any of the three relationship subsystems it was in the mother–infant dyad (M-F-HW-, M + F-HW-). In the other there tended to be high levels of interactive involvement across all three dyads or else only the mother–infant subsystem was not particularly interactive (M + F + HW +, M-F + HW +). To determine if in fact these family subtypes might be variants of each other we classified these two sets of family types as set I and set III, classified the remaining four family types from our configurational system (M-F + HW-, M-F-HW +, M + F + HW-, M + F-HW +) as set II, and proceeded to cross classify the three sets over time. Would families falling into sets I and III at each age of measurement be disproportionately likely to be classified in the same set at another point in time?

The results of our prediction analysis (Hildebrand, Laing, & Rosenthal, 1977) revealed significant stability from 1 to 3 (DEL = .25, $p <$ .004), from 3 to 9 (DEL = .16, $p <$ .05), and from 1 to 9 months (DEL = .28, $p <$ .0001) (see Table 4.10). In other words, families in which all dyads were disengaged or only the mother–infant dyad was highly engaged tended to remain this way over time, with the same being true of families in which all three dyads were highly involved or only the mother–infant dyad was not particularly interactive. Although it was certainly not the case that families were absolutely consistent over time, there was clearly a pattern of consistency suggesting trait-like as opposed to state-like ways in which the family triad functioned during the infant's first year.

In some households, it would appear, a truly interactive triadic family system seems to exist. Not only are mother and father interactively involved with the infant, but the two parents, as husband and wife, also tend to be in relatively frequent communication with one another. Moreover, it appears that it is in these families that the involved father enables the mother to spend time apart from her baby while still maintaining contact with her husband. This pattern in the data reminded us of what we so often observed in homes during our late afternoon and early evening observations. Father's appearance at the end of the day freed the mother to attend to other tasks, most often the preparation of the meal, which mothers often commented provided them with a respite from the demanding task of baby

TABLE 4.10
Stability of Family Sets*

| | | 3 Mos. | | | 9 Mos. | | |
|---|---|---|---|---|---|---|---|
| | | *I* | *II* | *III* | *I* | *II* | *III* |
| | I | 11 | 3 | 4 | 8 | 4 | 5 |
| 1 Mos. | II | 6 | 9 | 7 | 7 | 6 | 7 |
| | III | 4 | 4 | 8 | 4 | 2 | 8 |
| | | DEL = .25, $p < .003$ | | | DEL = .16, $p < .05$ | | |
| 9 Mos. | I | 27 | 16 | 11 | | | |
| | II | 19 | 23 | 11 | | | |
| | III | 11 | 10 | 34 | | | |

*I = M + F + HW + or M − M + HW +;
II = M − F − HW − or M + F − HW − ;
III = all other states: M − F + HW − ; M − F − HW +
M + F + HW − , M + F − HW +

care. It was not the case, however, that mothers, in taking these "psychological vacations" from child care, absented themselves from the family, but rather that they engaged in nonbaby activity while interacting with their husbands who were actively involved with their child. Recall from our earlier analyses that it was such marital interaction at 1-month postpartum that fostered subsequent father involvement (see Fig. 4.4).

In the second family type, systemic processes appear decidedly different. Either all individuals are disengaged from one another, relatively speaking, or just mother and baby tend to be actively involved with one another. Important to note is that the resultant mother–infant interaction that does transpire appears to take place in relative isolation of other family relationships. It is not as if husband and wife are highly involved as mother deals with the infant or as if father is independently involved with the child. Rather, we seem to have a family in which the father/husband is relatively detached both from his parent and spousal roles. Consistent with this interpretation are the earlier reported cross-sectional correlational findings indicating that marital and father–infant interaction tend to be positively correlated. Thus, in households in which fathers are not very involved with the infant they also tend, as husbands, not to be highly involved with their wives. It would seem, then, that in our two family types we have two kinds of men, one set who actively participate in the family and another set who are generally uninvolved. The data pertaining to the prenatal marital quality of households subsequently classified as interactively disengaged (M-F-HW-) and interactively engaged (M + F + HW + ) suggests that to some degree these two types of family systems are identifiable prior to the baby's birth and, indeed, it may well be differences in marital relationships prior to the transition to parenthood that contribute to the development of these two distinct types of families.

## SUMMARY AND CONCLUSIONS

The very length of this chapter and the nature of the analyses conducted underscore the complexity of the family system, a social organization comprised not only of developing individuals but relationships as well. Trying to characterize the nature of this system not simply at one point in time but rather over time, and especially across a major turning point in the family, enhances our appreciation of the limits of our ability to grapple with such dynamic complexity. Although we set out to apply principles of a system's perspective to the family across the transition to parenthood and end up convinced that such systematic inquiry enhances understanding of individual and relationship development, the interdependence of relationships and even the nature of the mother–father–infant triad, it remains clear that additional inquiry is called for.

With respect to individual development, we found it noteworthy that in our investigation, as well as in many others, there is very limited evidence to indicate that adults change in some fundamental way upon becoming parents. Despite the plethora of claims that such development takes place, the fact of the matter is that the empirical data are anything but convincing. As we noted earlier, future research must be planned with more consideration given to the specific aspects of adult psychological functioning that are expected to change and with more attention paid to individual differences in adult development.

The benefits of considering variation in developmental processes were revealed in our analysis of stability and change in infant temperament. Some infants, we discovered, were rather consistent over time in their propensity to cry whereas others changed rather dramatically. Not only was it the case that those whose crying increased relative to others were more likely by the end of their first year to be insecurely attached to their parents, but it also appeared that change in observed negative emotionality seemed to be related to characteristics of parents whereas stability seemed to be a function of characteristics of infants. Such findings raise questions about the actual processes, interactional or otherwise, that mediate the relation between characteristics of parents and changes in infant negative emotionality and about how families cope if their infants are relatively impervious to environmental input with respect to features of their temperaments.

Both stability and change were evident when we turned to consider relationship development, particularly the marital relationship. Although marriages that seemed to be functioning best prior to the birth of a first child remained that way after the transition to parenthood, it was nevertheless the case that feelings of love for the spouse declined whereas feelings of ambivalence about the relationship increased. Complementing these affective changes were changes in spousal interactions and activities. Recall that joint leisure activity declined whereas household division of labor became more traditional and that conflict increased whereas problem-solving communication decreased. Although it is tempting to infer that one set of changes caused the other, a system's perspective alerts us to the fact that the changes just chronicled are, in all likelihood, bidirectionally and reciprocally related.

During the period when spousal relationships are changing, we noted that patterns of parent–infant interaction remained remarkably consistent, at least insofar as the relative involvement of men and women in the family is concerned. Like other studies, our research reveals that men serve principally as secondary parents, with mothers assuming primary responsibility (on average) for caring for their infants. Although fathers may be considered the playmate in the family and mother the caregiver, it would be mistaken to infer that fathers are more playful than mothers. Despite the fact that a greater percentage of father's interactive involvement is devoted to stimulating and arousing exchanges with the baby, such behavior is far more frequently displayed by mothers.

Parent–infant relationships, we also found, do not function in a vacuum. Even though fathers are much less involved with their infants than are mothers, their degree of involvement covaries with the functioning of the marital relationship—and more so than does mother–infant interaction, at least when measured in the triad. Particularly when spouses are interactively involved very early in the infant's first year, father–infant interaction seems to be promoted. Although the quantity of paternal involvement seems to be influenced by what goes on in the marriage, it is the quality of the infant–mother relationship that is related to the marital relationship. Recall that mothers of infants insecurely attached to them experienced a more pronounced decline in the quality of their marital relationships across the transition to parenthood than did mothers of secure infants. The fact that infant–mother attachment security also systematically covaried with changes in mothers' personal opinions of themselves and was related to maternal personality measured prenatally cautions us from concluding that marriage directly and unidirectionally affects the infant–mother attachment bond. From a system's perspective it seems far more appropriate to conclude that the infant–parent relationship is multiply determined and that infant, parent, and marital processes—and no doubt others as well—contribute to the overall functioning of the family system of which the infant-parent relationship is just one part.

The exploratory analyses of the family triad that we reported nicely illustrate some of the ways in which parts and wholes apparently fit together in the family system. It was particularly intriguing to discover two general types of family systems that appeared to have alternate states. In one that we characterized as engaged high levels of interaction took place in all three dyads or else just the mother–infant dyad evinced limited interactive involvement. In the other that we characterized as disengaged either low levels of interaction were observed across all three dyads or just the mother–infant subsystem was highly interactive. Although it was men in particular who seemed to play clearly different roles in these households, we should point out that it was maternal personality as well as both spouses' marital appraisals that distinguished the most engaged and most disengaged families prior to the infant's birth.

Although it is apparent from even this brief summary that our investigation was systematic, focusing on elements of the family system (individuals), subsystems comprised of interacting elements (relationships), and the interrelation of relationships subsystems, we remain ambivalent about the extent to which this research is truly systemic in nature. Systems theorists are inclined to define systems in terms of very general principles such as self-stabilization, self-organization, and hierarchical organization (e.g., Sameroff, 1982). It remains unclear to us at the present time that any of these basic characteristics of a system or of the family system have been revealed by our investigation. The basic reason for this is that it has never been clear to us, as noted at the outset, how such conceptualizations are to be operationalized in the research process. Focusing on individuals, relationships, the interdependence of relationships, and the family triad represents an important beginning, but in our minds only a beginning. The challenge for future inquiry remains one of applying these more abstract principles considered to define a system in ways that move beyond what we have accomplished and, in so doing, illuminate processes of family development.

## ACKNOWLEDGMENTS

Work on this chapter and the research described herein were supported by grants from the National Institute of Child Health and Human Development (R01HD15496), the Division of Maternal and Child Health of the Public Health Service (MC-R-424067), and by an NIMH Research Scientist Development Award to the first author (K02-MH00486).

# REFERENCES

Ainsworth, M. D. S., Blehar, M. C., Waters, E., & Wall, S. (1978). *Patterns of attachment.* Hillsdale, NJ: Lawrence Erlbaum Associates.

Ainsworth, M. D. S., & Wittig, B. A. (1969). Attachment and exploratory behavior of one-year-olds in a strange situation. In B. M. Foss (Ed.), *Determinants of infant behavior* (Vol. 4). London: Methuen.

Aldous, J. (1977). Family interaction patterns. *Annual Review of Sociology, 3,* 105–135.

Antonucci, T., & Mikus, K. (in press). The power of parenthood: Personality and attitudinal changes during the transition to parenthood. In G. Michaels & W. Goldberg (Eds.), *The transition to parenthood: Current theory and research.* New York: Cambridge Press.

Baltes, P., Reese, H., & Lipsitt, L. (1980). Lifespan developmental psychology. *Annual Review of Psychology, 31,* 65–110.

Bates, J. E. (1987). Temperament in infancy. In J. D. Osofsky (Ed.), *Handbook of infant development* (2nd ed., pp. 1101–1149). New York: Wiley.

Bates, J. E., Freeland, C. A. B., & Lounsbury, M. L. (1979). Measurement of infant difficultness. *Child Development, 50,* 794–803.

Bateson, G. (1979). *Mind and nature.* New York: Dutton.

Baumrind, D., (1982). Are androgynous individuals more effective persons and parents. *Child Development, 53,* 44–75.

Belsky, J. (1981). Early human experience: A family perspective. *Developmental Psychology, 17,* 3–23.

Belsky, J. (1984). The determinants of parenting: A process model. *Child Developoment, 55,* 83–96.

Belsky, J. (1985). Experimenting with the family in the newborn period. *Child Development, 56,* 407–414.

Belsky, J. Gilstrap, B., & Rovine, M. (1984). The Pennsylvania Infant and Family Development Project, I: Stability and change in mother–infant and father–infant interaction in a family setting at one, three, and nine months. *Child Development, 55,* 692–705.

Belsky, J., Lang, M. E., & Rovine, M. (1985). Stability and change in marriage across the transition to parenthood: A second study. *Journal of Marriage and the Family, 47,* 855–865.

Belsky, J., & Pensky, E. (in press). Marital change across the transition to parenthood. *Marriage and Family Review.*

Belsky, J., & Rovine, M. (1987). Temperament and attachment security in the Strange Situation: An empirical rapprochement. *Child Development, 58,* 787–795.

Belsky, J., Spanier, G. B., & Rovine, M. (1983). Stability and change in marriage across the transition to parenthood. *Journal of Marriage and the Family, 45,* 553–556.

Belsky, J., & Volling, B. (1987). Mothering, fathering, and marital interaction in the family triad during infancy: Exploring family system's processes. In P. Berman & F. Pedersen (Eds.), *Men's transition to parenthood: Longitudinal studies of early family experience* (pp. 37–64). Hillsdale, NJ: Lawrence Erlbaum Associates.

Benedek, T. (1970). Parenthood during the life cycle. In E. J. Anthony & T. Benedek (Eds.), *Parenthood: Its psychology and psychopathology.* Boston: Little, Brown.

Bibring, G. L., Dwyer, T. F., Huntington, D. C., & Valenstein, A. F. (1961). A study of the psychological processes in pregnancy and the earliest mother–child relationship. *Psychoanalytic Study of the Child, 16,* 9–44.

Boles, H. C. (1981, August). *Impact of a first child on sense of self.* Paper presented at the American Psychological Association, Los Angeles.

Braiker, H., & Kelley, H. (1979). Conflict in the development of close relationships. In R. Burgess & T. Huston (Eds.), *Social exchange and developing relationships.* New York:

Academic Press.

Brazelton, T. B. (1973). *Neonatal behavioral assessment scale*. London: William Heinemann Medical Books Ltd.

Brim, O., & Wheeler, S. (1966). *Socialization after childhood: Two essays*. New York: Wiley.

Brody, G., Pillegrini, A., & Sigel, I. (1986). Marital quality and mother-child and father-child interactions with school-aged children. *Developmental Psychology, 22*, 291–296.

Bronfenbrenner, U. (1979). *The ecology of human development*. Cambridge, MA: Harvard University Press.

Buss, A. H., & Plomin, R. (1984). *Temperament: Early developing personality traits*. Hillsdale, NJ: Lawrence Erlbaum Associates.

Cattell, R. B., Eber, H. W., & Tatsuoka, M. M. (1970). *Handbook for the Sixteen Personality Factor Questionnaire (16PF)*. Champaign, IL: Institute for Personality and Ability Testing.

Christensen, A., & Margolin G. (1988). Conflict and alliance in distressed and nondistressed families. In R. Hinde & J. Stevenson-Hinde (Eds.), *Relationships within families*. (pp. 263–282). Oxford: Oxford University Press.

Clarke-Stewart, K. A. (1978). And daddy makes three: The father's impact on mother and young child. *Child Development, 49*, 466–478.

Cowan, C., Cowan, P., Coie, L., & Coie, J. (1978). Becoming a family: The impact of a first child's birth on the couple's relationship. In L. Newman & W. Miller (Eds.), *The first-child and family formation* (pp. 296–326). Chapel Hill, NC: Carolina Population Center.

Cowan, C. P., Cowan, P. A., Heming, G., Coysh, W. S., Curtis-Boles, H., & Boles, A. J. (1985). Transition to parenthood: His, hers, and theirs. *Journal of Family Issues, 6*(4), 451–481.

Cox, U., Connor, Y., & Kendell, R. (1982). Prospective study of the psychiatric disorders of childbirth. *British Journal of Psychiatry, 140*, 111–117.

Curtis-Boles, H. (1983, August). *Self changes in the early stages of parenting*. Paper presented at the American Psychological Association, Anaheim.

Cutrona, C. (1982). Nonpsychotic postpartum depression: A review of recent research. *Clinical Psychology Review, 2*, 487–503

Deutsch, H. (1945). *Psychology of women* (Vol. II). New York: Grune & Stratton

Durrett, M., Otaki, M., & Richards, P. (1984). Attachmenanthmother'perceptioosupporfrom ..the father. *International Journal of Behavioral Develope ment, 7, s* 167–176.f n t d t.

Durrett, M., Richards, P., Otaki, M., Pennebaker, J., & Nyquist, L. (1986). Mother's involvement with infant and her perception of spousal support, Japan and America. *Journal of Marriage and the Family, 48*, 187–194.

Easterbrooks, M. A., & Emde, R. (1986, April). *Marriage and infant: Different systems linkages for mothers and fathers*. Paper presented at the International Conference on Infant Studies, Beverly Hills, CA.

Elder, G. (1981). History and the life course. In D. Bertaux (Ed.), *Biography and society: The life history approach in the social sciences* (pp. 77–115). Beverly Hills, CA: Sage.

Elliot, S., Rugg, A., Watson, J., & Brough, D. (1983). Mood changes during pregnancy and after the birth of a child. *British Journal of Clinical Psychology, 22*, 295–305.

Emery, E. (1982). Interparental conflict and the children of discord and divorce. *Psychological Bulletin, 92*(2), 310–330.

Engfer, A. (1986). Antecedents of behaviour problems in infancy. In G. A. Kohnstamm (Ed.), *Temperament discussed: Temperament and development in infancy and childhood*. (pp. 165–180). Lisse, West Germany: Swets & Zeitlinger.

Engfer, A. (1988). The interrelatedness of marriage and the mother child relationship. In R. Hinde & J. Stevenson-Hinde (Eds.), *Relationships within families* (pp. 104–118). Oxford: Oxford University Press.

Fawcett, J. T. (1978). The value and cost of the first child. In W. B. Miller & L. F. Newman (Eds.), *The first child and family formation* (pp. 244–265). Chapel Hill, NC: Carolina

Population Center.

Fedele, N., Goldberg, E., Grossman, F., & Pollack, W. (in press). Psychological issues in adjustment to first parenthood. In G. Michaels & W. Goldberg (Eds.), *The transition to parenthood: Current theory and research.* New York: Cambridge University Press.

Feldman, S. S., Biringer, Z. C., & Nash, S. C. (1981). Fluctuations of sex related self-attributions as a function of stage of family life cycle. *American Psychological Association, 17*(1), 24-35.

Feldman, S. S., & Nash, S. (1984). The transition from expectancy to parenthood: Impact of the firstborn child on men and women. *Sex Roles, 11,* 61-78.

Feldman, S. S., Nash, S. C., & Aschenbrenner, B. (1983). Antecedents of fathering. *Child Development, 54,* 1628-1636.

Goldberg, W. A., & Easterbrooks, M. A. (1984). The role of marital quality in toddler development. *Developmental Psychology, 20,* 504-514.

Goldberg, W. A., Michaels, G. Y., & Lamb, M. E. (1985). Husbands' and wifes': Adjustment to pregnancy and first parenthood. *Journal of Family Issues, 6*(4), 483-503.

Goldsmith, H. H., Buss, A. H., Plomin, R., Rothbart, M. K., Thomas, A., Chess, S., Hinde, R. A., & McCall, R. B. (1987). Roundtable: What is temperament? Four approaches. *Child Development, 58,* 505-529.

Gough, H. G., & Heilbrun, A. B., Jr. (1980). *The adjective check list manual.* Palo Alto, CA: Consulting Psychologists Press.

Greenbaum, C. W., & Landau, R. (1982). The infants exposure to talk by familiar people: Mothers, fathers, and siblings in different environments. In M. Lewis & L. Rosenthal (Eds.), *The social network of the developing infant.* New York: Plenum.

Grossman, F., Eichler, L., & Winickoff, S. (1980). *Pregnancy, birth, and parenthood.* San Francisco: Jossey-Bass.

Grossman, F. K., Pollack, W. S., Golding, E. R., & Fedele, N. M. (1987). Affiliation and autonomy in the transition to parenthood. *Family Relations, 36,* 263-269.

Grossman, K., Grossman, K., Huber, F., & Wartner, U. (1981). German children's behavior towards their mothers at 12 months and their fathers at 18 nonths in Ainsworth's Strange Situation. *International Journal of Behavioral Development, 4,* 157-182.

Gunnar, M. R., Mangelsdorf, S., Kestenbaum, R., Lang, S., & Larson, M. (1987, October). *Temperament and attachment: A second look at rapprochement.* Paper presented at conference on Developmental Psychopathology, University of Rochester, New York.

Gutmann, D. (1975). Parenthood: Key to the comparative psychology of the life cycle? In N. Datan & L. Ginsberg (Eds.), *Life-span developmental psychology.* New York: Academic Press.

Havighurst, R. J. (1973). History of developmental psychology: Socialization and personality development through the life span. In P. B. Baltes & K. W. Schaie (Eds.), *Life-span developmental psychology: Personality and socialization.* New York: Academic Press.

Hildebrand, D., Laing, J., & Rosenthal, H. (1977). *Prediction analysis of cross-classifications.* New York: Wiley.

Hobbs, D. (1965). Parenthood as crisis: A third study. *Journal of Marriage and the Family, 27,* 677-689.

Hobbs, D. (1968). Transition to parenthood: A replication and extension. *Journal of Marriage and the Family, 31,* 720-727.

Hobbs, D., & Wimbish, J. (1979). Transition to parenthood by black couples. *Journal of Marriage and the Family, 39,* 677-689.

Hoffman, L. (1978). Effects of the first child on the woman's role. In W. Miller & L. Newman (Eds.), *The first child and family formation* (pp. 340-367). Chapel Hill, NC: Carolina Population Center.

Hopkins, J., Marcus, M., & Campbell, S. (1984). Postpartum depression: A critical review. *Psychological Bulletin, 45,* 498-575.

Huston, T., & Robins, E. (1982). Conceptual and methodological issues in studying close relationships. *Journal of Marriage and the Family, 44,* 901–925.

Jackson, D. (1976). *Jackson Personality Inventory.* Goshen, NY: Research Psychologists Press.

Jacobson, J. L., Jacobson, S. W., Fein, G. G., & Schwartz, P. M. (1984). Factors and clusters for the Brazelton scale: An investigation of the dimensions of neonatal behavior. *Developmental Psychology, 20,* 339–353.

Kaij, L., & Nilsson, A. (1972). Emotional and psychotic illness following childbirth. In J. Howells (Ed.), *Modern perspectives in psycho-obstetrics.* New York: Brunner/Mazel.

Kotelchuck, M. (1976). The infant's relationship to the father: Experimental evidence. In M. E. Lamb (Ed.), *The role of the father in child development.* New York: Wiley.

Lamb, M. E. (1976). Twelve-month-olds and their parents: Interactions in a laboratory playroom. *Developmental Psychology, 12,* 237–244.

Lamb, M. E. (1977a). The development of mother-infant and father-infant attachments in the second year of life. *Developmental Psychology, 13,* 639–649.

Lamb, M. E. (1977b). Father-infant and mother-infant interaction in the first year of life. *Child Development, 48,* 167–181.

Lamb, M. E., Frodi, A. M., Hwang, C.-P., & Frodi, M. (1982). Varying degrees of paternal involvement in infant care: Attitudinal and behavioral correlates. In M. E. Lamb (Ed.), *Nontraditional families: Parenting and child development* (pp. 117–138). Hillsdale, NJ: Lawrence Erlbaum Associates.

Lamb, M. E., Frodi, A. M., Hwang, C.-P., & Steinberg, J. (1982). The effects of gender and caretaking role on parent-infant interaction. In R. Emde & R. Harmon (Eds.), *Development of attachment and affiliative systems.* New York: Plenum Press.

LaRossa, R., & LaRossa, M. M. (1981). *Transition to parenthood: How infants change families.* Beverly Hills, CA: Sage.

Leifer, M. (1977). Psychological changes accompanying pregnancy and motherhood. *Genetic Psychology Monographs, 95,* 55–96.

Lewis, C. (1986). *Becoming a father.* Milton Keynes, England: Open University Press.

Lewis, M., & Weinraub, M. (1976). The father's role in the infant's social network. In M. E. Lamb (Ed.), *The role of the father in child development.* New York: Wiley.

Lidz, T. (1976). *The person: His or her development throughout the life cycle* (2nd ed.). New York: Basic Books.

Lowenthal, M., Thurnher, M., & Chiriboda, D. (1976). *Four stages of life.* San Francisco: Jossey-Bass.

Main, M., & Weston, D. (1981). Security of attachment to mother and father: Related to conflict behavior and the readiness to establish new relationships. *Child Development, 52,* 932–940.

Matheny, A. P. (1986). Stability and change of infant temperament: Contributions from the infant, mother, and family environment. In G. Kohnstamm (Ed.), *Temperament discussed.* Berwyn, PA: Swets North America.

Matheny, A. P., Jr., Riese, M. L., & Wilson, R. S. (1985). Rudiments of infant temperament: Newborn to 9 months. *Developmental Psychology, 21,* 486–494.

McHale, S. M., & Huston, T. L. (1985). The effect of the transition to parenthood on the marriage relationship. *Journal of Family Issues, 6*(4), 409–433.

McLaughlin, S., & Micklin, M. (1983). The timing of first birth and changes in personal efficacy. *Journal of Marriage and the Family, 45,* 47–55.

Meyer, H. (in press). Marital and mother-child relationships: The impact of developmental history, parental personality characteristics, and child's difficultness. In R. Hinde & J. Stevenson-Hinde (Eds.), *Relationships within the family.* Oxford: Oxford University Press.

Miller, J. G. (1978). *Living systems.* New York: McGraw-Hill.

Minuchin, P. (1985). Families and individual development: Provocations from the field of family therapy. *Child Development, 56,* 289–302.

Moss, P., Boland, G., Roxman, R., & Owen, C. (1986). Marital relations during the transition to parenthood. *Journal of Reproductive and Infant Psychology, 4,* 57–67.

Neugarten, B. (1968). Adult personality: Toward a psychology of the life cycle. In B. Neugarten (Ed.), *Middle age and aging.* Chicago: University of Chicago Press.

O'Hara, M. W., Neunaber, D. J., & Zekoski, E. M. (1984). Prospective study of postpartum depression: Prevalence, course, and predictive factors. *Journal of Abnormal Psychology, 93,* 158–171.

Parke, R. D. (1978). Perspectives in father-infant interaction. In J. Osofsky (Ed.), *Handbook of infancy,* (pp. 549–590). New York: Wiley.

Parke, R. D., & Sawin, D. B. (1975, April). *Infant characteristics and behavior as elicitors of maternal and paternal responsivity in the newborn period.* Paper presented to the Society for Research in Child Development, Denver, CO.

Parke, R. D., & Sawin, D. B. (1980). The family in early infancy: Social interactional and attitudinal analyses. In F. A. Pedersen (Ed.), *The father-infant relationship: Observational studies in a family setting* (pp. 44–70). New York: Praeger.

Parke, R. D., & Tinsley, B. J. (1987). Family interaction in infancy. In J. Osofsky (Ed.), *Handbook of infant development* (2nd ed., pp. 579–641). New York: Wiley.

Pedersen, R., Yarrow, L., Anderson, B., & Cain, R. (1978). Conceptualization of father influences in the infancy period. In M. Lewis & L. Rosenblum (Eds.), *The social network of the developing infant.* New York: Plenum.

Peterson, F. L., Peterson, K. J., Redman, E. S., Nicholls, C., & Blasenak, B. (1986, August). *Transition into parenthood: A pilot project of the expectant couples enrichment class.* Paper presented at the American Psychological Association, Washington, DC.

Pettit, G. S., & Bates, J. E. (1984). Continuity of individual differences in the mother-infant relationship from six to thirteen months. *Child Development, 55,* 729–739.

Phillips, D., & Parke, R. D. (1981). *Father and mother speech to prelinguistic infants.* Unpublished manuscript, University of Illinois, Champaign, IL.

Power, T. G., & Parke, R. D. (1982). Play as a context for early learning: Lab and home analyses. In I. E. Sigel & L. M. Laosa (Eds.), *The family as a learning environment.* New York: Plenum.

Richards, M., Dunn, J., & Antonis, B. (1977). Caretaking in the first year of life: The role of fathers' and mothers' social isolation. *Child: Care, Health, and Development, 3,* 23–26.

Riese, M. L. (1987). Temperament stability between the neonatal period and 24 months. *Developmental Psychology, 23,* 216–222.

Rossi, A. (1968). Transition to parenthood. *Journal of Marriage and the Family, 30,* 26–39.

Rothbart, M. K. (1981). Measurement of temperament in infancy. *Child Development, 52,* 569–578.

Rothbart, M. K. (1986). Longitudinal observation of infant temperament. *Developmental Psychology, 22,* 356–365.

Russell, C. S. (1974). Transition to parenthood: Problems and gratifications. *Journal of Marriage and the Family, 36,* 294–302.

Russell, G., & Russell, A. (1987). Mother-child and father-child relationships in middle childhood. *Child Development, 58,* 1573–1585.

Ryder, R. (1973). Longitudinal data relating marital satisfaction and having a child. *Journal of Marriage and the Family, 35,* 604–607.

Sagi, A., Lamb, M., Shoham, R., Duir, R., & Lewkowicz, K. (1985). Parent-infant interaction in families on Israeli Kibbutizm. *International Journal of Behavioral Development, 8,* 273–284.

Sameroff, A. (1982). Development and the dialectic: The need for a systems approach. In W. Collins (Ed.), *The concept of development: Minnesota Symposium on Child Development* (Vol. 15, 83–103). Hillsdale, NJ: Lawrence Erlbaum Associates.

Sarbin, T., & Allen, V. (1968). Role theory. In G. Lindzey & E. Aronson (Eds.), *The handbook of social psychology* (2nd ed., Vol. 1). New York: Guilford.

Shainness, N. (1963). The psychologic experience of labor. *New York State Journal of Medicine, 63,* 2923-2932.

Shereshefsky, P. M., & Yarrow, L. J. (1973). *Psychological aspects of a first pregnancy and early postnatal adaptation.* New York: Raven.

Sirigano, S., & Lachman, M. (1985). Personality change during the transition to parenthood: The role of perceived infant temperament. *Developmental Psychology, 21,* 558-567.

Soloman, J. (1982). *Marital intimacy and parent-infant relationships.* Unpublished doctoral dissertation, University of California, Berkeley, CA.

Sroufe, L., Jacobvitz, D., Mangelsdorf, S., DeAngelo, E., & Ward, M. (1985). Generational boundary dissolution between mothers and their preschool children: A relationship systems approach. *Child Development, 56,* 317-325.

Thomas, A. (1984). Temperament research: Where we are, where we are going. *Merrill-Palmer Quarterly, 30,* 103-109.

Thomas, A., & Chess, S. (1977). *Temperament and development.* New York: Brunner/Mazel.

Thomas, A., Chess, S., & Birch, H. G. (1968). *Temperament and behavior disorders in children.* New York: NYU Press.

Turner, R. (1978). The role and the person. *American Journal of Sociology, 84,* 1-23.

Waldron, H., & Routh D. (1981). The effect of the first child on the marital relationship. *Journal of Marriage and the Family, 43,* 785-788.

Walsh, F. (1981). Conceptualizations of normal family functioning. In F. Walsh (Ed.), *Normal family processes* (pp. 3-25). New York: Guilford.

Washington, J., Minde, K., & Goldberg, S. (1986). Temperament in preterm infants: Style and stability. *Journal of the American Academy of Child Psychiatry, 25,* 493-502.

White, L. K., & Booth, A. V. (1985). The transition to parenthood and marital quality. *Journal of Family Issues, 6*(4), 435-449.

Yogman, M. J. (1983). Development of the father-infant relationship. In H. Fitzgerald, B. Lester, & M. Yogman (Eds.), *Theory and research in behavioral pediatrics* (Vol. 1). New York: Plenum.

Yogman, M. J., Dixon, S., Tronick, E., Als, H., & Brazelton, T. B. (1977, March). *The goals and structure of face-to-face interaction between infants and their fathers.* Paper presented to the Society for Research in Child Development, New Orleans.

# 5 Some Amplifying Mechanisms for Pathologic Processes in Families

G. R. Patterson
L. Bank
*Oregon Social Learning Center*

We maintain that antisocial child behavior, and perhaps most forms of child psychopathology, are the outcome of social processes. These processes have several important characteristics: (a) they unfold over time, (b) each child moves through a sequence of recognizable steps, and (c) the movement is from relatively trivial to more severe forms of the pathology. For children, these processes have their beginnings in the daily social exchanges with family members, and in effect, these social exchanges are the key mechanism driving many forms of child pathology. After a period of weeks or months, the effects of this training generalize to settings outside the home. This, in turn, sets the occasion for a set of predictable reactions from the child's social environment. When practiced at school, antisocial behaviors produce immediate reinforcers for the child, but in the long run, lead to two dramatic social failures: The child is rejected by normal peers and fails academically. These social failures define the second step in the processes. The child's reactions—sadness and depressed mood—to these failures defines part of the third step. This concatenation of actions and reactions unfolding over time defines what we mean by *process*. We believe that the series of steps defining the coercion process form a transitive progression such that a significant proportion of children found at the later stages have passed through the earlier stages. The progression moves from relatively minor to relatively major problems in child adjustment. Data is provided in a later section that provide a test for this idea.

## Early Starters

For a small number of boys, the coercion process begins in the preschool years and persists into adolescence. We hypothesize that such an early beginning characterizes a substantial number of the boys at risk for chronic delinquency (multiple offenses). The empirical literature provides surprisingly consistent support for this assumption. For example, in the study by Spivak (1983) cited by Farrington (1987), 83% of the adolescent frequent offenders had been rated as badly behaved by teachers when the boys were in Grade 1. Farrington also cited the studies by Ensminger, Kellam, and Rubin (1983), who obtained the comparable figure of 45%; and for the study by Craig and Glick (1968) the figure was 56%.

## Late Starters

The sequence leading to delinquency does not, of course, have to begin during the preschool years. In fact, it may start as late as early adolescence. Slightly more than one third of delinquent adolescents are thought to be late starters (Farrington, 1981). The present writers hypothesize that for the late starters the process is initiated by a prolonged disruption in family social interactional patterns. In a later section, we examine some of the disruptor variables and parent traits thought to serve this function.

The idea that some children may begin the process early and others late, whereas some who start may drop out, places some unique constraints on any attempts to "model" such a process. Over time, family members and family structures reflect two opposing tendencies. There is a sense in which the occurrence of family events or structures are stable over substantial periods of time (e.g., for a year or two), but there is also a sense in which a significant number of individuals or families show substantial changes over the same time interval. Perforce, a model describing families must be dynamic, describing not only what changes come about and why some things are stable. The major function of this chapter is to identify some of those variables thought to be related to change and to stability. Structural equation modeling (SEM) is the analytic format used to address these issues.

## The Data and the Sample

The sample consisted of two cohorts of roughly 100 families each of Grade 4 boys. Of the 10 highest crime areas in the city, 4 were randomly selected (each year). All of the families of Grade 4 boys living in these areas were contacted and asked to participate in the study. Seventy-four percent of the families actually participated; teachers' ratings showed no differences between participants and refusers. The sample is almost entirely Caucasion and of lower social status: 75% are working class or unemployed. The families receive up to $300 each time they participate in the 23-hour assessment. Full-scale probes have been carried out at Grades 4 and 6. We maintained contact with families who had moved, and thus far, less than 1% of the sample has been lost. The details of the recruitment and sampling procedures are described in Capaldi and Patterson (1987). The assessment and psychometric procedures involved in building each of the constructs are detailed in Capaldi and Patterson (1988).[1]

## OUTLINE OF THE PROCESS MODEL
## AND HYPOTHESES TO BE TESTED

The process model is really about two very general questions: What starts the process and what keeps it going?

### What Starts It?

Whether the process begins when the child is a toddler or later as a preadolescent, we believe the immediate determinants are the same. It begins because parents have not been able to maintain a moderate level of child compliance. Typically, this means parents use ineffective discipline and monitoring. The covariation between disrupted discipline practices in the home and child antisocial, behavior was modeled in Patterson (1986a), replicating an earlier analysis by Patterson, Dishion, and Bank (1984) and more recently replicated for a sample of single-parent families by Baldwin and Skinner (1988).

These findings raise an important question. Why are parenting practices such as discipline and monitoring disrupted in the first place? In this chapter, we briefly explore the contributions of three types of variables that seem to relate to disruptions in parenting skills: (a) a lack of parental social skills, (b) the contribution of parental traits such as antisocial behavior or child traits such as difficult temperament, and (c) the impact of disruptor variables such as stress (e.g., unemployment) or martial conflict. In a later

---

[1]The details of the measurement of indicators for each construct are available from Capaldi and Patterson (1988). The convergent discriminiative matrices for each of the modeling figures used in this Chapter can be obtained by sending the reference for this Chapter and the number of the figure to Oregon Social Learning Center, 207 E, Fifth Ave., Suite 202, Eugene, Oregon, 97401.

section we briefly examine the relationships of some of these constructs and use SEM to model their relations to parenting practices.

All three sets of variables play a role in determing the onset of the process for preschoolers. For the children who start the process later, the disruptor variables play a key role (e.g., dramatic increases in martial conflict or in stressors such as unemployment will be associated with disruptions in discipline and monitoring practices). To test this idea, we examine data showing that when the parenting practices change over time, they are accompanied by commensurate shifts in the level of antisocial behavior of the child.

## What Maintains It?

The increases in antisocial behaviors produce reactions from the social environment that have massive implications for the target child, and for the family too. The sequence of effects, laid out in Fig. 5.1, begins with the transaction between parents and child. To describe the first step, we have adapted material prepared by Sameroff and Fiese (1987). Their summary of our coercion model seems ideally suited to the present discussion. We have simply added two additional steps to their transactive sequence. The process begins with the toddler having difficulties learning normal levels of compliance to parental house rules and requests. It may be that the child's temperament makes him or her more difficult than most to train; but the fact is that the parents fail to respond effectively. Scolding and explosive, irritable, and inconsistent discipline produce a child who becomes increasingly noncompliant. This further compounds the discipline difficulties and both child and parents gradually show an escalation in all forms of coercive behavior (yelling, hitting, whining, crying, sarcasm, etc.). The child's behavior is now noticeably different from other children and individuals outside the family label him or her as antisocial.

The parent changes the child and also behaves in such a way as to permit that child to obtain similar training from his or her siblings. Based on our clinical experience, we see the effects of the interchanges as being bidirectional between child and parents, as well as between the child and siblings; that is, all family members are being trained to be coercive. In a later section, we review the literature and our own data that relate to the bidirectionality hypothesis.

It might be noted in passing that the problem child seems to occupy some special family niche. Comparison of interaction patterns for normal and clinical samples showed that the parents of antisocial children were significantly more coercive than parents of normal children only in their

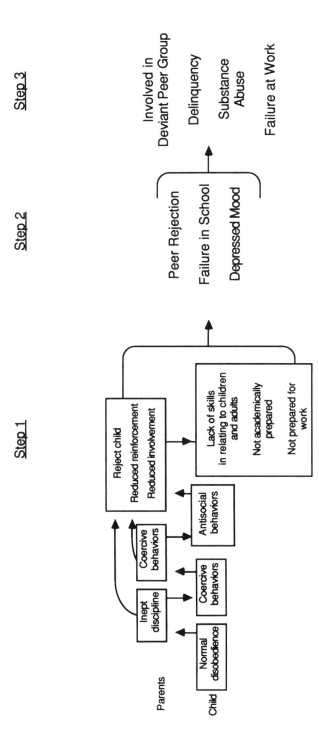

FIG. 5.1. Concatenated coercion model.

171

interactions with the problem child (Patterson, 1986b). Their interactions with the siblings of the problem child were well within the normal range. In general, they seem to tolerate very high levels of coercion among all children in the family.

Daily discipline confrontations and increasing conflict with siblings take their toll. The parents' avoidance reactions reflect those of peers, teachers, and mental health workers who must interact with such children. Parents tending to avoid interactions with the children are less reinforcing. These differences in interactions have been observed both in the home (Patterson, 1982) and in playground interaction with peers (Dodge, Schlundt, Schocken, & Delugach, 1983; French, 1987; Walker, Shinn, O'Neill, & Ramsey, 1987).

In a general sense, the parents reject the child. The rejection may even begin before the birth of the child, as seen in some of the families we work with. But the obdurate, aversive quality of the child's behavior quickly adds fuel to this position. An earlier correlational study by Patterson (1984a) showed that measures of discipline confrontations, conflicts with siblings and difficulties at school all significantly contributed to accounting for variance in a construct assessing parental rejections.

Requests to do homework are met with abuse and with noncompliance. Similar reactions occur at home and school in conjunction with efforts to get the child to sit at his or her desk, follow rules for particular settings or complete homework. In a learning situation, the child is simply not attending; much of his or her energy is observed to be invested in nontask behaviors (Hops & Cobb, 1974; Walker et al., 1987).

Reactions of the peer group and the school to the child's deviant behavior define the second step in the progression. The relation between one step and another in the progression is a probable one. Not all children who are taught to be antisocial at home are rejected by normal peers: however, as we see, the majority of them are. Not all children who are rejected or who fail in school are antisocial, but again, a substantial number of them are. In a later section we explore in detail the probable relation among a series of steps in the coercion model. The exploration includes an estimate for the likelihood that there is more than one path to a given step in the model.

In summary, rejection by normal peers and by parents as well as academic failure are thought to function as maintenance variables. Presumably each of these outcomes serves to increase the risk that the child will remain in the process. In that these variables were generated by the process, they have been tentatively identified as positive feedback loops. In a later section, we employ SEM to examine the candidacy of rejection by peers as a positive feedback loop.

## Additional Hypotheses to be Explored

There are many implicit assumptions that are required to make the process model a workable one. Those that are explored in the present report are listed here:

1. Parent–child stabilities. To understand change, one must, at the beginning, establish some modicum of stability. In a later section, we examine two hypotheses that relate to this issue. First, we examine the assumption that the construct measuring antisocial behavior is stable when measured at Grades 4 and 6.

If one has some stability, then one is in a position to question its source. The assumption tested here is that the stability in child behavior is a function of corresponding stability in parenting practices. The third assumption is that there is a synchronistic relation between the measures of child and parent behavior at both points in time. All three hypotheses are tested in a section that follows.

2. Generalization from home to school. One of the critical hypotheses illustrated in Fig. 5.1 is that the effects of training in the home for antisocial behaviors will generalize to the school and the community. We briefly review the findings that relate to this assumption.

Support for the assumption of a second step would require that a construct measuring antisocial behavior covary significantly with construct scores measuring academic failure, depressed mood and peer rejection.

Figure 5.1 also implies a connection between steps two and three. This is tested by demonstrating that measures of peer rejection, antisocial behavior, and academic failure obtained at Grade 4 will predict involvement in the deviant peer group and in delinquent behavior at Grade 6.

3. Stationarity assumption. As a working hypothesis, we believe that the stationarity assumption does not apply to the coercion process. The parameters that govern the early stages of a family conflict are different from those that govern the later stages of extended coercive exchanges. In keeping with this position, the observation studies of antisocial boys in a residential setting by Rausch (1965) showed that their interactional sequences did not fit a simple Markov chain. In our own studies, we find that the risk of high amplitude aggression varies as a function of the length of the coercive chain (Reid, Taplin, & Lorber, 1981).

No further effort is made in the present report to examine the stationarity assumption as it applies to microanalyses of social interaction. But the reader will note that, at a macrolevel, there are developmental shifts in terms of which variables contribute significantly to antisocial behavior. As already noted, peer rejection and school failure are assumed to maintain the child in the process. As we see later, these are thought to be delayed causal variables. By adolesence, it is expected that commitment to a deviant peer group will begin to make significant contributions to accounting for delinquent behavior. Although the family is primarily responsible for the initiation of the process, it shares joint responsibility with the peer group later in the process.

## STEP 1: TRANSACTIONS
## BETWEEN PARENTS AND CHILD

The etiology for the majority of antisocial children has its beginnings in parent–child and child–sibling interactions (Patterson, 1982). If one carries out functional analyses of child behaviors such as teasing, hitting, yelling, arguing, and so forth, it becomes apparent that their occurrence is controlled by the behavior of other family members. The responses are reliably elicited (in a probabilistic sense) by the reactions of other family members. The responses in turn elicit predictable reactions from siblings and from parents (Patterson, 1977). These functional analyses strongly emphasize the necessity for thinking of these responses as defining a *dyadic trait* for coercion (Patterson, 1984b). The contribution of these exchanges to children's antisocial behavior has been examined in SEM analyses of two samples by Patterson, Reid, and Dishion (in press). The model was replicated for yet a third sample by Baldwin and Skinner (1988).

The assumption is that as the training progresses, the behaviors of antisocial children, parents, and siblings are altered in similar ways. In effect, family members and antisocial children alternate in the roles of aggressors and victims, each eliciting and inadvertently reinforcing the coercive behavior of the other. The general perspective is, of course, very much in keeping with the bidirectionality of effects position taken by Bell and Harper (1977) and the transactional position described by Sameroff (1982).

It is assumed that during social exchanges between parents and children or children and siblings, contingencies operate continuously. The effect of these contingencies is to produce slight, but significant, changes in the future likelihood of each partner's behaviors. For example, a study by Snyder and Patterson (1986) showed that a single negative reinforcement (escape conditioning trial) embedded in ongoing interaction in the home produced significant alterations in the strength of child response. The data showed that these contingencies altered the future likelihood of the response occurring after the parent behavior that served as the stimulus during the earlier trial. The application of contingency analyses to social interaction sequences in families is discussed in detail in Patterson et al. (in press).

The key assumption here is that for most of us these fluctuations vary

Time-I                          Time-3

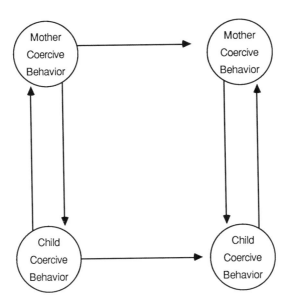

FIG. 5.2. Continuities and bidirectional effects for coercive exchanges between mothers and sons.

around a mean value. Small shifts toward deviancy are not significant. The reactions of other family members function as inhibiters; the mother may become less stressed and provide fewer controlling stimuli and less reinforcement. There may be a 10% or 20% increase in the likelihood of a child's crying, yelling, or temper tantrums for a few days, but eventually the child's values return to their baseline level. The contingencies may shift for a few days because of visiting grandparents or an illness. In keeping with this, the test—retest values for family members' reactions to children's coercive behaviors have been shown to be quite stable over time intervals such as 2 to 4 weeks (Patterson et al., in press). Figure 5.2 represents the stability of these patterns over 2 years.

These studies support the idea that the target child and family members are significantly affected by the behavior of the other. The findings set the stage for a more interesting second generation of questions concerning differences in the *magnitude* of these effects. Why are not the mother, father, and siblings at equal risk as is the problem child to be labeled *deviant* or *antisoical?* Is the magnitude of the effect greater from family members to the target child than from target child to family members? In this section, we explore some of the methodological problems encountered when using SEM analyses to estimate the magnitude of bidirectional effects.

We maintain that the study of bidirectional effects will eventually reflect a developmental model in which the magnitude of the effects shifts as a function of the child's age. For example, it might be that the young, irritable infant may elicit irritable reactions from the mother to the same degree (Engfer & Gavranidou, 1985), as the mother's depression and lack of social skills exacerbates the mother's irritable reactions. As the child reaches school age and his or her level of coercive skill has increased, the magnitude of effects may reflect the relatively greater contribution of child to family members, as suggested in the carefully designed study by Anderson, Lytton, and Romney (1986). In a 2 × 2 factorial design, mothers of both normal and conduct-disordered boys were observed in a laboratory setting. Only the main effect term for child classification was significant; conduct-disordered boys were significantly more noncompliant with both their own mother and with the mothers of normal boys. The findings imply that the magnitude of effects would be greater for child to mother than mother to child.

As a working hypothesis, we assume that although the child may have a significant impact on the mother, the contribution could be overshadowed by the inhibiting effect of interacting with a noncoercive spouse, friends, or relatives. For mothers of older coercive children, the contribution of external variables such as adequacy of the marital relationship, depression, and other stressors are the prime determinants. We believe that a mother's social exchange patterns with her child might be highly stable over time. At this point, we have no basis for predicting whether the coercive patterns for the boys will be more or less stable than for their mothers. The data in Fig. 5.2 present the findings based on home observations of the second cohort of our longitudinal study of at-risk families observed in their homes for three sessions during Grades 4 and 6.[2]

The structural variables that measure coercive exchanges include: (a) *start-up,* the likelihood of initiating a coercive event given a context in which the other person is neutral or positive; (b) *synchronous negative,* the

---

[2]Throughout this chapter, data from the first cohort of 102 families in the Oregon Youth Study have been used for analysis. During Wave 1, observations of Cohort I families, the targeted boy was the focus for one 10-minute period rather than the intended two 10-minute periods. Because of this oversight, the indicators for the Child Coercion construct at Grade 4 failed to converge satisfactorily. Just prior to publication of this chapter, however, data for the two waves of observation in the second cohort became available for analysis. The coercion indicators for boys at Grade 4 converged as expected when sufficient observation time was used, and we have, therefore, based this analysis on Cohort II rather than Cohort I data.

likelihood of reacting in a negative manner given the other person has just behaved negatively; and (c) *continuance,* the likelihood of acting negatively given a negative antecedent behavior by the same individual (within the prior 6-second window). The variables assessed both the child's reactions to the mother and her reactions to the child. The coercive interactions were sampled separately from a series of three observations in the home where the interaction sequences of the family members were recorded in real time (Dishion, Gardner, Patterson, Reid, & Thibodeaux, 1983).

## Stability of Coercive Style

Ideally, the cross-lagged paths from mom to child and child to mom across the 2-year span could be tested while embedded in the model in Fig. 5.2. Note that in this context, both mother and son stabilities from Grade 4 to 6 would be estimated as would be the anticipated reciprocal mother-son "synchronous" effects at each point in time. Unfortunately, such a model cannot be easily identified. For the present chapter, data from the second cohort of 105 mothers and sons were used to test a model with *spans* instead of paths. In other words, the hypothesis being tested is one of correlations among the latent variables. This hypothesis is clearly less powerful than that depicted in the desired model in Fig. 5.2, but, on the other hand, it is testable. This analysis resulted in a satisfactory fit, chi-square (52) = 54.48, $p = .38$, with the two stabilities and mother−child relation at Grade 6, all reaching statistical significance with correlations in the .6 to .75 range. The mother−child relation at Grade 4 and the correlation of earlier mother coercion to later child coercion were in the expected direction ($p < .2$). The earlier child coercion relation to later mother coercion did not materialize at all. This analysis is consistent with the hypothesized model in Fig. 5.2.

The reciprocal (bidirectional) synchronous effects can be identified through the use of what is known as "instrumental variables" in sociological literature (Duncan, 1975; Kohn & Schooler, 1978). An instrumental variable is one that temporally precedes the bidirectional effect, but can be causally linked to only one of the variables of interest. For example, the maternal grandparents' socioeconomic status or parenting practices might have an impact on the child through the mother, but not directly on the child. The problem is further complicated by the need to specify all pertinent variables in a model to avoid potentially spurious results. We do not yet have an instrumental variable solution to the current problem of reciprocal effects, although we have taken steps in that direction (Vuchinich, 1987; Vuchinich, Bank, & Patterson, 1988).

## Magnitude of Effects

Once a satisfactory set of instrumental variables is successfully tested with the reciprocal effects model, it is possible to fix the magnitude of those effects in more complex models. This strategy may provide the most acceptable solutions to problems such as the current one. One further wrinkle, however, has recently been introduced by Bielby and Matsueda (1987); their studies in Monte Carlo have demonstrated that reciprocal effects solutions may have sufficient power to conclude that significant, equal-magnitude bidirectional effects exist, but that usage of instrumental variables may unreliably observe differing magnitudes of effect.

## PARALLEL CONTINUITIES:
## MAINTENANCE OF PROCESS

The coercive exchanges of family members and target child are embedded in a larger matrix of variables. The contextual variables that seem most relevant are parental discipline and monitoring practices. When effectively employed, they serve as inhibitors for daily increases in coercive child behaviors. A severe disruption in the performance of these parenting skills would be shortly accompanied by increases in coercive child behavior.

### Discipline and Monitoring

From the perspective of the coercion model, a set of macrotype variables determines whether or not coercive microsocial processes will occur (Patterson, 1982). These variables describe faulty family-management practices such as discipline and monitoring. An irritable, explosive parental style during discipline exchanges is ineffective in controlling child noncompliance or any of the other coercive behaviors (whining, teasing, hitting, yelling, temper tantrums). Instead of clear commands to stop, the parent makes vague threats; then, without backing up these threats, the parent scolds and lectures. In the face of this nattering, the problem child is significantly more likely to continue noncompliant behavior than is the normal child faced with similar parental reactions.

Why is it that in some families parental efforts to intervene actually make things worse? Normal families tend to set specific consequences for misbehavior and follow through with punishments when appropriate. In families with coercive parenting styles, however, the child learns that threats to punish do not imply a parental willingness to follow through. The pre- and postanalyses of family interaction in treated families showed that training parents to follow through and consistently use effective backup punishments reduced the likelihood of punishment acceleration[3] to nearly normal levels (Patterson, 1982).

---

[3]Punishment acceleration is defined as the difference between two conditional probabilities, $p^2 - p^1$, when $p^1$ is the likelihood that a child will behave in a coercive fashion if his immediately

Our clinical attempts to intervene in these families showed that parents of problem children were also less effective in monitoring or tracking the child. Parents of antisocial boys generally do not know where their sons go or what they do outside of the home. The effect of this is to reinforce a wide range of antisocial behaviors and attitudes. The deviant peer group performs this crucial function.

The sequence of events is imagined to be something like this: Coercive parenting styles train the child to respond in antisocial ways; the child generalizes these coercive styles to interactions at school with teachers and peers. The normal peer group finds it difficult to inhibit these unacceptable behaviors and rejects the child. The only youngsters remaining who will accept the rejected boy are members of a deviant peer group. Poor parent monitoring permits the child to engage in increasingly illegal activities. Within the deviant peer group, antisocial behavior is positively reinforced. In a later section, we briefly examine some of the variables associated with this drift to a deviant peer group. The problem has been analyzed in detail in Dishion (1987) and Dishion, Patterson, and Skinner (1988).

## Parallel Continuities

If both parental errors (of commission and omission) are involved, then measures of child antisocial behavior should be highly stable between Grades 4 and 6. This stability in child behavior will be paralleled by an equal stability in the two aspects of parenting practices, leading to what we term the *parallel continuities hypothesis*. The hypothesis to be tested is whether child antisocial behaviors are stable over a 2-year interval and whether this is a parallel stability for parent discipline and monitoring practices.

The empirical findings from over a dozen longitudinal studies reviewed by Olweus (1979, 1980) led him to conclude that measures of antisocial behavior had about the same test–retest reliabilities as do measures of children's intelligence. These findings lead us to believe our multiagent/multimethod procedures for defining child antisocial behavior are highly stable over a 2-year interval.

The hypothesis was tested using longitudinal data from Cohort I assessed at Grades 4 and 6. The results are summarized in Fig. 5.3. The data showed that the stability coefficient for the Child Antisocial Behavior construct was of an appreciable magnitude (.61) and highly significant. The findings

---

preceding behavior was coercive; $p^2$ is the likelihood that the child will continue to behave coercively if his parent responded coercively to his initial negative behavior. In other words, does a parent's inept discipline (for example, nattering and abusive behavior), increase the probability of continued negative behavior from the child?

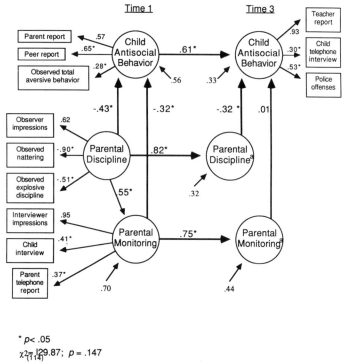

FIG. 5.3. Parallel continuities in parent and child behavior and some synchronous relationships.

strongly support the hypothesized stability in the measures of child behavior.

The hypothesis of parallel continuities requires that the measures of parental behavior also be stable over time. In keeping with this requirement, the stabilities for both constructs measuring parent behavior were significant and of a magnitude equal to or slightly greater than that obtained for the child behavior. The findings are consistent with those from earlier studies. For example, Schaefer and Bayley (1960) found substantial stabilities in mothers' reports about their irritable reactions to their children (.64) over a 6- to 11-year interval. Similarly, Dunn, Plomin, and Daniels (1986) showed that mothers were quite stable in how they reacted to target children and siblings when they were 12 months and 24 months of age.

## Synchronous Effects

We believe that the breakdown in parent practices causes the initial changes in child aggression. The causal status of these variables can only be tested in designs that employ experimental manipulations; such a study is currently being completed. For the moment, we can examine only the correlations between parent and child behavior; if the hypothesis is correct, then the correlations should be significant. In the language employed by Dwyer (1983) and others who write about longitudinal designs, the relatively immediate impact of changes in parent behavior on child behaviors is called a *synchronous effect* (rather than a *lagged effect*).

The hypothesized synchronous effects of parent behavior on child behavior required significant paths between the two parenting constructs and the child antisocial construct at both times. The model presented in Fig. 5.3 cannot be used as an effective test for this hypothesis, the reason being that at Time-3, the two paths are estimated relative to the contribution of the measure of antisocial behavior at Time 1. This problem has been noted by Gollob and Reichardt (1987) and is discussed in greater detail in a section that follows. Suffice it to say here that an adequate test would require examining the contribution of parenting practices to the Child Antisocial Behavior construct where an estimate of stability for antisocial is available from both Time-1 to Time and then also from Time to Time + 1. As a less than satisfying means of getting around this problem we used separate multiple regression analyses at both times. They showed that the two parenting variables accounted for 27.4% of the variance in child antisocial behavior at Grade 4 and 26.9% at Grade 6. At both times, the parenting skills made significant contributions. The findings support the idea that parenting behaviors are significantly related to child behaviors at both times. The data also provide a good overall fit to the a priori specified stabilities in parent and child behaviors and the synchronous relation between them. This is shown by the nonsignificant chi-square value for the model in Fig. 5.3 ($p = .263$).

These findings imply a good deal of stationarity, the relative contributions of monitoring and discipline seem highly stable over a 2-year period. However, it should be kept in mind that, for the older age group, it is assumed that deviant peers would now begin to make a unique and significant contribution to antisocial behavior. Enthusiasm for an adequate fit will be greater if the future model fits when it takes into account the stability estimate for the antisocial construct at both points in time.

## More About Synchronicity: Changes in Mean Level

However useful correlational data might be in understanding the covariates of ordinal rankings of subjects' scores, they do not convey information about shifts in mean level. The earlier discussion about late starters suggests that those parents who show a disruption in their parenting practices have children who demonstrate commensurate increases in their level of antisocial behavior.

The data in Fig. 5.4 reflect changes in the level of antisocial composite scores that accompany changes in parental monitoring scores. Good parenting was arbitrarily set at .5 SD above the mean for that age group and poor parenting was set at .5 SD below the mean. Only 14 families showed a shift from good parenting at Grade 4 to poor parenting at Grade 6. The shift to disrupted parenting was accompanied by an increase in antisocial child behavior. The change in child behavior for this group was significant ($t = 2.71$, $p < .01$). The juvenile court data showed that the likelihood of one or more police offenses was .21 for this group.

Fifteen families showed an improvement in parenting skills from Grade 4 to Grade 6. This was accompanied by the predicted reduction in antisocial behavior for the child. The change in mean level approached significance ($t = 1.43$, $p < .2$). A perusal of the juvenile court data showed that the likelihood of one or more police offenses was .06 for this group.

Data for both the "improvers" and the "worseners" support the hypothesis that changes in parent monitoring were accompanied by the predicted changes in child antisocial behavior. Families displaying inept monitoring at both Grades 4 and 6 ($N = 11$) were characterized by a mean antisocial score of $+.54$ and a likelihood of .27 for a police offense. The 61 families who showed normal levels of monitoring at both assessment probes were characterized by a mean score for antisocial behavior of $-.20$ and a .06

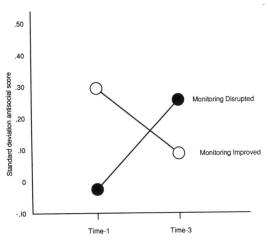

FIG. 5.4. Changes in antisocial behavior as a function of changes in monitoring (Cohort II).

likelihood for a police offense. Apparently, improvements in monitoring between Grades 4 and 6 can reduce the likelihood of police contacts to normal levels, whereas decrements in parental monitoring during the period can result in significantly greater likelihood of police contact.

Fig. 5.5 summarizes the comparable data for changes in parental discipline. The same decision rules used in the analyses of monitoring were applied to this data set. As before, those families with disrupted discipline at both points ($N = 17$) were characterized by very high antisocial scores (mean $= .91$) and those families with good discipline at both points ($N = 63$) had very low antisocial scores (mean $= -.26$).

Very few families showed substantial shifts in discipline. Because of the small Ns, no statistical analyses were carried out. There were modest reductions in mean levels of antisocial child behavior for the eight families in which discipline practices improved. The 13 families with disrupted practices showed moderate increases in antisocial behaviors. These findings are consistent with the hypothesis.

A curious aspect of the data is the difference in mean level at Grade 4 for the improvers and the worseners. Families in which discipline practices are about to worsen start with children who are already more antisocial than

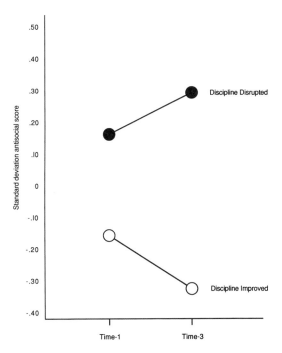

FIG. 5.5. Changes in antisocial behavior as a function of changes in discipline (Cohort I).

children in families about to get better. This may be some of the best evidence we have of a process at work. For example, families already in the coercion process have moderately antisocial children. For these families, the discipline practices and the child will get worse.

The next round of analyses for synchronistic effects require data from longitudinal studies that employ random assignment and intervention procedures as a form of experimental manipulation. As noted earlier, we view SEM with longitudinal data as a useful means for identifying developmental variables worthy of manipulation.

## VARIABLES RELATING TO RISK
## FOR INITIATING THE PROCESS

Our hypothesis suggests that certain dispositions in the child and the parent place the family at risk for initiation of the coercion process. For example, some children have a difficult temperament and presumably are more difficult for the parent to socialize. On the other hand, there may be certain traits in the parents that are also associated with risk for disrupted childrearing practices. The traits we have explored thus far are parental social competence, antisocial behavior, and depressed behavior.[4]

This section examines the hypothesis that the effect of child and parent dispositions on family-management practices will be mediated by disruptor states such as stress and marital conflict. In a sense, the real contribution of the child and parent traits may be to place the family at increased risk for stress and for marital conflict. Presumably, it is stress and marital conflict that directly disrupt childrearing practices.

### Temperament

It is assumed that some children are more difficult to socialize than others. For example, the irritable and inconsolable infant might be significantly more likely than the normal infant to be at risk for disrupted parenting practices. As shown in the longitudinal study by Werner and Smith (1977), this risk is exacerbated when it occurs in conjunction with marginally skilled parents. The empirical findings by Werner and Smith imply an interactive rather than a main effects model; that is, the unskilled mother in conjunction with the difficult infant constituted a risk for later adolescent delinquency.

The longitudinal study of infants by Lee and Bates (1985) showed the

---

[4]Donald Fiske (in press) discusses the social interactional, as compared to more traditional, approaches of personality psychology.

emergence of a stable factor as early as 6 months that was also clearly defined at 13 and 24 months. This factor was defined at each age by fussiness, overall difficulty, changeable and unsoothable ratings by the mother. These ratings correlated significantly with observed mother–child interactions in the home. In keeping with the present formulation, these infants were generally more difficult to discipline.

Although more methodological work needs to be done in defining early temperament, recent studies, such as Wilson and Matheny (1983), suggest good convergence across methods (observation & mother ratings). The programmatic studies by Rothbart (1977) suggest that parent ratings can be used to differentiate temperament in surprisingly young infants.

In that our own longitudinal study began with boys in Grade 4, it was necessary to use retrospective data to define temperament. Both of the parents provided an account of difficulties with the child up to the age of four. The interview items and psychometric properties of the scale are described in Capaldi and Patterson (1985).

Prior analyses (Patterson & Forgatch, in press) showed that child deviancy contributed to long-term increases in single mother stress. These findings led to the hypothesis that a measure of the difficult child as a toddler would contribute to parents' reports of their current stress.

## Antisocial and Socially Unskilled Parents

*Antisocial Parents.* In the Patterson and Dishion (in press) report, there was a low but significant correlation between parent and child antisocial trait scores. For mothers, the correlation was .34 ($p < .001$), and for fathers, .24 ($p < .001$). The measure of parent antisocial trait is defined by state arrest record, self-reported aggression on the Pd and Ma scales of the MMPI, and records from the department of motor vehicles. State arrest records apply to only a few mothers, skewing the distribution and rendering it nonusable (this is not the case for fathers, however). (For details on the psychometric properties of this construct, see the report by Capaldi & Patterson, 1988.)

Earlier analyses had shown that mother and father antisocial traits covaried significantly with both disrupted discipline and measures of stress (Patterson & Dishion, in press). However, we had never simultaneously examined the contribution of the parent antisocial trait to stress and to marital adjustment. In this context, the contribution of the antisocial parent to disrupted disciplinary practices may appear quite different.

*Social Competence.* The majority of parents referred to us for treatment because of antisocial sons generally tended to be socially un-skilled people. Most of the families were from the lower social status groups. Our impression is that for these families, effective parenting was prevented because parents were relatively innocent of parenting skills. We assume that social status covaries with social competence and that lower social status families have a higher incidence of unskilled parenting practices. In our studies of parent social competence we have used interviewers' impression of social skill, and parent education and occupation as indicators.

The studies showing a correlation between social status and a higher incidence of negative outcomes are consistent with this hypothesis. For example, recent national survey studies such as the one carried out by Elliott, Ageton, Huizinga, Knowles, and Canter (1983) showed that the incidence of severe self-reported crimes correlated significantly with social status. The lower social status groups were characterized by a high incidence of crimes such as burglary, homicide, theft, and so on. The review by Dohrenwend and Dohrenwend (1972) showed a higher incidence of stressors and psychiatric disturbances for the lower classes. The review by Antonovsky (1972) of 30 or more studies showed the inescapable conclusion that one's social class influenced one's chances of staying alive: A ratio of roughly 1:1.4.

Our studies hypothesize that parent social competence covaries with child rearing skills. Lower social status, then, should be characterized by a higher prevalence of disrupted parenting practices. Studies that are relevant to these issues show that most are based on monomethod (interviews with parent or with child), and that for every study supporting the hypothesis, another can be found that does not. We assume that multiagent/ multimethod assessments will presently provide data that more consistently support the hypothesis. One study using such methods, but disproportionately sampling the lower classes (Patterson et al., in press), found significant correlations between all measures of family-management practices and the Parent Social Competence construct.

In later studies, we systematically use confirmatory factor analyses to differentiate between social skills and social status. Although we may do a disservice to the field by combining two well-established concepts such as social skill and social status, the fact that the indicators converge so well is thought to be a sufficient basis for beginning the modeling studies in this way.

*Stress and Marital Adjustment.* The details for the definition of the two disruptor variables are described in the report by Capaldi and Patterson (1987). The Marital Adjustment construct is defined by the parents' self-report on the Dyadic Adjustment inventory and by a score from the home observation data: the proportion of spouse–spouse interactions that are positive. Stress is defined entirely by parent self-reports by daily hassles, medical problems, life events, financial problems, mother working, and number of children in the family. Earlier studies have convinced us that the models should be constructed separately for mothers and fathers. At the time of this writing, only the analyses for mothers have been completed. In modeling the interrelationships among the child and parent traits, we had no theoretical model to work from. For that reason, the model in Fig. 5.6 must be thought of as strictly post hoc. It was based on our scanning the convergent/discriminant validity matrix. By its very nature, such a model demands replication before it can be taken seriously. This is currently being done for the forthcoming publication by Patterson et al. (in press).

The findings show that the antisocial mother perceives her Grade 4 boy to have been a difficult toddler. The significant span may represent a causal process (genetic or otherwise), but for the present we do not know this to be the case so no path is shown.

Antisocial mothers tend to be less socially competent. Again, the highly significant relation is indicated with a span because we do not know what causes what. These parental dispositions in turn seem to relate to problems in marital adjustment. It is the relatively unskilled mothers who are most

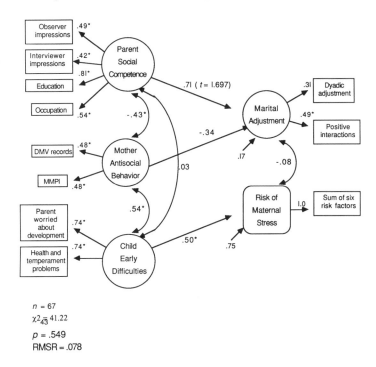

$n = 67$

$\chi^2_{43}\ 41.22$

$p = .549$

RMSR = .078

FIG. 5.6. Relations among child and mother traits and two disruption variables.

likely to have marital adjustment problems, and being antisocial seems to add to the risk. Notice that the two parent dispositions account for most of the variance in the measure of marital adjustment.

Only the parents' retrospective account of early child difficulties covaried significantly with their reports of currently being stressed. As mentioned earlier, previous findings suggest a significant path from mothers' antisocial trait to stress (Patterson & Dishion, in press). However, this relation may be mediated by how difficult the child is to deal with. If antisocial mothers are at greater risk for having a difficult infant–toddler, they are also more likely to report themselves as being more stressed.

## WHAT DISRUPTS DISCIPLINE PRACTICE?

The next section concerns how child and parent traits work together to disrupt maternal family-management skills. If we can understand what disrupts discipline then we will, perhaps, understand late starters. The models are examined separately for intact and single parent families.

### Amplifier Hypothesis

We began the longitudinal study with the assumption that stressors such as unemployment or the slow buildup in marital conflicts would explain the disruptions in discipline that produce late-starting antisocial boys. Although this may still be the case, the correlational studies reviewed in this section suggest a more complex model. The alternate model has been suggested by some of the work of G. Elder and his colleagues, and labeled the amplifier hypothesis. The present context suggests that socially un- skilled or antisocial parents become increasingly disrupted in their discipline practices when placed under stress or when involved in marital conflict. Not all families' discipline practices are disrupted by severe stressors or even by severe marital conflict. These disruptors seem to amplify an existing lack of skills or antisocial traits that in turn may disrupt otherwise marginally adequate discipline practices. We also assume that divorce or separation amplifies difficulties primarily for less socially skilled and antisocial mothers. The bivariate correlations examined by Patterson et al. (in press) suggest that the discipline practices are most sensitive to disruption by stressors or by marital conflict.

Elder, Caspi, and Downey (1983) showed that fathers with a tendency to be irritable became increasingly explosive in their discipline confrontations with their sons when subjected to prolonged economic stress during the Great Depression. Explosive and irritable discipline was also associated with increases in their sons' antisocial behavior. The stressors had much less effect on the discipline practices of (previously) nonirritable fathers. Further support for the amplification hypothesis is provided in the findings from the longitudinal study by Block, Block, and Gjerde (1986). They showed that families whose members tend to be somewhat coercive prior to the advent of parental stress may be most vulnerable. Patterson and Dishion (in press) also found support for the amplifier hypothesis using concurrent data sets for fathers and, to a lesser extent, for mothers. The effect of stress on discipline practices was mediated by the parental antisocial trait.

## Intact Families

Patterson et al. (in press) used SEM for a sample of intact families assessed at Grade 4 to determine if stress and marital conflict formed direct paths to discipline. Although the chi-square showed an adequate fit ($p = .22$) between the data set and the a priori model, there were several surprises. Neither of the paths from stress and marital adjustment to discipline was significant.

As shown in Fig. 5.7a, a mediational model for intact families fares only slightly better. Again, there was a good fit of the model to the data, but the model only accounted for 16% of the variance in the Discipline construct. The effect of stress on parenting practices was mediated by the two constructs measuring parental traits. The mediated disruption model makes only a modest contribution to our understanding of discipline practices.

## Single-Parent Families

Although suggestive, these findings were disquieting because of the small amount of variance accounted for by discipline. However, it is expected that single-parent and clinical samples will be characterized by higher levels in both the relevant parent traits and in the levels of stress and conflict. Our post hoc reaction was to test a model of disruption effects with a sample that is being disrupted, for example, a clinical sample or a sample of divorced mothers. The models summarized in Fig. 5.7 examined the data for a set of single mothers participating in the Oregon Youth Study of at-risk families. For the sake of comparison, the same model is presented first for intact families and then for single-parent families.

In keeping with the amplifier idea, the effects of both stress and mothers' antisocial trait on discipline practices were mediated by the level of social competence. Presumably, single mothers who were only marginal in social competence would perform at even lower levels if they were antisocial. It seemed that the highly stressed and antisocial mothers were characterized by reduced levels of social competencies. This latter group would be most at

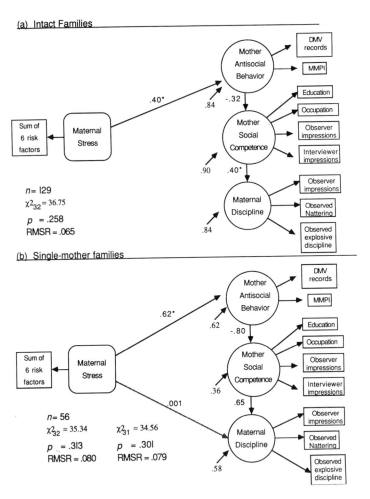

FIG. 5.7. Disruption models for single-mother ($N$ = 54) and intact ($N$ = 127) families.

risk for disrupted discipline. Figure 5.7b shows that for this model, all path coefficients are highly significant. Furthermore, the model accounts for 46% of the variance in the Discipline construct. Direct paths from stress to discipline and social competence were statistically nonsignificant.

The disruptor model significantly increases our understanding of what factors for single-mother households are associated with disruptions in discipline. It seems to be the socially competent mothers who are least at risk. This factor is even more important than knowing the level of stress. Presumably, a highly stressed single mother who is neither antisocial nor socially incompetent will be able to manage the discipline confrontations. Notice, too, that it is the acting-out single mother who is most at risk for a lack of social skills. Prevention procedures for these at-risk families might focus directly on teaching parenting skills and indirectly on training for social skills such as problem solving.

We are currently attempting to replicate the model for a larger sample of recently separated mothers (Forgatch & Patterson, 1988). We are also examining the interactive contribution of parent level of social competency and changes over time in marital adjustment as they relate to changes in discipline practices. The disruptor model suggests that when parents or marginal social competence become embroiled in marital conflict, they will also show major increases in disrupted discipline. Discipline practices within the single-parent subset may be particularly vulnerable to family conflict.

## Implications for Early and Late Starters

It makes a profound difference whether the family is disrupted early or late in the child's developmental history. If the process is initiated before the age of 5 or 6, then the second step is an omission in the development of absolutely critical social survival skills. The coercive child will not be taught adequate levels of social skills for forming relations with peers nor the skills to develop and maintain an intimate relationship with an equal (Youniss, 1980). Coercive children will also fail to develop academic and work-related skills. We return to the details of why this is so in a later section. Suffice it to say that current intervention procedures have shown that the antisocial symptoms can be changed, but it is not clear that these omissions in survival skills can be remediated (Kazdin, 1985).

Being a late starter implies that the child may already have passed safely through the first few years of training in social skills by peers. He also may have developed some modest skills in coping with academic and work requirements. When the process does start, it begins in the same way. Disruptions in parental monitoring and discipline are accompanied by rapid rises in noncompliance, temper tantrums, yelling, arguing, and so forth. But the late-starter youth who then joins the deviant peer group already has some modicum of relational and work-oriented skills. We believe that these skills form a basis for predicting nonchronicity in delinquent behaviors and early drop out from the deviant peer group to begin working and begin a family. Chronic delinquents are more likely to avoid both of these alternatives and remain in the deviant peer group (Elliott, Huizinga, & Ageton, 1985). The slender findings available from the Cambridge longitudinal study are in keeping with these predictions from the process model. The data showed that late starters tended to have about half the conviction rates as early starters (West, 1969).

## FROM STEP 1 TO STEP 2
## IN THE PROGRESSION

The coercion process is thought to unfold over time in a sequence of actions and reactions. In the first step, the child essentially acquires an antisocial trait. The second step describes the reactions of the social environment to this behavior.

For problem children, basic training in the home is characterized by faulty parental practices in several key areas of functioning other than just discipline or monitoring. The families also fail to provide the prosocial skill training necessary for adjustment in our culture. In addition, his patterns of coercive interaction make it difficult or impossible for the teachers and normal peer group to correct these omissions. As we see, rather than inhibiting the coercive process, their reactions amplify it.

The coercive child has not learned the prosocial skills necessary to form close relationships with either adults or peers. Furthermore, he is not taught how to work or to engage in disciplined effort of any kind. In that he has not learned to accept critical feedback or suggestions for changing behavior, he is also not ready to be taught these prosocial skills by anyone outside the family. When such a child is placed in the school setting, he is at grave risk to be identified as a double failure. Several days of contact will be sufficient for him to be identified as one to be rejected or at least isolated by normal peers (Coie & Kupersmidt, 1983; Dodge, 1983). Within a year or two he is also likely to be identified as an academic failure.

Both our clinical experience and the extensive literature reviewed in Kazdin (1985), Wilson and Herrnstein (1985), and Patterson et al. (in press) offer strong support for the double failure hypothesis. This formulation leads to several testable hypotheses. First, there should be direct correlations between the training in the home for antisocial behaviors and measures of peer rejection and academic failure. Our first test of these ideas used SEM of *concurrent* data collected at Grade 4 (Patterson et al. in press). It would be expected that by Grade 4, those antisocial boys who had started the process earlier would show concurrent breakdown in both peer relations and in academic skills.

The first hypothesis tested was that discipline practices in the home could covary with a generalized measure of antisocial behavior that sampled problem behaviors in both the home and the school. As illustrated in Fig. 5.8, the data support the hypothesis, showing a significant covariation between the observation-based measure of parent discipline practices in the home and reports from the school and the home about the child's antisocial behavior.

The double-failure hypothesis would require significant paths from the

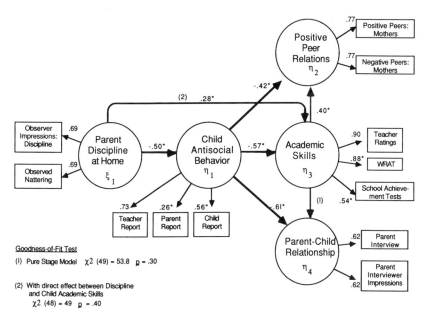

FIG. 5.8. From home to school: Social failure (from Patterson et al., in press).

Child Antisocial Behavior construct to constructs measuring peer relations and academic failure. Both path coefficients were significant, supporting the hypothesis. Simply knowing that the child is antisocial is a sufficient basis for accounting for from 30% to 40% of the variance in the various measures of social failure. The statistically nonsignificant chi-square ($p$ = .30) indicates that there was an adequate fit between the a priori clinical model and the data set.

The model is consistent with the idea that the effects of inept discipline in the home are significantly related to antisocial behavior and these, in turn, are significantly related to three different kinds of social failure. The addition of a direct path from discipline to academic skills was statistically significant and resulted in a much better fitting model than the first alternative.

An adequate design for testing the prediction that events unfold from step one to step two would require that we obtain measures of antisocial behavior prior to school entry and measures of peer relations and academic failure at ages 7 and 8. Recent analyses by Dishion (1987) provide a somewhat weaker design, but the findings are consistent with the hypothesis. They showed highly significant correlations between measures of antisocial behavior (and parent discipline) obtained at Grade 4 and measures of peer relation obtained at Grade 6. In addition, Patterson, Capaldi, and DeBaryshe (1988) showed that the effect of child antisocial behavior in Grade 6 significantly affected academic achievement at the same time.

## PROGRESSION FROM STEP 2 TO STEP 3

If the child continues to wend his way through this concatenated sequence of experiences, then the progression will presumably lead to yet another set of outcomes. These new outcomes are his reactions to their reactions. As outlined in the coercion formulation, his reaction to his dual failure is one of sadness or increased depressed mood. His reaction to finding little or no support from peers and from home is to drift into the deviant peer group (Patterson et al., in press). In this section, we briefly review the data relating to the Grade 6 boys' commitment to the deviant peer group.

It should be emphasized that the movement from one step to another sounds more discrete than it really is. It probably is not the case that in Grade 1 the child is labeled *antisocial* and then waits 5 or 6 years for the deviant peer group to form. It is more likely that as his antisocial behavior increases, the percentage of peers rejecting him keeps apace. One change more or less matches the other. Similarily, as he is rejected, he probably begins to interact more with the two or three other children in the group that also tend to be rejected by all others. By adolescence there will be a sizeable collection of persons that hang out together. From the vantage point of our adult concerns, we label them as a *deviant peer group*. By that time we can also obtain crude measures of a child's involvement in such a group and enter this new variable in our models.

The child's coercive style of interpersonal interactions and his accompanying lack of social skills leads to his rejection by normal peers. We believe that eventually he finds or is selected by the group of deviant peers. Presumably, the deviant peer group becomes recognizable at some time during preadolescence (as a guess, ages 10–12). Other investigators have pointed out that members of this group share a general attitude that is antiadult, -school, and -authority (Elliott et al., 1985; Elliot & Voss, 1974). In our own formulation, we have assumed that it is the child's rejection by normal peers, his antisocial behavior, and a failure in parent monitoring that contribute to this drift (Patterson et al., in press). Monitoring was identified as an important variable in an earlier pilot study of normal adolescents and their families (Patterson & Dishion, 1985).

To test this hypothesis, Dishion et al. (1988) analyzed the data collected for Cohorts I and II in the at-risk sample for Grades 4 and 6. The Monitoring construct was defined by child and parent telephone reports as well as by interviewers' global impressions about the adequacy of tracking.

Peer relations were defined at Grade 4 by two indicators based on peer nominations; at Grade 6, two indicators based on teacher ratings were used. The Deviant Peer construct was defined at both Grades 4 and 6 by reports from child, teachers, and parents. The psychometric properties of these constructs are summarized in the volume by Capaldi and Patterson (1988). In our own studies, we have found that the Child Antisocial Behavior and Positive Peer Relations constructs are so highly interrelated that knowing one provides a very good basis for predicting the other (Patterson et al., 1984). For this reason the Child Antisocial Behavior construct was not included in the model.

Dishion et al. (1988) found an acceptable fit between the a priori model and the data set. Even more gratifying was the fact that both early and later rejection by normal peers (in Grade 4) made significant contributions to deviant peer involvement to Grade 6. Parent monitoring made a significant contribution at both grades. Boys who were poorly monitored were most at risk for becoming involved. This latter result replicates the findings from the Patterson and Dishion (1985) study. These two variables accounted for 85% of the variance in the Grade 6 peer relations construct. These contributions were made relative to the contributions made by knowing the peer relations construct score at Grade 4. In that its (relative) path coefficient was only .02, one could say that the two variables accounted for all the information contributed by the stability of the deviant peer measure.

It is, perhaps, noteworthy that in the Eugene–Springfield metropolitan areas, where this study has been taking place, virtually all students attend a middle school for Grades 6 through 8. Thus, all study boys changed schools between Grades 4 and 6, and many of them were in middle schools with few peers from their elementary school years. Evidence cited earlier suggested that antisocial, peer-rejected boys, when interacting with previously unknown normal peers, were likely to be quickly identified as deviant and rejected once again (Coie & Kupersmidt, 1983; Dodge, 1983). On the other hand, clinical intervention and subsequent improvements in parental monitoring can make a difference in outcome for these problem boys (Bank, Patterson, & Reid, 1987).

The findings are consistent with the hypothesis that antisocial boys who are rejected by normal peers in Grade 4 are at risk for drifting into and remaining in a group of deviant peers. This drift is further exacerbated by a failure in Grade 6 in parental monitoring.

## A DEVIANCY AMPLIFIER:
## A CASE OF DELAYED EFFECTS?

We are interested in the possibility that some variables may be generated as by-products of the process and then function as delayed causal variables that feed back into the process and make it worse. Thus far, we have completed the appropriate analyses for only one such construct — Positive Peer Relations. This section examines the SEM analysis appropriate to this issue.

As noted earlier, it is hypothesized that some variables, such as childrearing practices, have relatively rapid effects on child behaviors (synchronistic), while others, such as rejection by peers, may have a delayed causal effect. Low self-esteem and academic achievement are other variables being considered as candidates for causing delayed effects.

## Limited Shopping for Social Opportunity

The delayed effect hypothesis raises the interesting question of why some events may have an immediate effect and others a delayed effect. That is, what is the mechanism? The hypothesis offered here — but not yet tested — is that each of these variables sets limits on the opportunities the children have for certain critical socialization experiences.

Rejection by normal peers is akin to a mandate that stipulates more restricted future experience. There will be restrictions on certain settings, on certain activities, and on the availability of certain groups of children. Each limitation or set of missed opportunities should enhance the possibility that they will remain fixed in the antisocial process.

It is assumed that each of us selects a social group and social settings that provides a rough match for our level of prosocial and antisocial skills. As suggested by Scarr (1985a, 1985b), person and setting shopping activities may reflect both genetic predispositions and our past history of reinforcement for certain activities. From our social interactional perspective, the child shops among persons and settings to maximize a mutuality for positive reinforcement and to minimize punishment or being ignored. Presumably, the individual selects the group and the group selects the individual. With increasing age, one would expect members of the child's peer groups to be increasingly homogeneous in terms of activities, values, and interests.

With each year that the normal peer socialization process is omitted, the coercive child becomes more obviously deviant. There are simply more and more things missing from what one expects of a child of that age. For example, these children are less likely to learn athletic skills. They not only have difficulty cooperating in a group, but respond negatively to any and all kinds of corrective negative feedback. This means they will lack the prowess at throwing a baseball or basketball that serves as one of the major positive skills determining peer acceptance for younger boys (Hops, 1983). They are unlikely to be members of a scouting troop. They know in advance that they will be rejected by its members and, besides, their parents would not make the effort required. Missing in these unfortunate boys is the development of normal prosocial skills. Possessing these skills makes the normal 10-year-old socially complex and obviously different from a 6-year-old boy. The peer socialization process and its importance is beautifully described in the studies of peer group influence by Youniss (1980).

## Positive Feedback Loop?

We are aware of no ready means in the social sciences for identifying positive feedback loops. The procedures presented here seem reasonable but it is our first attempt to consider this problem, so there might well be some egregious error in logic or arithmetic that will lead us to search for other alternative approaches.

There is strong support for the hypothesis that peer rejection correlates significantly with antisocial behavior (Hartup, 1983). The SEM data reviewed in the early sections of this report are also consistent with this idea. The experimental studies by Coie and Kupersmidt (1983) and Dodge (1983) take these correlations one step further. Their manipulations establish the fact that the relation is indeed *causal*: in the short run, *antisocial behaviors produce peer rejection*.

We think this variable may play a dual role, with both effects unfolding over a considerable period of time. As already noted, peer rejection in Grade 4 does something (unspecified) that eventually leads to a deviant peer group at Grade 6. It seems to take a year or two before this effect becomes significant. It is hypothesized that the same variable may also have a delayed effect in contributing to antisocial behavior; again, the effect is obtained over a period of a year or two.

It is hypothesized that rejection by normal peers leads to restrictions in social experiences that ensure the child's continuance in the coercion process. There are no alternative paths that will open before him to lead him back to the normal socialization process. He is unlikely to learn some redeeming social skill such as a sport. He is unlikely to be touched by a great teacher who discovers the hidden talent that is there. He continues on his way towards a career as an antisocial adult.

If we collect all of these assumptions together and express them in a correlational model with longitudinal data, the model would have to meet certain requirements. It requires first that we have an estimate of the stability for the dependent variable, antisocial behavior. As noted earlier the Child Antisocial Behavior construct is highly stable from Grade 4 to 6. The path coefficient was estimated for the latent constructs as defined in Fig. 5.9. To provide the most conservative estimate possible, while also controlling for problems of method variance, we chose to follow an indicator mismatching procedure (Bank, Patterson, Dishion, & Skinner, in

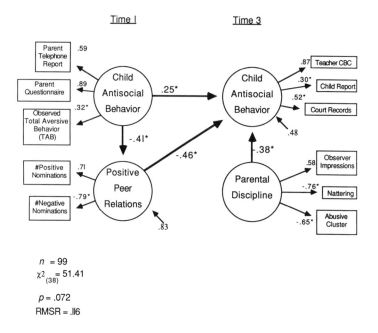

FIG. 5.9. Rejecting peers as a delayed effect.

press). Notice that there is no overlap in the indicators that define antisocial behavior at the two points in time. The resulting stability coefficient was .65.

The next requirement is to put in the most powerful synchronous variable at Grade 6. The general model stipulates that parental discipline is the most powerful single determinant for child antisocial behavior. In the figure, the path coefficient describing this relation is .38.

There are three contributions to the variance for antisocial behavior at Grade 6. Parent discipline practices is one; another is reflected in the autocorrelation or stability coefficient. As pointed out by Gollob and Reichardt (1987), a latent construct measure at any given time reflects in part a causal process that was operating in the preceding week, month, or year. The third contribution might be made by peer rejection measured at Grade 4, our candidate for the position of feedback variable.

The three path coefficients tell their own story. They are to be interpreted as standard partial beta coefficients that describe the contribution of each variable *relative* to the other two. As shown, the relation between peer relations at Grade 4 and child antisocial behavior at Grade 6 is not only significant, but also the largest magnitude path coefficient (.46) in the model. Knowing that the child is rejected by normal peers at Grade 4 is an even more powerful estimate of variance in child antisocial behavior at Grade 6 than is knowledge of parental discipline at Grade 6. Rejection by peers at Grade 4 was presumably produced by the child's antisocial behavior occurring at that time; one might then think of the process as analogous to a positive feedback loop. For the moment, we cannot think of any further requirements or tests that could be employed to reject the idea. The three variables together account for 52% of the variance in the measure of the latent construct at Grade 6. The chi-square showed an acceptable fit between the a priori model and the data set.

Our next step is to find a way of testing the shopping hypothesis. Another possibility is to examine the likelihood that the relation between peer rejection at Grade 4 and antisocial behavior at Grade 6 is mediated by involvement with deviant peers. One could well imagine deviant peers as providing both modeling and positive reinforcement for antisocial behaviors and thus contributing directly to strengthening this behavior.

One outcome of the analysis was something of a surprise. The original estimate for the stability coefficient for antisocial behavior was .65. However, in Fig. 5.9, this value has been reduced to .25. We have labeled this phenomenon the *disappearing stability variance* and plan to address this problem in detail in a subsequent report. We have encountered this phenomenon in several different analyses, and believe it is not artifactual. For the moment, we assume that if the variables introduced explain why a behavior is maintained (stable), then they will account for significant portions of the stability variance. For example, in Fig. 5.9, parent discipline is itself stable over time, and at any point makes a significant contribution to maintenance of antisocial behavior. Its contribution at Time-2 accounted for a significant portion of the stability variance in the measure of antisocial behavior.

One way of thinking about this is to assume that at Grade 4, both the Child Antisocial Behavior and Positive Peer Relations constructs share some predictive power in explaining what is going to happen to antisocial behavior at Grade 6. A multiple regression analysis could compare the relative contribution of both variables in accounting for variance in the measure of antisocial behavior at Grade 6. As shown, in the context of the model, prior knowledge about peer relations is a better predictor of later aggression than is knowledge of the earlier level of antisocial behavior. Incidentally, one of the utilities of the SEM approach is that it permits us to examine such a possibility after the errors of measurement and correlated error terms have been disentangled (cf. Dwyer, 1983). We remain mildly skeptical but enthusiastic about this line of analyses. The metaphor provides such a beautiful fit to many clinical and developmental problems that it is certainly worth pursuing.

## A PROGRESSION FOR DELINQUENT BEHAVIOR?

Progressions

As already noted, the steps in the coercion sequence probably do not have rigid boundaries delineating one from the other. But they are useful heuristics in that we can delineate one step from another and calculate very rough probability statements about the likelihood of movement from one to the other. This section examines some of the data relevant to the hypothesis that the sequence may in fact be a progression. One key characteristic of a progression of particular interest is its transitivity. As used here, the transitive progression implies that the majority of the children who are at the last step (chronic delinquents) have also moved through the prior three steps. A closer inspection of this idea will show that transitivity relates to a single path, while violations relate to the possibility of alternate paths to the same outcome. Both are useful pieces of information. In this section, we examine some means for describing these possibilities, particularly the idea that there may be more than one path to delinquent behavior.

We assume that the child moves through the sequence over time. The longer the child is in any given stage, the greater his risk for moving on to another, more extreme step in the series. The manner in which the hypothesis is stated suggests the use of event history analysis or some general application of continuous time sequence analysis as described by Gardner and Griffin (1988). When our data set is complete, we plan to use such analyses. As a preliminary step, however, we should be able to calculate the likelihood of moving from one step to another. This was one of the features of a progression emphasized in the early writings of Guttman (1944). To illustrate this, we summarized the coercion model as a sequence of four steps. The first step for our sample began at Grade 4 with a measure of antisocial behavior. The accompanying rejection by peers was the second step. According to the model, this should lead to involvement in a deviant peer group by Grade 6; the fourth step will be official records of police offenses. Presumably, all Grade 6 boys who have had a police contact would have moved through all prior stages.

Most textbooks on delinquency talk about multiple causes. As a working hypothesis, we believe that most of these variables can be ordered with a single model to define one, perhaps two, paths leading to chronic offending (Patterson et al., in press). If the data support the coercion model, it would also suggest that there are only a very limited number of paths to the same outcome. It is our hunch that there are only two main paths to chronic delinquency.

Guttman (1944) assumed that a transitive progression implied a single underlying process. This idea can be used to study the interesting clinical phenomena that are essentially low baserate events; for example, setting fires, assault, and hallucinations. We can begin by ordering antisocial symptoms such as noncompliance, temper tantrums, fighting, stealing, and setting fires by frequency of occurrence (e.g., Patterson, 1982). Patients observed to engage in low baserate symptoms, such as setting fires, have also exhibited all of the higher rate symptoms that precede it in the progression? If this is so, we may understand fire setting by studying the higher rate, easier to study, symptoms such as stealing and fighting.

There is no single index that summarizes all of the information in a progression. Guttman's coefficient of reproducibility was one approach to deriving such an index; the critiques by Robinson (1973) and others attest to the failure of this effort. Instead of a single index, we rely on three kinds of simple conditional probability statements as a means for extracting the information from a progression. What is the base-rate probability for the events in the sequence? What is the conditional likelihood of moving from an earlier to a later stage in the progression? If one is at a later stage, what is the conditional likelihood of having arrived there by moving through the entire sequence of steps, and also what is the likelihood of an alternative path?

## A Potential Progression

A potential progression can be formed by arranging events in order from most to least frequent. The next step is to decide what kind of measures will go into the sequence. If all of the measures are based on the same method of assessment (e.g., mother interview data), then the progression may be confounded. For this reason, multiagent/multimethod indicators were used for each of the three constructs in the progression. The third step makes it almost impossible to carry out a formal search for a single index. It is necessary to set up decision rules that will identify those boys who are at risk and those who are not at each step. Different cutting scores could result in greatly varied outcomes. We arbitrarily set the mean value for antisocial behavior as the cutting score for step one, .25 SD above the mean for peer rejection for step two, and .50 SD above the mean for association with deviant peers for step three.

The data in Fig. 5.10 summarize the information used to describe a progression of the coercion model for delinquency. The data were collected from the first cohort of 102 boys at Grades 4 and 6. Many, but not all, antisocial boys are rejected by the normal peer group (.60). A test of significance would require that the conditional value be significantly greater than the base-rate value for peer rejection (.34). Notice, however, that if the cutting score had been set at the 70th or 90th percentile, then a larger proportion of the boys would have been rejected.

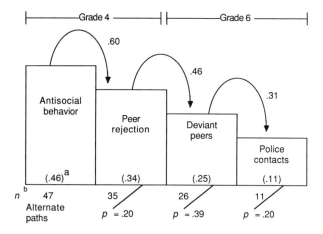

FIG. 5.10. Transitive progression to delinquency.

If the child was rejected to Grade 4, then the likelihood was .46 that he would be in a deviant peer group by Grade 6. A comparison of that value with the (arbitrarily set) base rate of .25 suggests that rejected boys are at significant risk for drifting into a deviant peer group.

If the boy was in a deviant peer group at Grade 6, the likelihood was .27 that he would have committed at least one police offense by Grade 6. Even at the early stage of adolescence, belonging to a deviant peer group is associated with a grave risk for delinquent behavior. It should be noted that for the 28 boys who were both antisocial and peer rejected in Grade 4, the likelihood of continuing the progression to the deviant peer group was .57. Furthermore, for those 16 boys who came through all of the first steps, the likelihood of police contact by the end of Grade 6 was .44. The likelihood of moving one from one step to the next is usually about double the base-rate value. At any given step, the boy is at about twice the risk for the next step as are boys not in the process.

*Alternate Paths.*  It was hypothesized that a simple probabilistic analysis of sequences could provide a crude means for estimating the likelihood of other paths to the same outcomes. This could, of course, be a means for cueing the investigator to prepare an alternative model. With the arbitrary setting of base-rate values noted earlier, we can still obtain useful information about limitations in our current model. This is done by simply calculating at each step the proportion of subjects who were not in the preceding step. For example, 80% of the boys rejected by peers were above the mean on the antisocial score; by definition, 20% were rejected for some other reason (for example, being hyperactive or withdrawn). The conditional probability values for alternate paths is more accurately thought of as a summary statement for our ignorance than a precise estimate of other paths. However, the idea of alternate paths is a useful heuristic, so the phrase is included here (correcting the probability value for errors of measurement might make it more useful).

As shown by the data, 39% of the children in the preadolescent deviant peer group were either misclassified at step two or had arrived by some other path. For example, such misclassified boys could be low achievers who were not antisocial; they could also be neglected or poorly monitored boys.

Only 11 boys had committed one or more police offenses for delinquent behavior by the summer following Grade 6. Seven of these were correctly identified by the model; they had been identified as being at risk in each of the preceding three steps. All four of the remaining delinquents had been correctly identified as being at risk at two of three steps; one was not classified as antisocial, one was not classified as peer rejected, and two were not classified as associating with deviant peers.

Notice that in Fig. 5.10., 20% of the youths who became delinquent had not been identified as being in a deviant peer group. This is consistent with the idea that the progression may be transitive; 80% of those at step four had come through step three. We might, however, introduce the more rigorous requirement that transitivity implies that all of the preceding steps be filled. In this case, only 64% met the requirement.

It may be that our application of the transitivity concept from psychophysical scaling is inappropriate. Technically,a transitivity requires that if one says that $a$ is greater than $b$ and that $b$ is greater than $c$, then $a$ must be greater than $c$. Given this, then $a$, $b$, and $c$ define points on at least an ordinal scale. Nothing in the present discussion implies scaled intervals. Nor do we meet the requirements for precise specification among the three steps. We do not mean to give a false sense of precision to the discussion. It is just that, at the moment, we have not come up with a better metaphor for thinking about developmental progressions and how the concept of transitivity might apply to them.

*Prediction.*    It is probably premature to discuss the model as a prediction device in that most of the children who will become delinquent have not as yet been caught by the police. What we have currently are the earliest of the early starters; according to the literature reviews already noted, these youngsters are probably most at risk for becoming chronic offenders. The peak age for committing, and being caught committing, delinquent behavior is around ages 15 to 16. The boys in our sample were only ages 12 to 13 when the police records were examined. By age 18, the expected base rate value of delinquency for this high-risk sample is expected to be greater than .30.

With those qualifications, the hit rate for the model was 87%, with a false positive error of 59% and a false negative error of 36%. Our prediction is that most of the youths who are caught in the next year (being caught is a chance event, according to the literature) will fit all three prior steps in the model and thus reduce the false positive error. As they stand, the descriptive findings provide solid support for the application of the coercion formulation to understanding delinquent behavior (Patterson et al., in press).

## IMPLICATIONS

We have made an argument for the idea that the child antisocial trait may have its beginning in the disrupted interactions with other family members. Their inadvertent reinforcement strengthens a wide variety of coercive behaviors such as noncompliance and temper tantrums that lead to fighting, stealing, and so forth. Presumably, the quality of the exchanges of the child with family members is controlled by the kind of family management skills employed by the parent. The data presented here showed that, over a 2-year period, the stability is antisocial behavior was matched by a roughly equivalent stability in parenting practices.

We assumed a bidirectional effect for the parent–child exchanges with some asymmetry in favor of the effect of the parent on the child. A procedure currently being explored estimates the magnitude of the effect of child on parents relative to the effect of the parent on the child. At the time of this writing, the analyses have not been completed.

As a general case, we are saying that a trait such as antisocial behavior is generalizable across time and settings, but that it also is more than that. A high trait score signifies that the child is caught up in a process that, if it continues, will dramatically alter the social environment in which the child lives. To understand the process, we must understand the details of where the antisocial behaviors come from and what maintains them. Most significantly, however, we must also have data describing the reactions of key members of the social environment (family, peers, teachers) to the antisocial behaviors. Presumably, it is the reaction of the parents, the peers, and teachers to the child's explosive temper tantrums, noncompliance, and fighting that determines the long-term maintenance of the process itself, as well as the maintenance of the antisocial trait behaviors.

A decade of longitudinal studies has shown that such juvenile behaviors as temper tantrums, fighting, and stealing are, in fact, prototypic and significantly correlated with later adolescent delinquency. Therefore, in designing prevention programs, one major concern is identifying at-risk antisocial boys before they have developed court records. However, the fact that the antisocial traits reflect an ongoing process has profound implications for the timing of prevention programs. The information about the process tells us when we must intervene; that is, critical points in the child's development that yield best results for clinical interventions.

The process notion implies that if prevention began early enough, it would not have to focus on the remediation of peer relational skills or academic skills. For early starters, effective prevention might start when the child is age 4 to 6. This would require a minimum of effort in reducing antisocial behavior, and successful outcomes should mean that the child would not have to go through the trauma of being rejected and failing in school.

On the other hand, if the intervention were to start at some later, fixed starting point such as Grades 3 and 4, then according to the process notion, many of them would already have an extensive history of failure with peers and several years of partial failure in school subjects. The remediation effort would have to include not only the parent training component to reduce the antisocial behavior, but components for peer relational skills as well. It would also have to include a third component to remediate one or more academic skills. It should be mentioned that, to date, there are *no* intervention or prevention studies that have used all three components together. The parent training component alone typically costs an average of 20 hours of professional time to treat children ages 6 through 12 (Patterson, Chamberlain, & Reid, 1982). Interventions that combined all three components would presumably double or triple the hours of professional time needed.

In some fundamental sense, the families of antisocial children may be representative of a constantly changing, highly unstable system. Clinically they give the impression that each family member is a practicing Hobbesian. All family members seem intent on maximizing their own self-interest. The outcome is a collection of individuals and a process that moves increasingly away from, rather than toward, a stable family process. As we noted at the outset of this chapter, these clinical families may be an instance where the ordinary inhibitors of deviancy are in abeyance. Each move toward increasing deviancy is amplified rather than inhibited. It seems to us that this is the maximization of immediate self-interest versus maximizing long-term gains for the group that differentiates deviancy-producing from growth-enhancing families.

## ACKNOWLEDGMENTS

The writers gratefully acknowledge the support provided by MH 37940, funded through the NIMH sections for Studies in Antisocial and Violent Behavior and the National Institute of Alcoholism and Alcohol Abuse. These funds provided for the collection of the data used in the present chapter. The modeling analyses for deviant behaviors were funded by MH 37940; the analyses for peer relations and achievement by HD 22679 through NICHD. The writers owe a special debt to the arduous efforts of Deborah Capaldi and her staff to provide the high quality data, and to Martie Skinner and her cadre of LISRELETTES who carried out the modeling studies.

## REFERENCES

Anderson, K. E., Lytton, H., & Romney, D. M. (1986). Mothers' interactions with normal and conduct-disordered boys: Who affects whom? *Developmental Psychology, 22,* 604–609.

Antonovsky, A. (1972). Social class,, life expectancy, and overall mortality. In E. G. Jaco (Ed.), *Patients, physicians, and illness: A sourcebook on behavioral science and health* (2nd ed., pp. 5–30). New York: The Free Press.

Baldwin, D. V., & Skinner, M. L. (1988). *A structural model for antisocial behavior: Generalization to single-mother families.* Manuscript submitted for publication.

Bank, L., Patterson, G. R., Dishion, T. J., & Skinner, M. (in press). The glop problem in structural equation modeling. In G. R. Patterson (Ed.), *Depression and aggression: Two facets of family interaction.* Hillsdale, NJ: Lawrence Erlbaum Associates.

Bank, L., Patterson, G. R., & Reid, J. B. (1987). Delinquency prevention through training parents in family management. *Behavior Analyst, 10,* 75–82.

Bell, R. Q., & Harper, L. V. (1977). *Child effects on adults.* Hillsdale, NJ: Lawrence Erlbaum Associates.

Bielby, W. T., & Matsueda, R. L. (1987, August). *Detecting reciprocal effects in nonrecursive models: An application of power analysis.* Paper presented at the annual meeting of the American Sociological Society, Chicago, IL.

Block, J. H., Block, J., & Gjerde, P. F. (1986). The personality of children prior to divorce: A prospective study. *Child Development, 57,* 827–840.

Capaldi, D., & Patterson, G. R. (1985). *Early problems with target child* (OSLC Technical Report). Eugene, OR: Oregon Social Learning Cente

Capaldi, D., & Patterson, G. R. (1987). An approach to the problem of recruitment and retention rates for longitudinal research. *Behavioral Assessment, 9,* 169–177.r.

Capaldi, D., & Patterson, G. R. (1988). *Psychometric properties of fifteen latent constructs from the coercion model.* Manuscript submitted for publication.

Coie, J. D., & Kupersmidt, J. B. (1983). A behavioral analysis of emerging social status in boys' groups. *Child Development, 54,* 1400–1416.

Craig, M. M., & Glick, S. J. (1968). School behavior related to later delinquency and nondelinquency. *Criminologica, 5,* 17–27.

Dishion, T. J. (1987). *A developmental model for peer relations: Middle childhood correlates and one-year sequelae.* Unpublished doctoral dissertation, University of Oregon, Eugene,

OR.

Dishion, T. J., Gardner, K., Patterson, G. R., Reid, J. B., & Thibodeaux, S. (1983). *Family process code* (Tech. Rep.). Eugene: Oregon Social Learning Center.

Dishion, T. J., Patterson, G. R., & Skinner, M. L. (1988). *Peer group selection process from middle childhood to early adolescence.* Unpublished manuscript, Oregon Social Learning Center, Eugene, OR.

Dodge, K. A. (1983). Behavioral antecedents: A peer social status. *Child Development, 54,* 1386–1399.

Dodge, K. A., Schlundt, D. C., Schocken, I., & Delugach, J. D. (1983). Social competence and children's sociometric status: The role of peer group entry strategies. *Merrill-Palmer Quarterly, 29,* 309–336.

Dohrenwend, B. S., & Dohrenwend, B. P. (1972). Social class and the relation of remote to recent stressors. In M. Roff, L. N. Robins, & M. Pollack (Eds.), *Life history research in psychopathology* (Vol. 2, pp. 170–185). Minneapolis: University of Minnesota Press.

Duncan, O. D. (1975). *Introduction to structural equation models.* New York: Academic.

Dunn, J. F., Plomin, R., & Daniels, D. (1986). Consistency and change in mothers' behavior toward young siblings. *Child Development, 57,* 348–356.

Dwyer, J. H. (1983). *Statistical models for the social and behavioral sciences.* New York: Oxford University Press.

Elder, G. H., Caspi, A., & Downey, G. (1983). Problem behavior in family relationships: A multigenerational analysis. In A. Sorensen, F. Weinert, & L. Sherrod (Eds.), *Human development: Interdisciplinary perspective* (pp. 93–118). Hillsdale, NJ: Lawrence Erlbaum Associates.

Elliott, D. S., Ageton, S. S., Huizinga, D., Knowles, B. A., & Canter, R. J. (1983). The prevalence and incidence of delinquent behavior: 1976-1980. National estimates of delinquent behavior by sex, race, social class, and other selected variables. *National Youth Survey Report No. 26.* Boulder, CO: Behavioral Research Institute.

Elliott, D. S., Huizinga, D., & Ageton, S. S. (1985). *Explaining delinquency and drug use.* Beverly Hills, CA: Sage.

Elliott, D. S., & Voss, H. L. (1974). *Delinquency and dropout.* Lexington, MA: Lexington Books.

Engfer, A., Gavranidou, M. (1985, July). Antecedents of perceived behavior problems in children 4 and 18 months of age: A longitudinal study. Paper presented at the workshop on temperament and development in childhood, Leiden, The Netherlands.

Ensminger, M. E., Kellam, S.a G., & Rubin, B. R. (1983). School and family origins of delinquency. In K. T. Van Dusen & S. A. Mednick (Eds.), *Prospective studies of crime and delinquency* (pp. 73–97). Boston: Kluwer-Nijhoff.

Farrington, D. P. (1981, November). *Delinquency from 10 to 25.* Paper presented at the meeting of the Society for Life History Research, Monterey, CA.

Farrington, D. P. (1987). Early precursors of frequent offending. In J. Q. Wilson & G. C.Loury (Eds.), *From children to citizens: Vol. III. Families, schools, and delinquency prevention* (pp. 27–50). New York: Springer-Verlag.

Fiske, D. (in press). From inferred personalities toward personality in action. *Journal of Personality.*

Forgatch, M. S., & Patterson, G. R. (1988). *The effects of stress, social, and antisocial behavior on family management in single-mother families.* Manuscript in preparation.

French, D. C. (1987). Children's social interaction with older, younger, and same-age peers. *Journal of Social and Personal Relationships, 4,* 63–86.

Gardner, W., & Griffin, W. (1988). *Predicting delinquency and antisocial behavior with sequential analysis.* Manuscript in preparation.

Gollob, H. F., & Reichardt, C. S. (1987). Taking account of time lags in causal models. *Child Development, 58,* 80–92.

Guttman, L. A. (1944). A basis for scaling qualitative data. *American Sociological Review, 9,* 139–150.

Hartup, W. W. (1983). Peer relations. In P. Mussen & E. M. Hetherington (Eds.), *Social and personality development: Handbook of child psychology: Vol. IV. Socialization, personality, and social development* (pp. 103–196). New York: Wiley.

Hops, H. (1983). Children's social competence and skill: Current research practices and future directions. *Behavior Therapy, 14,* 3–18.

Hops, H., & Cobb, J. A. (1974). Initial investigation into academic survival-skill training: Direct instruction and first-grade achievement. *Journal of Educational Psychology, 66,* 548–553.

Kazdin, A. E. (1985). *Treatment of antisocial behavior in children and adolescents.* Homewood, IL: Dorsey.

Kohn, M. L. & Schooler, C. (1978). The reciprocal effects of the substantive complexity of work and intellectual flexibility: A longitudinal assessment. *American Journal of Sociology, 84,* 24–52.

Lee, C. L., & Bates, J. E. (1985). Mother-child interaction at age two years and perceived difficult temperament. *Child Development, 56,* 1314–1325.

Olweus, D. (1979). Stability of aggressive reaction patterns in males: A review. *Psychological Bulletin, 86,* 852–875.

Olweus, D. (1980). Familial and temperamental determinants of aggressive behavior in adolescent boys: A causal analysis. *Developmental Psychology, 16,* 644–660.

Patterson, G. R. (1977). Accelerating stimuli for two classes of coercive behaviors. *Journal of Abnormal Child Psychology, 5,* 334–350.

Patterson, G. R. (1982). *A social learning approach to family intervention: III. Coercive family process.* Eugene, OR: Castalia.

Patterson, G. R. (1984a). Siblings: Fellow travelers in coercive family processes. In R. F. Blanchard (Ed.), *Advances in the study of aggression* (pp. 173–215). New York: Academic Press.

Patterson, G. R. (1984b). Microsocial process: A view from the boundary. In J. C. Masters & K. Yarkin-Levin, (Eds.), *Boundary areas in social and developmental psychology* (pp. 43–66. Orlando, FL: Academic Press.

Patterson, G. R. (1986a). The contribution of siblings to training for fighting: A microsocial analysis. In D. Olweus, J. Bloc, & M. Radke-Yarrow (Eds.), *Development of antisocial and prosocial behavior: Research, theories, and issues* (pp. 235–261). Orlando, FL: Academic Press.

Patterson, G. R., Capaldi, D., & DeBarsyshe, B. (1988). *Child antisocial behavior: A significant antecedent to academic failure.* Manuscript in preparation.

Patterson, G. R., Chamberlain, P., & Reid, J. B. (1982). A comparative evaluation of parent training procedures. *Behavior Therapy, 13,* 638–650.

Patterson, G. R., & Dishion, T. J. (1985). Contributions of families and peers to delinquency. *Criminology, 23,* 63–79.

Patterson, G. R., & Dishion, T. J. (in press). Multilevel family process models: Traits, interactions, and relationships. In R. A. Hinde & J. Stevenson-Hinde (Eds.), *Relations between relationships within families.* Oxford, England: Oxford University Press.

Patterson, G. R., Dishion, T. J., & Bank, L. (1984). Family interaction: A process model of deviancy training. In L. Eron (Ed.), special edition of *Aggressive Behavior, 10,* 253–267.

Patterson, G. R., & Forgatch, M. S. (in press). Three stages in a mother-child stress process. In G. R. Patterson (Ed.), *Depression and aggression: Two facets of family interaction.*

Hillsdale, NJ: Lawrence Erlbaum Associates.

Patterson, G. R., Reid, J. B., & Dishion, T. J. (in press). *A social learning approach to family intervention: IV. Antisocial boys.* Eugene, OR: Castalia.

Rausch, H. L. (1965). Interaction sequences. *Journal of Personality and Social Psychology, 2,* 487–499.

Reid, J. B., Taplin, P. S., & Lorber, R. (1981). A social interactional approach to the treatment of abusive families. In R. Stuart (Ed.), *Violent behavior: Social learning approaches to prediction, management, and treatment* (pp. 83–101). New York: Brunner/Mazel.

Robinson, J. P. (1973). Toward a more appropriate use of Guttman scaling. *Public Opinion Quarterly, 37,* 260–267.

Rothbart, M. K. (1977, March). *Measurement of temperament in infancy.* Paper presented at the meeting of the Society for Research in Child Development, New Orleans, LA.

Sameroff, A. J. (1982). Development and the dialectic: The need for a systems approach. In W. A. Collins (Ed.), *Minnesota symposium on child psychology* (Vol. 15, pp. 83–103). Hillsdale, NJ: Lawrence Erlbaum Associates.

Sameroff, A. J., & Fiese, B. H. (1987). *Conceptual issues in prevention.* Manuscript submitted for publication.

Scarr, S. (1985a). Constructing psychology: Making facts and fables for our times. *American Psychologist, 40,* 499–512.

Scarr, S. (1985b, April). *Personality and experience: Individual encounters with the world.* Paper presented at the Henry A. Murray Lectures in Personality, Michigan State University, East Lansing, MI.

Schaefer, E. S., & Bayley, N. (1960). Consistency of maternal behavior from infancy to preadolescence. *Journal of Abnormal Social Psychology, 61,* 1–7.

Snyder, J. J., & Patterson, G. R. (1986). The effects of consequences on patterns of social interaction: A quasi-experimental approach to reinforcement in natural interaction. *Child Development, 57,* 1257–1268.

Spivak, G. (1983). *High risk early behaviors indicating vulnerability to delinquency in the community and school.* Washington DC: National Institute of Juvenile Justice and Delinquency Prevention.

Vuchinich, S. (1987, November). *Statistically demonstrating reciprocal effects.* Paper presented at the annual meeting of the National Council for Family Relations, Atlanta, GA.

Vuchinich, S., Bank, L., & Patterson, G. R. (1988). *Parental discipline and antisocial behavior in adolescent boys: A longitudinal study.* Manuscript in preparation.

Walker, H. M., Shinn, M. R., O'Neill, R. E., & Ramsey, E. (1987). A longitudinal assessment of the development of antisocial behavior in boys: Rationale, methodology, and first-year results. *Remedial and Special Education, 8*(4), 7–16.

Werner, E. E., & Smith, R. S. (1977). *Kauai's children come of age.* Honolulu: University Press of Hawaii.

West, D. J. (1969). *Present conduct and future delinquency.* London: Heinemann.

Wilson, J. Q., & Herrnstein, R. J. (1985). *Crime and human nature.* New York: Simon & Schuster.

Wilson, R. S., & Matheny, A. P. (1983). Assessment of temperament in infant twins. *Developmental Psychology, 19,* 172–183.

Youniss, J. (1980). *Parents and peers in social development: A Sullivan-Piaget perspective.* Chicago: University of Chicago Press.

# 6 Commentary: Process and Systems

Frances Degen Horowitz
*The University of Kansas*

"Systems" has become a popular code word for saying we really must think more complexly about development. The question is whether each of these authors has taken us past the general message of the code word. I think so — although each has done it differently and, I think, with differential degrees and types of success. In my remarks I would like to take the discussant's perogative to make some comments about the chapters by Oyama, Fentress, and Thelen, to identify common and different themes, and then to take on the systems issue from my own perspective as it relates to these three chapters.

## NATURE-NURTURE

Susan Oyama's chapter (chapter 1, this volume), like her book *The Ontogeny of Information* (Oyama, 1985), is a bold attempt to move us, once and for all, off of a "terminology set" with respect to nature and nurture; a set that has been decidedly unproductive for our field. As she notes so eloquently, everyone gives lip service to rejecting the oppositional question of nature versus nurture, even as a growing number of serious investigators are busy parcelling out percentages to one or the other source of influence; others give a due to the environment but finally assure us that it is the gene that drives the organism to select its environment (Scarr & McCartney, 1983). Certainly it is not lost on anyone, I hope that these comments are made in the midst of the setting for the fascinating Minnesota Twin Studies efforts, which have revealed remarkable similarities in behav-

211

ior in twins reared apart. The periodic Sunday Supplement reports of the findings in this research program have the inevitable effect, even if not intended by the investigators, of reinforcing the strong and growing tendencies in our society today to attribute to genes the programs for developmental expression along with some pretty heavy political baggage and social policy implications.

Whether Oyama's sounding alarms are sufficient to cause the kind of profound rethinking of our terminology that might be desired remains to be seen. The goal is not unlike that chosen by the feminist movement for raising consciousness, sensitizing us to the use of generic gender language so that all children are always "he" and all people are always "him." I suspect the task Oyama has set for herself and for us may be somewhat more formidable, so deeply rooted are we in the nature–nurture dichotomy in our field. She, herself, notes the magnitude of the problem in referring to the seeming "metaphysical urge to contain ontogenetic variety within genetic boundaries."

I find myself strongly disposed to Oyama's basic premises and, comfortable with her approach to developmental systems. Her "constructivist interactionism" is not unlike the structural/behavioral model of development that I have been examining with respect to some essential assumptions (Horowitz, 1987). As Rich Weinberg will verify, when his publisher wrote for permission to reprint my structural/behavioral model in his and Scarr's textbook (Scarr, Weinberg, & Levine, 1986) the request came with the suggestion that the dimension of my model that is labeled *organismic* be changed to *genetic* because it seemed a simply synonymous change: After all, isn't organismic equivalent to genetic? In fact, in my model organismic and genetic are not equivalent for the very reasons that Oyama would object to such synonym-making. But that kind of synonym assumption is endemic in our field.

*New Jargon—Old Problems.* Equally endemic but not at all insidious in its implications is the use of "systems" in talking about development. It is as if we have recently discovered von Bertalanffy and general systems theory (von Bertalanffy, 1968), and found a glove that fits the groping hand looking for ways in which to address the obvious complexity of behavioral development. Although I think the systems theory approach has much to offer and have used it extensively myself in my own recent discussion of developmental theories (Horowitz, 1987), my caution is against a new jargon to address old problems and a possible over use of systems concepts when large portions of behavior may not be best understood in general systems terms.

Fentress (chapter 2, this volume) has chosen a "dynamic network analysis" as the envelope for his discussion of developmental systems;

Thelen's (chapter 3, this volume) choice is "dynamical systems principles"; as stated, Oyama elected "constructive interactionism." My own reading of these three chapters is that Fentress and Thelen are circling around the same ring in the circus whereas Oyama is focusing on a different but partially overlapping ring. By this I mean that Oyama seems to be referring to a systems concept that is broader than the individual organism whereas Thelen and Fentress' systems concepts about development relate more specifically to an individual ontogeny.

I was surprised that while Gottlieb's and Marler's work and related work of others were mentioned across the three chapters, nowhere was there reference to the work of Z.-Y. Kuo (1967) — the Chinese psychologist so liberally credited by Gottlieb. To quote from my own work (Horowitz, 1987):

> Kuo considered processes of development not in terms of the usual nature-nurture analysis, but with respect to the interaction of the organisms and its environment in which there were was mutual modification; the result was a modified and reorganized organism, and a modified and reorganized environment. (p. 90)

Kuo believed, and had some data to support this belief, that the organism has many different behavioral developmental possibilities — he called them behavior potentials. This involved:

> the recognition that there are a large number of possibilities or potential behavioral patterns in each newborn organism given the limits of the normal morphological structure of the species. This is not equivalent to asserting that there are inborn behavioral predispositions, but rather sets out the notion of a potential of behavioral gradient patterns that have different probabilities of development. Learning, in this scheme, is a central but not a sole mechanism determining which potentialities develop and at what level. . . . Kuo repeatedly emphasized that each organism and each species has many behavior potentials. Those that are actualized are "chosen" by the processes and the set of environmental conditions that obtain. The import of this perspective cannot be underestimated because it places the controlling elements neither in the organism nor in the environment but in the process. (Horowitz, 1987, pp. 90–91)

And, it is the emphasis upon the constructive process that, I believe, is at the heart of Oyama's effort to break the dichotomous nature–nurture mind set . . . a mind set that Kuo also attacked, both theoretically and empirically.

Kuo emphasized and had experimental data demonstrating that prenatally there was a confluence of factors: Thelen's notion of "controlling parameters," and von Bertalanffy's (1968) "leading parts" are similar. All are compatible with Fentress' proposition that prenatal precursors play a critical role in setting the determining probabilities that one set of behaviors will emerge out of the process as opposed to another set of behaviors. This is not unreasonable and the experimental work of Gottlieb and others have been supportive of these ideas (see Gottlieb, 1983).

Fentress' proposal that in a dynamic network annalysis experience serves as helping to select among alternative pathways and also maintains behavioral and neural networks and shapes the nature of generalization is entirely compatible with Kuo and Gottlieb's discussions. Those, in turn, are compatible with Oyama's thesis. In turn, one recalls Donald Hebb's (1949) cell assembly and phase sequence analysis. Its gross aspects are increasingly verified in current neuroscience research. Fentress' notions about the role of environment in fostering neural networks is Hebbian in its essential characteristics.

*Process.* I was particularly heartened by the emphasis in all three of these chapters on "process." It has seemed to me for some time now that many of our debates on such issues as continuity and discontinuity are misfocused on specific phenomena. I believe that the real issue is not the continuity and discontinuity of phenomena but, rather, the continuity and discontinuity in process. Thelen, it seems to me, has addressed this particularly well, especially with respect to transitions and shifts.

A question that is repeatedly addressed in developmental theories is the one that relates not only to the appearance of novel behavior but to the appearance of novel behaviors in the repertoire of an individual which are, in rough outline, the same novel behaviors that appear in the repertoires of all the normal individuals of the species. Of paramount importance in our understanding of the processes that produce regularity in novelty is Oyama's comment that "invariant aspects of the environment are not developmentally irrelevant" (chapter 1). Gravity is invariant but it is not irrelevant to the shaping of the behavioral repertoire. Thelen emphasizes the notion of control parameters. In development there is an orderly change in the nature and relative weights of the variables that constitute the control parameters—albeit with large individual differences. We need to be able to track the rate of change and the variation in the relative weights of the different change rates. We must do this with respect to the individual components of the control parameters. If we can measure all of these things, including the invariant aspects of the environment, then we can begin to make progress toward the systematic accounting of process and how it plays out over time and phenomena to encompass development even though there will always be an amount that is indeterminate. It is the tracking of changing parameters in process that will give us our major advances in understanding development.

*Development and Systems.* As you can see, I think there is a marvelous fitting together of these three chapters and there is much more to say about each and about them together. I would like, however, to conclude my discussion by sharing with you two aspects of my own thinking about development and systems. In doing so I want to present two diagrammatical representations for aiding the discussion, although in doing so I run the danger of the misconceptions that can arise when complex material is presented out of its fullest context.

Figure 6.1 reflects my attempt to show all the elements of developmental systems that I think a developmental theory must specify. Many of these elements are to be found in whole or in part in one of the three chapters under discussion. This is neither the proper place nor is there time to consider each of the labels. I want to focus, however, the top and bottom labels on the outline—Universals I and Universals II and nonuniversals. I think that any developmental systems theory must deal with the regularities of development that appear in all normal members of the species as they develop (i.e., universals), as well as those aspects of the behavioral

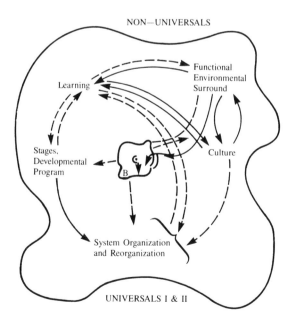

FIG. 6.1. The elements that must be taken into account in a developmental theory model. (from Horowitz, 1987)

repertoire which are not necessarily found in each member of the species (i.e., nonuniversals). Additionally, I think it is important to note that even in the case of the universal behaviors there are often differences in the degree to which these behaviors are elaborated in the repertoire, the content that characterizes the behavior, and the contexts in which these behaviors are expressed.

Language is an example. All normal children learn language. But, the language they learn is the language of their community—the content is the one specifically "taught" to them. The degree to which language is elaborated and the manner in which it functions is specific to cultural norms and expectations and individual differences. Language is an example of what I would call a Universal II behavior—it has a high probability of development in the normal organisms, it has a relatively long developmental trajectory, it varies greatly as a function of specific experience embedded in a sociocultural context and in relation to individual differences.

Universal I type behaviors are similar to Universal II type behaviors except that they have even higher probabilities of expression, typically have short developmental trajectories, and are less variable as a function of sociocultural contexts. Some of the basic perceptual behaviors involved with sensory functions are of this type.

The nonuniversal behaviors are those that may be elaborations of the universal behaviors or variants or new forms of behavior. They do not have high organismically (i.e., species typical) determined probabilities of development in the behavioral repertoire but are learned as a function of experience provided in a sociocultural context. It is quite likely that a very large proportion of the content of the human behavioral repertoire that is acquired is of the nonuniversal kind. It is highly dependent on learning opportunities either provided for the individual or created by the individual with these learning opportunities embedded in complex sociocultural systems involving cross-generational transmission processes as well as the more straightforward linear S–R associations.

I believe that it is very important for any developmental systems approach to encompass the development of both universal and nonuniversal behaviors. This means that there must be within the systems approach a developmental analysis of learning. Even in the analysis of emergent universal behaviors such as walking those aspects of the acquisition that involve learning components and the operation of contingent feedback principles must be amenable to a learning analysis.

The fact is that we have a large set of laws that account for the acquisition of responses in learning terms. These laws tend to be somewhat developmental but they need not be so. It is quite conceivable that the laws are amenable to refinement in a context of a systems analysis in terms of the role of contingent experience or information feedback mechanisms under conditions of changing control parameters. For this reason I think it is time to stop the silly and simplistic caricatures of learning and of S-R analyses as incompatible with a systems approach. It is very clear that in a systems approach one can talk of open and of closed systems. Closed systems tend to be linear and may even come into existence as the result of linear processes. Ultimately, the challenge is to have the fullest account of developmental processes. This account would consider the contribution that the laws of learning make to the course of those processes; it would also consider the manner in which the processes change in the context of the organization and reorganization of systems.

Figure 6.2 is familiar to many of you (see Horowitz, 1987). I share it to make a point that relates to Thelen's discussion of shifts and transitions. What you see here are the dimensions of organism and environment to which I referred earlier. I do not go into the nature of these dimensions. It is, however, theoretically possible to consider the likelihood that different combinations of organismic and environmental variables determine where, on this surface of developmental outcome, an individual is at a given point in time. This would represent the individual's developmental status — a joint function of organismic and environmental factors.

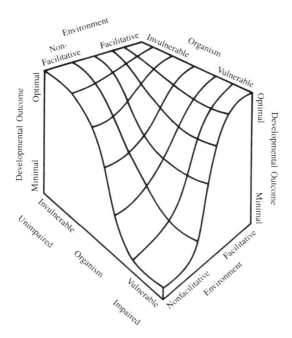

FIG. 6.2. The structural/behavioral model to account for developmental outcome (from Horowitz, 1987).

Thelen's notions with respect to changes in control parameters are very compatible with my ideas about points or junctures where the variables and/or the relative weights of critical variables or "control parameters" change. It is at these change points that I believe we may be able to define stages or what Robert Emde (Emde, Gaensbauer, & Harmon, 1976) called biobehavioral shifts or what David Feldman (1980) described as stage with respect to task demands. I think it is theoretically possible to consider that these relationships may someday be described by mathematical equations. When the variables in the equations change and/or when their relative weights change, that is when shifts, transitions, or stage endings and beginnings can be said to occur. I think Thelen's use of control parameters is related to von Bertalanffy's (1968) concept of leading part. These concepts have much utility in helping guide us where to look for the controlling variables in behavioral change.

To summarize, I respond very favorably to the three chapters partly because they speak to my biases, but also because I think they go a considerable distance to introduce into the rhetoric about systems some of the specifics that make it possible to test hypotheses and conduct critical experiments. I would only caution that any systems analysis cannot ignore established bodies of laws. Kuhn's (1970) notion of a scientific revolution, if one is on the Kuhn wave length these days, requires that established laws be incorporated into and accounted for by the new theories. No science progresses by disposing of its established facts; rather progress comes from incorporating them into better, more complete accounts of the phenomena and processes of interest.

## REFERENCES

Emde, R. N., Gaensbauer, T. J. & Harmon, R. J. (1976). Emotional expression in infancy. A biobehavioral study. *Psychological Issues, A Monograph Service* (Vol. 10). New York: International Universities Press.

Feldman, D. (1980). *Beyond universals in cognitive development.* Norwood, NJ: Ablex.

Gottlieb, G. (1983). The psychobiological approach to developmental issues. In P. H. Mussen (Ed.) *Handbook of Child Psychology* (4th ed., Vol. II, pp. 1-26). M. M. Haith & J. J. Campos (Ed.), *Infancy and developmental psychobiology.* New York: Wiley.

Hebb, D. O. (1949). *The organization of behavior.* New York: Wiley.

Horowitz, F. D. (1987). *Exploring developmental theories: Toward a structural/behavioral model of development.* Hillsdale, NJ: Lawrence Erlbaum Associates.

Kuhn, T. (1970). *The structure of scientific revolutions.* Chicago: Chicago University Press.

Kuo, Z.-Y. (1967). *The dynamics of behavioral development.* New York: Random House.

Oyama, S. (1985). *The ontogeny of information.* Cambridge: Cambridge University Press.

Scarr, S., & McCartney, K. (1983). How people make their own environments: a theory of genotype - environment effects. *Child Development, 54,* 424–435.

Scarr, S., Weinberg, R. A., & Levine, A. (1986). *Understanding development.* San Diego: Harcourt Brace Jovanovich

von Bertalanffy, L. (1968). *General system theory* (rev. ed.). New York: Braziller..

# 7 Commentary: General Systems and the Regulation of Development

Arnold J. Sameroff
*Brown University*

Symposia at the University of Minnesota have been accurate barometers of thinking about the relation of general systems principles to development. The original Concept of Development Symposium organized by Dale Harris (1957) included general systems theory in the planning stage by issuing an invitation to Ludwig von Bertalanffy, but unfortunately he was unable to attend. It was not until 25 years later that general systems theory was formally acknowledged in the second Minnesota symposium with the theme of concepts of development (Sameroff, 1981). And now only 7 years later there is an entire symposium devoted to an assessment of systems and development. It seems that it is far easier for the field to accept technical advances than theoretical ones. The instantaneous adoptions of new assessment techniques (Ainsworth, Blehar, Waters, & Wall, 1978; Brazelton, 1973) are in marked contrast to the decades necessary to adapt to new conceptual frameworks. Piaget's ideas that had been published in the 1930s were understood only in the 1960s. General systems views of the same epoch are only now being treated seriously. Unfortunately it is unusual for a theory in psychology to be accepted on its own merit. It must be validated by some more "basic" discipline, if not in detail, then in metaphor. The active organism metaphor so clearly documented in embryological research (Waddington, 1957; Weiss, 1969) was used to justify Piagetian concepts. Cybernetic models documented in information science disciplines are now serving to accomplish the same end for general systems approaches (see Thelen, this volume).

I rarely refer to systems without the delimiter "general." Systems thinking, in general, is different from general systems thinking, in specific.

219

Systems thinking alone is vaguely restricted to the proverbial idea that "no man is an island," that is, everything is connected to everything else. *General systems* refers to a specific category of theory that *specifies* how everything is connected to everything else. The general version seeks properties that can be described independently of the concrete data of individual disciplines. It has been described as lying midway between "the specific that has no meaning and the general that has no content" (Boulding, 1956). The goal of developmental theorists, in general, and the participants of this symposium, in particular, is to produce a developmental systems theory that would be useful in interpreting past products of developmental research and organizing fruitful future efforts.

A discussion of general systems approaches to behavioral development can be viewed from two perspectives attributable to Boulding (1956). The first approach is to seek processes in development that are analogous to those in other disciplines. For example, in almost all disciplines there are populations of elements to which new ones are added or born and old ones are subtracted or die. Moreover, these elements exchange information or energy with each other and with an environment. The second approach is to include the development of behavior in a hierarchy of complexity with the developmental concerns of all other scientific disciplines. For example, psychological processes are composed of biological processes and compose social processes. One could combine these two perspectives by creating a general systems theory of development that is hierarchically organized and has each level operating on the same set of general principles. Such efforts have been elaborated by Werner (1957), Piaget (1971), and other writers (Sameroff, 1983, 1987).

Comprehensive theoretical efforts at explanation have been labeled *paranoid psychology* by Sheldon White (1983), revealing his judgment of individuals with a theory that explains everything. However, his contrasting category of *bewildered psychology* is equally negative in that its practitioners have great difficulty in going beyond the data in hand. In this discussion, I attempt a mild version of paranoia that would not be too bewildering to the reader. I reiterate some of the principles of general systems theory that I have found most useful in explaining old data, including some that have resolved some theoretical contradictions. Then I assess some presentations on systems and development to determine the degree to which the authors converge on these systems principles. Finally, I offer my own view of the organization of development as it relates to a general system theory.

## GENERAL SYSTEMS THEORY

Although there are a large number of general systems theories that incorporate a multitude of levels and processes (Miller, 1978), I have settled on five principles that capture the core issues in such perspectives (Sameroff, 1983): wholeness and order, self-stabilization, self-reorganization, hierarchic interaction, and dialectical contradiction. In turn, each of these general systems principles have specific analogs in developmental theories (see Table 7.1). Wholeness and order provide the basis for continuity and identity; self-stabilization for development; self-reorganization for evolution; hierarchic interaction for discontinuity; and dialectical contradiction for motivation.

*Wholeness and Order.* The reason that wholes are more than the sum of their parts is that relationships are added that can never be assigned to single elements. This antireductionistic principle has its gestalt examples in the circle or melody which can be composed of a variety of different elements or tones yet still retain its identity if the relationships among the elements are unchanged. More interesting examples can be found in arbitrary systems that have been organized through evolution such as the genetic code or language. All living proteins result from combinations of 20 permutations of 4 biochemical bases. There is no intrinsic explanation why each one of the orderings of chemical bases on the DNA molecule encodes a specific amino acid. The origin of the genetic code was a probablistic outcome of evolutionary processes that with other probabilities could have produced other codes for the same amino acids or other codes for other amino acids. Similarly, there is no intrinsic explanation why a specific ordering of sounds encodes a specific meaning in a language. The existence of a wide array of languages that can express the same meanings demonstrates both the arbitrariness of the origins of part–whole relationships, and the specificity of their contemporary interactions. Wholes and their parts create a system with dual constraints, neither will have continuity and identity without the other. Language would not exist without sound or other units to which meaning can be attached, and units of sound would not cohere without a semantic system that relates those meanings.

The developmental analog of wholeness and order is continuity and identity. As in the organismic metaphor of the cell, continuity is in the relationship of the parts rather than in their specificity. The parts of the

TABLE 7.1
Theoretical Principles

| General Systems | Developmental Systems |
|---|---|
| Wholeness & order | Continuity and identity |
| Self-stabilization | Development |
| Self-reorganization | Evolution |
| Hierarchical interaction | Discontinuity |
| Dialectical interadiction | Motivation |

body are in constant transformation as nutrients flow in and excretions flow out. At the psychological level the organizational view of attachment is an example where the specific behaviors may change while the representation may remain the same (Sroufe & Waters, 1977). A family is defined independently of the specific actors, although this definition is itself in flux with the evolution of serial parenting in multimarriage families.

*Self-Stabilization.* Dynamic systems respond to contextual perturbations either by homeostatic or homeorhetic processes. Systems have a set point (e.g., the setting of a thermostat) that they try to maintain by altering internal conditions to compensate for changes in external conditions. Human thermoregulation is an example of a homeostatic process that is organized primarily biologically but can be facilitated by behavioral processes (e.g., putting on a coat or turning on the air conditioner). Egocentrism, perceptual constancy, or the use of attributions are examples of psychological homeostatic processes used to reinterpret environmental perturbations as congruent with existing mental organization.

For developmental systems homeorhesis (Waddington, 1962) is a more important self-stabilizing process than the more well-known process of homeostasis. In homeorhesis the system stabilizes around a trajectory rather than a set point as in physical growth. There is an organized time course over which growth accelerates and decelerates until adulthood. Underweight preterm infants are not permanently stunted because for these infants the time course is accelerated to provide a catch-up opportunity so that the child achieves normal physical development by the end of the second year. Swaddled infants who show motor lags when initially unwrapped, soon show normal age-appropriate locomotion skills no different from unswaddled infants. This is another example of homeorhetic processes that act as self-righting tendencies.

What we observe as development is a product of self-stabilization. An active organism subject to an ordered series of perturbations will respond with an ordered series of adaptations. Most attention has been devoted to internal sources of perturbations, usually labeled as *maturation.* As the genotype regulates biological changes in the body, there is a continuous process of adaptation while each change is assimilated into the system's functioning. The genetic timetable of activity is stimulated in a transactional process by resulting changes in the body's biochemistry. Since the demise of learning theory, far less attention has been paid to the ordered series of external perturbations that also serve to organize and regulate development. I have labeled the regulatory system for experience the *environtype* (Sameroff, 1985). The environtype includes a developmental agenda for raising children in which graded changes in the child trigger changes in the environment. Some of these triggers are age-graded and tied to specific points in time. At 3 years of age, for example, children are placed in new physical environments (i.e., nursery schools) with new socializing agents (i.e., teachers) and a new peer group. Other graded changes are tied by different cultures to different developmental milestones, (e.g., walking, talking, or puberty). The individual's adaptation to these sets of organized internal and external perturbations is what we label *development*. In contrast, evolution is a response to stable unorganized perturbations (see Fig. 7.1).

*Self-Reorganization.* Adaptive self-reorganization occurs when the system encounters new constants in the environment that cannot be balanced by existing system mechanisms. Adaptation is defined locally as change that permits the system to maintain its setpoints best in new circumstances. Adaptation frequently has the connotation of progress but such teleology is foreign to general systems thinking. A misreading of the theory of evolution gave rise to the idea that psychological development is toward some better state of existence (Kessen, 1987). The modern synthesis in the theory of evolution (Mayr, 1970) defines it as a probablistic process rather than a deterministic one. Evolution results from changes in distributions of genetic material in a population produced by changes in individual reproductive success as a consequence of changed environmental conditions.

Piaget's (1971) concept of adaptation is a psychological example of this process expressed through assimilation and accommodation. To the extent that the system cannot assimilate the new environmental conditions with existing regulatory subsystems, accommodation must occur in the form of new subsystems derived either from new relations between existing subsystems or by the establishment of a higher order subsystem with new

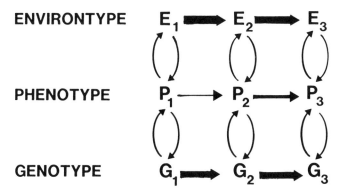

FIG. 7.1. Regulation model of development with transactions among genotype, phenotype, and environtype (from Sameroff, 1985).

functions. The Piagetian example is better suited to homeorhetic self-stabilization than to evolutionary reorganization because human cognitive development is well-buffered by both biological and educational constraints. On the other hand, there was a period in human evolution when environmental change provided the opportunities for the advances in cognition that led to modern human abstract thinking abilities. Such processes may be still active as indicated by data that abstract intelligence scores have risen dramatically in the last generation in a wide variety of countries around the world (Flynn, 1984, 1987).

To understand the future of human evolution one must consider social factors, not biological factors, as the major motivating force. The evolution of the environtype, the familial and social external regulators of development, has progressed at a much faster rate than the evolution of the genotype, the internal biological developmental regulator. Wilson (1975) described human society as autocatalytic. Fueled by positive feedback from its own social products, the evolution of the human species began to operate independently of the typical environmental constraints that influenced the evolutionary progressions of all other species. Such changes can be still found in recent times in socially determined modifications of women's roles and in the changing organization of the family.

*Hierarchical Interactions.* From the perspective of general systems theory a system that has the first three principles, wholeness and order, self-stabilization, and self-reorganization, will change in the direction of hierarchic structuration (Laszlo, 1972). In the view of Nobel prize winner, Herbert Simon (1973) "nature loves hierarchies." He hypothesized that systems based on hierarchies are much more stable in evolution because a failure in organization will not destroy the whole system but only decompose it down to the next level of stable subsystems. Material hierarchies run from subatomic particles through people and nations to the universe. Cognitive hierarchies run from sensorimotor schemas through logical systems to social institutions.

Within principles of hierarchic interaction I have been able to find the most satisfying account of developmental discontinuities. In addition, there is an interesting resolution of the organismic versus mechanistic metaphor controversy to be discussed later. The judgment that a discontinuity has occurred in development is typically based on a lack of correlation between assessments at two points in time. The usual interpretation is that the individual got better or worse. Wohlwill (1973) pointed out that most such lack of correlations were because the assessments were measuring different kinds of functioning at the two points in time. Just because tests given to 3-year-old and a 12-year-old are both called intelligence tests or personality tests does not mean that intelligence or personality at the two ages consist of the same dimensions or functions.

Understanding discontinuities is based on what Pattee (1973) has described as alternative descriptions in hierarchic interactions. Each part of a system has a number of properties that can place it in relation to other parts. For example, in a concept formation task exemplars that vary on a number of dimensions can be sorted by color, shape, or size. The color, shape, or size can be considered alternative descriptions of the same part. In a hierarchy, superordinate levels, the whole, only utilize some properties (i.e., alternative descriptions) of the subordinate level, the part. A physiological example can be found in the hierarchical relationships of the body. The circulatory system includes the heart, which is composed of tissues that are composed of cells. A complete description of the heart would require a description of each tissue and cell part. However, from the perspective of the circulatory system, the significant alternative description of the heart includes only its pumping property. Many tissue and cell properties contribute to this functioning but these are irrelevant from the circulatory system's perspective. In fact, the heart can be replaced in the system by someone else's or even a machine without any tissues or cells as long as the pumping function is carried out. Alternative descriptions of the machine would include its rust resistance or hardness, but the significant one in the circulatory system is only its pumping ability.

At the behavioral level society is a system composed of institutional subsystems composed of individual subsystems. At the level of institutions, individuals are only valued if they fulfill some defined alternative role in the organization. Whether the individual is male or female, White or Black, young or old, physically handicapped or retarded, may be relevant or irrelevant for certain role demands. For those roles where there are overlapping descriptions (e.g., college professor and chessmaster) there will be continuity of performance, but for those roles where there are alternative descriptions (e.g., bowling team member and lawyer) there is little expectation for correlation in competencies. Other alternative descriptions may be pertinent to who sits together at lunch or who marries who, but then in these cases still other alternative descriptions will be irrelevant.

Discontinuity is found when alternative descriptions are important in different social contexts or different developmental periods. Much is made of the lack of correlation between developmental assessments during the first year of life and later intelligence scores. The ability to walk is an important developmental marker in the first 2 years of life, but has little relevance to later intellectual functioning unless it prevents a child from going to school. There may be continuity at the subsystem level, a motorically handicapped infant may still be a motorically impaired adult, but not necessarily at the superordinate level, the motorically handicapped adult can become a lawyer or a parent. In a similar vein, an individual who is very effective intellectually may be very incompetent socially, the proverbial nerd, because these different capabilities are alternative descriptions of the same individual from the perspective of different social institutions.

*Dialectical Contradiction.* The last principle discussed is the motivational force in behavioral change. I have discussed self-stabilization and reorganization as reactions to environmental perturbations. What I have not pointed out is that many of these perturbations, especially in development, are not random events. They are the result of the system's own activity. The basic premise of all constructivist theories of development is that individuals come to know the world through their own activity. It is through action that knowledge and development emerge. The contradiction is that by acting on the world one is constantly changing it, so that the act of knowing is already changing what one is trying to know.

Dialectical contradiction is most evident in evolutionary history. When bacteria first evolved they did not use oxygen but began producing it as a by-product. This by-product changed the atmosphere to permit the evolution of new species of bacteria that used oxygen for energy. At the same time, the new oxygen killed off the species of bacteria that originally produced the atmospheric changes. The action of a species produced consequences that eventually destroyed it, the ultimate contradiction.

Our activity in the world changes it so that it can never be the way it was before. Technological advances such as the discovery of fire, the invention of electricity or microchips all have nonreversible effects on evolution. Unintended developmental by-products such as pollution are further examples of the contradictory effects of human activity. Technological evolution spills over into social evolution. The rise of factories removed the father from the house reorganizing family life. The need for the mother to become the primary caregiver may have been a major basis for the institutionalization of sex-role differentiation in modern society. The contradictions between changed context and the system's current state of organization are what push for new levels of stabilization. Environmental protection laws and equal rights amendments are ways in which society reorganizes itself to adapt to these new circumstances.

Psychologically, dialectical contradiction has been most explicitly treated in Piaget's (1971) theory of cognitive development. Equilibration is the result of an individual's efforts to overcome contradictions between the subject's cognitive organization and the object. Each assimilation requires some accommodation to occur because no two experiences are ever identical: and each new accommodation means that the next experience will be assimilated somewhat differently because the subject will have been changed. Riegel (1976) enlarged the number of domains among which contradictions occurred to include the biological, the psychological, the social, and the physical setting. In his view, developmental changes that are thought to represent stages, such as adolescence, are the resolution of a cascade of dialectical contradictions between physical status, cognitive development, and social roles.

## SOCIAL DEVELOPMENT AND GENERAL SYSTEMS

With this short summary of principles for a general systems theory, we can turn to some of the presentations of this symposia to see how close is the fit between theory and data. My attention is most closely directed to the presentations of social interactions in the work of Patterson and Bank (chapter 5) and Belsky, Rovine, and Fish (chapter 4). Both chapters are either state of the art or extensions of the state of the art and test the frontiers of empirical work in social interaction. In each case, I examine to see if principles of wholeness and order, self-stabilization, self-reorganization, hierarchic interaction, and dialectical contradiction can be applied.

In the Patterson and Bank chapter a main point was that the behavior or personality of the child could not be explained out of the family context. Wholeness and order was found in family interaction patterns. Self-stabilization was evident in the recurring negative interactions among family members in the coercive families whenever noncompliance occurred. Self-reorganization was seen in the development of the coercive family style itself. The initial perturbing effects of normal noncompliance produced a coercive parenting style that increased rather than decreased the noncompliant behavior. These reorganizations could be seen in a series of stages as the family moved toward the production of an antisocial child.

The Patterson and Bank analyses did not consider hierarchical relationships between the child and family. Although the family is clearly a part of the analysis, it is only considered as a collection of interacting individuals, either in terms of parent–child or child–child behavioral changes. It is a problem in the field of social development in general that there is little bridging to the family systems literature where much attention is paid to family level characteristics but little attention to individual characteristics. On the other hand, Patterson and Bank use their data to throw some interesting light on the issue of alternative descriptions.

In principle, each system in which the individual participates can incorporate a different aspect of the person. The school can relate to the child's academic performance, whereas the family can relate to the child's social performance. However, the choice of alternative descriptions might be an active rather than a passive process. Individuals can emphasize one or another of their characteristics in different situations. In the case of the antisocial child, the description given importance and exaggerated by the family interactions comes to dominate the child's behavior in other contexts. Instead of emphasizing their academic prowess in the school setting, children from coercive families emphasize disruptive antisocial behavior that alienates them from both teachers and schoolmates.

Dialectical contradictions permeate the Patterson and Bank data. In two major cases, the efforts of both parents and child produce opposite effects. The inept coercive childrearing that parents use to produce compliance in the child produces instead the contradictory behavior of noncompliance. This contradiction in outcome is produced by a discrepancy between the parent's good intentions and poor childrearing knowledge. A similar contradiction occurs between the child's later attempts to engage peers in social relationships at school and the resulting rejection. The child is provided with only one aggressive model of social interaction by his or her family that does not serve to attract friends at school. The dialectical problems in these instances can be resolved only through therapeutic interventions where both the parents and child experience consciousness raising. The Patterson and Bank intervention strategies that help parents and children to change their interactive behavior and outcomes are good demonstrations of how the environtype can reorganize to alter family experience through action of the social context, in this case the social service system.

The Belsky et al. study of family formation also lends itself well to a general systems analysis. Belsky et al. are explicit about the use of general systems principles especially around hierarchical relationships. Individuals are seen as participating in dyads that are organized into families. The family subsystems are based on alternative descriptions of the members. The marital dyad emphasizes different aspects than the parenting dyads (i.e., mother–father vs. mother–child or father–child).

Self-stabilization is explicitly analyzed by observing the marital dyad before and after the perturbation of childbirth. The effect of this normative event can be assessed as a developmental change for the population as whole, or individual differences can be studied among couples who are better or worse at restabilizing. The normative event presents a major opportunity for self-reorganization as the new constant perturbation, the child, becomes a permanent part of the system. However, as with most such developmental changes there is little attempt to specify what is new in the system's behavior when the focus of the research is on how well the parents maintain the old. One cannot correlate caregiving before and after the birth of the child, because there is no caregiving before. These are examples of discontinuity in behavior that can only be given continuity in generalized assessments of age or stage appropriate personal competence.

Hierarchical interactions are the exciting core of the Belsky et al. analysis.

They are able to ask questions about the effects of parts on systems and subsystems, of wholes on parts and of subsystems on parts. Specifically, they examine the role of each individual in their dyadic relationships and then the role of the dyadic relationships in the family. Moreover, they can then examine the effect of perturbations or changes in each family member on their behavior in dyads and the dyads behavior in the family group. Such imaginative analyses show the power of general systems perspectives for illuminating the dynamic processes that mediate observed behavioral outcomes. Without some explicit realization of the importance of context for understanding individual behavior, Belsky and his associates never would have collected the interaction data that made systems analyses possible.

The Belsky et al. and Patterson and Banks studies are only segmented peeks at child development. My major criticism of both chapters is that neither takes a developmental orientation toward the child. In the Belsky et al. project, the child can be replaced by a pet animal without changing the study. The basic research question was how does the marital dyad respond to the addition of a new family member that needs care and attention. In the Patterson and Bank chapter, the behavior of the child is the outcome but it is not treated developmentally. There is no attention to the characteristics that the school-age child brings to the situation that may be different from the preschool- or high school-age child, nor the different effects that family coercion might have on children of different ages. But one cannot do everything in any single study, even a study based on appreciation that everything might be relevant to the outcomes.

The difference between a study based on general systems theory principles and one that is not may not be in any empirical detail, but it will be in the conceptual frame. When a general systems researcher examines infants or school-age children, the design is based on an active decision not to study other ages because of the scope of the work or the questions asked. When nonsystems researchers use the same design it is usually because they do not consider developmental status to be a relevant dimension. Similarly, researchers that ignore family structure, social class, or ethnic background usually do so by default rather than by choice. The data are increasingly clear that the default option can rarely be justified. In almost every domain of child functioning, contextual factors make significant contributions (Sameroff, 1987). To ignore these factors is no longer the reflection of a different point of view, it is just bad science.

## A STORY OF PSYCHOLOGY

One of the current concerns among psychologists is with the future of psychology as a science. As a profession it is marked by extremely rapid growth because of the increasing consciousness of the public that much of mental health and illness are consequences of human behavior. However, as a science the field has become highly fractionated because the more rigorous among us have come to believe that less and less of what we do can be explained behaviorally. The physiological psychologists have continued their search for the explanations of behavior in the biological reductionism of their neuroscience colleagues. On the other end, the cognitive psychologists have seen their efforts as more germane to the construction of artificial intelligence in the service of computer manufacturers rather than the explanation of real intelligence in human beings. This centrifugal activity has left the core of psychology as a science increasingly devoid of content. Is there any prospect for psychology maintaining an identity as a discipline?

If one looks at the past history of the field, psychology's periods of unity have arisen when there was a shared metaphor. Learning theory held that role until the 1960s. Any well-educated psychologist could understand any other well-educated psychologist because they all spoke the same language. If one studied physiology, personality, or cognition, one used the same terms of reference. Everyone attended all colloquia because the common language resulting from the common metaphor led to a common ability at discourse.

Currently, there is little scientific romance within psychology as a whole. The most evidence of professional energy is in the efforts of subdisciplines to find legitimacy elsewhere. Clinical psychologists seek to become psychiatrists, physiological psychologists seek to become biologists, and cognitive psychologists seek to become mathematicians. The newest unification is the proposed marriage between cognitive science and neuroscience, not as common metaphors, but in the belief that they are dealing with an identical empirical reality. The most popular view among them is that neural circuitry and logic are the same thing, and this identity will explain anything else of interest in the epiphenomenon of behavior.

I find the use and understanding of metaphor as a much more fundamental scientific enterprise than the study of biology or mathematics. In an essay entitled "Education by Poetry," Robert Frost commented:

"I have wanted in late years to go further and further in making metaphor the whole of thinking. . . . What I am pointing out is that unless you are at home in metaphor, unless you have had your proper poetical education in the metaphor, you are not safe anywhere. Because you are not at ease with figurative values, you don't know the metaphor in its strength and its weakness. You don't know how far you may expect to ride it and when it may break down with you. You are not safe in science; you are not safe in history. . . .

We still ask boys in college to think, but we seldom tell them what thinking means; we seldom tell them it is just putting this and that together; it is saying one thing in terms of another. To tell them is to set their feet on the first rung of a ladder the top of which sticks through the sky. (cited in Johnson, 1987)

My personal attraction to general systems theory is because of its conspicuous focus on metaphor as its core concern. It satisfies my need to see unity in a diversely, perversely chaotic universe. It is part of an effort to recapture my experience as a graduate student when all psychologists spoke the same language. However, then we thought the language was truth rather than metaphor. The decline in the importance of learning theory occurred when we realized that it was only one metaphor among many. Developmentalists were enlisting in the cause of a more satisfying metaphor, the organismic one. Although many took the linear view that the false mechanistic model was to be replaced by the true organismic one, the dialectical contradiction between the two models offered the opportunity for a more comprehensive synthesis.

## MECHANISM, ORGANISM, AND GENERAL SYSTEMS THEORY

Mechanistic and organismic metaphors have been presented as contrasting bases for developmental models (Reese & Overton, 1970). In general, the organismic model has been seen as the better approach for understanding developmental psychology, but this is not surprising, for it takes as its metaphor living biological systems (Piaget, 1971; Werner, 1957). However, mechanistic orientations have continued to exert their influence in the form of information processing theories and especially computer models of cognition (Simon, 1979). Another view is the possibility that organismic and mechanistic models are alternative descriptions of the same phenomena. The universe can be interpreted as being both mechanistic and organismic. Despite the admonitions of Reese and Overton (1970) and Pepper (1942) against mixing metaphors, appeals to unify such perspectives are frequently made (D. Kuhn, 1978; McCall, 1981).

To add to the complexities of interpreting development has been the request of life-span psychologists to replace mechanism and organism with contextualism (Baltes, 1979; Lerner & Busch-Rossnagel, 1981). The contextualists' emphasis on the importance of the structure of the environment is a necessary addition to the emphases of the other two models rather than as a substitute for them. Development and evolution may be probabilistic but they are not arbitrary. Every step in development is based on what already exists. The organismic model provides a basis for the continuity of development, just as the contextualist model provides a basis for discontinuity.

General systems theory may provide a framework for the combination of models previously suggested. Each system exists in a context of hierarchical relationships and environmental relationships. The analysis of hierarchical interfaces combines both organismic and mechanistic elements. Within such a more general view, interpretations can be made as to why a system appears to function mechanistically from one perspective, organismically from a second perspective, contextually from a third, and perhaps, dialectically from a fourth. An analogous overview permitted physicists to explain why from one empirical perspective light appeared to have properties of a wave, whereas from another perspective it appeared to have the properties of a particle.

Although it may be true that any living system is an interconnected network with many components contributing to any observed activity, the relationship between a whole and its parts is one of abstraction. The whole abstracts some aspect of its parts as a criterion for system membership. Such abstracting properties of hierarchies are a common characteristic of perceptual and cognitive systems. Perceptual constancy is the phenomenon when despite an object's changing proximal pattern of stimulation (e.g., perception of a cube being rotated in space), it is still treated as the same cube. Color categories are another such example. In spite of the continuous distribution of light wave frequencies, hues are treated discontinuously.

The Piagetian theory of cognitive development is a sequence of such abstractions in which the content of experience is depreciated relative to some abstracted formal properties as one goes further and further in intellectual development. In order to demonstrate that liquid quantity can be conserved, the child must ignore the different appearances of the liquid in two glasses and infer an underlying logical reality that makes them the same. Yet, at the perceptually based peroperational level, the liquids are different.

All reality is organic in that it varies with the constant activity of its components, but in the realm of contemplation, mechanical categorization must intrude. This philosophical point about cognition is equally true for biology, chemistry, and physics. The genetic code is interpreted categorically even though the electrical potentials that characterized the atoms in the DNA molecules are in constant flux. Bonner (1973) described the relationships among hierarchical levels in embryology as a series of developmental tests. Levels of the hierarchy act in an all or none fashion (i.e., an abstraction) to certain chemical regulators, despite the fact that the regulators are always present in some quantity. These biological systems have trigger-like mechanisms that go to a second state if the amount of regulator is above a threshold and remains in the current state if the amount is below the threshold.

The principles that have been described for a general systems theory of development can be seen to incorporate the properties of the dominant metaphors in developmental thinking. Such a wonderful theory can only foster my participation in paranoid psychology. As a more social function it permits a return to the days of yesteryear when there was a shared language of psychology.

Today we can read a volume such as this that includes presentations from empirical domains as disparate as motor organization and marital organization and the participants can understand them all. Our understanding may not necessarily include every detail, but it will include the metaphor and its properties. For each we can ask the same questions. What is the network of relationships? What are the parts and what are the wholes? What are the regulations and what are the constraints, both contextual and hierarchical? And of most importance to our developmental concerns, where did it come from and where is it going?

The general systems theory approach will lead us to seek common organizational parameters in every scientific explanation—a theory of context and a theory of development. The theory of context must show us the relation of parts to wholes and the mutual constraints imposed by hierarchical dual control. The theory of development must show us the processes of self-stabilization and the sources of perturbations that lead to reorganization. Each future step is constrained by prior organization but not determined by the past. Predicting the future will require knowing the systems, their environments, and their transactions in dialectical terms. This may seem a difficult task in its scope, on the other hand, to return to the simplicity of seeing the world through linear eyes would make any understanding of the future an impossibility. In my view on the basis of such general systems perspectives, we may really be on the rungs of a ladder "the top of which sticks through the sky."

## REFERENCES

Ainsworth, M. S., Blehar, M. D., Waters, E., & Wall, S. (1978). *Patterns of attachment: A psychological study of the strange situation.* Hillsdale, NJ: Lawrence Erlbaum Associates.

Baltes, P. B. (1979). Life-span developmental psychology: Some converging observations on history and theory. In P. B. Baltes & O. G. Brim, Jr. (Eds.), *Life-span development and behavior* (Vol. 2, pp. 6–37). New York: Academic Press.

Bonner, J. (1973). Hierarchical control programs in biological development. In H. H. Pattee (Ed.), *Hierarchy theory: The challenge of complex systems* (pp. 49–70). New York: Braziller.

Boulding, K. (1956). General systems theory—The skeleton of science. *Management Science, 2,* 197-–208.

Brazelton, T. B. (1973). Neonatal Behavioral Assessment Scale: *Clinics in developmental medicine* (No. 50). London: Heinemann; Philadelphia: Lippincott.

Flynn, J. R. (1984). The mean IQ of Americans: Massive gains 1932 to 1978. *Psychological Bulletin, 95*(1), 29–51.

Flynn, J. R. (1987). Massive IQ gains in 14 nations: What IQ tests really measure. *Psychological Bulletin, 101*(2), 171-191.

Harris, D. B. (1957). *The concept of development.* Minneapolis: University of Minnesota Press.

Johnson D. M. (1987, October). Robert Frost on Thinking [Letter to the editor], *Science, 237,* p. 447.

Kessen, W. (1987, August). *Developmental psychology: Present and future.* Paper presented at a meeting of the American Psychological Association, New York.

Kuhn, D. (1978). Mechanisms of cognitive and social development: One psychology or two. *Human Development, 21,* 92-118.

Laszlo, E. (1972). *Introduction to systems philosophy: Toward a new paradigm of contemporary thought.* New York: Harper & Row.

Lerner, R. M., & Busch-Rossnagel, N. A. (1981). Individuals as producers of their development: Conceptual and empirical basis. In R. M. Lerner & N. A. Busch-Rossnagel (Eds.), *Individuals as producers of their development: A life-span perspective* (pp. 1-36). New York: Academic Press.

Mayr, E. (1970). *Populations, species, and evolution.* Cambridge, MA: Belknap Press.

McCall, R. B. (1981). Nature-nurture and the two realms of development. A proposed integration with respect to mental development. *Child Development, 52,* 1-12.

Miller, J. G. (1978). *Living systems.* New York: McGraw-Hill.

Pattee, H. H. (1973). The physical basis and origins of hierarchical control. In H. H. Pattee (Ed.), *Hierarchy theory: The challenge of complex systems* (pp. 71-108). New York: Braziller.

Pepper, S. C. (1942). *World hypotheses.* Berkeley: University of California.

Piaget, J. (1971). *Biology and knowledge.* Chicago: University of Chicago Press.

Reese, H. W., & Overton, W. F. (1970). Models of development and theories of development. In L. R. Goulet & P. B. Baltes (Eds.), *Life-span developmental psychology: Research and theory* (pp. 137-186). New York: Academic Press.

Riegel, K. F. (1976). The dialectics of human development. *American Psychologist, 31,* 698-700.

Sameroff, A. J. (1981). Development and the dialectic: The need for a systems approach. In W. A. Collins (Ed.), *Minnesota symposium of child psychology* (Vol. 15). Hillsdale, NJ: Lawrence Erlbaum Associates.

Sameroff, A. J. (1983). Developmental systems: Contexts and evolution. In W. Kessen (Ed.), *History, theories, and methods.* Vol. I of P. H. Mussen (Ed.), *Handbook of child psychiatry* (pp. 237-294). New York: Wiley.

Sameroff, A. J. (1985, August). *Primary prevention and psychological disorder: A contradiction in terms.* Paper presented at the annual meeting of the American Psychological Association, Los Angeles.

Sameroff, A. J. (1987). The social context of development. In N. Eisenberg (Ed.), *Contemporary topics in developmental psychology* (pp. 273-291). New York: Wiley.

Simon, H. A. (1973). The organization of complex systems. In H. H. Pattee (Ed.), *Hierarchy theory: The challenge of complex systems* (pp. 1-28). New York: Braziller.

Simon, H. A. (1979). Information processing models for cognition. In M. R. Rosenzweig & L. W. Porter (Eds.), *Annual review of psychology* (Vol. 30, pp. 363-396). Palo Alto, CA: Annual Reviews.

Sroufe, L. A., & Waters, E. (1977). Attachment as an organizational construct. *Child Development, 34,* 817-848.

Waddington, C. H. (1957). *The strategy of the genes.* London: Allen & Unwin.

Waddington, C. H. (1962). *New patterns in genetics and development.* New York: Columbia University Press.

Weiss, P. A. (1969). The living system: Determinism stratified. In A. Koestler & J. R. Smythies

(Eds.), *Beyond reductionism: New perspectives in the life sciences* (pp. 3–55). Boston: Beacon Press.

Werner, H. (1957). The concept of development from a comparative and organismic point of view. In D. B. Harris (Ed.), *The concept of development* (pp. 125–148). Minneapolis: University of Minnesota Press.

White S. (1983). Developmental psychology, bewildered and paranoid: A reply to Kaplan. In R. M. Lerner (Ed.), *Developmental psychology: Historical and philosophical perspectives* (pp. 233–239). Hillsdale, NJ: Lawrence Erlbaum Associates.

Wilson, E. O. (1975). *Sociobiology: The new synthesis.* Cambridge, MA: Belknap Press.

Wohlwill, J. (1973). *The study of behavioral development.* New York: Academic Press.

# Author Index

# Subject Index